Published by
Edward Elgar Publishing Limited
The Lypiatts
15 Lansdown Road
Cheltenham
Glos GL50 2JA
UK

Edward Elgar Publishing, Inc.
William Pratt House
9 Dewey Court
Northampton
Massachusetts 01060
USA

A catalogue record for this book
is available from the British Library

Library of Congress Control Number: 2018931720

This book is available electronically in the **Elgar**online
Social and Political Science subject collection
DOI 10.4337/9781788112765

MIX
Paper from responsible sources
FSC® C013056
FSC www.fsc.org

ISBN 978 1 78811 275 8 (cased)
ISBN 978 1 78811 276 5 (eBook)

Typeset by Columns Design XML Ltd, Reading
Printed and bound in Great Britain by TJ International Ltd, Padstow

Contents

PART III EU EMBEDDED POLICIES ON ENTREPRENEURSHIP AND REGIONAL GROWTH

PART IV CASE STUDIES ON LOCAL POLITICAL ENTREPRENEURSHIP

PART V CONCLUDING REMARKS

Contributors

Alebaki, Maria – Aristotle University of Thessaloniki, Greece

Maria Alebaki is Adjunct Assistant Professor at the Department of Agricultural Economics. Her research interests include economic crisis and political entrepreneurship, agricultural policy and the tourism sectors for economic development.

Berggren, Caroline – University of Gothenburg, Sweden

Caroline Berggren is Associate Professor of Education at Gothenburg University. Her general research interest is social division based on class and gender with specific focus on the structure of education and the labour market in Sweden.

Gretzinger, Susanne – University of Southern Denmark, Denmark

Susanne Gretzinger is Associate Professor in Strategic Leadership and Marketing at the Institute of Border Region Studies. Her main research areas are strategic leadership and strategic network management.

Karlsson, Charlie – Jönköping International Business School, Sweden

Charlie Karlsson is Professor of Economics at Jönköping International Business School. In his research, he has focused on infrastructure economics, urban economics, the economics of technological change, regional economics, spatial industrial dynamics, entrepreneurship and small business economics, and the economics of R&D and higher education.

Leick, Birgit – University College Østfold, Norway

Birgit Leick is Associate Professor at the Faculty of Business, Languages and Social Sciences, University College Østfold, Norway. Her research interests take place at the nexus of business studies and regional studies with particular interest in firms, institutions and regional development, business strategies and inter-firm business networks and entrepreneurship theory and practice.

Olausson, Albin – Linköping University, Sweden

Albin Olausson is a PhD Candidate at The Department of Management and Engineering. His ongoing research focuses on local and regional development policies with particularly empirical focus on the municipal level and local policy formation and steering.

Parkhouse, Anna – University Dalarna, Sweden

Anna Parkhouse is Senior Lecturer of Political Science. Her research interests include the European Union as regional and global actor, the impact of the EU membership incentive on rule adoption in minority rights legislation and European policies on asylum seekers and refugees.

Petridou, Evangelia – Mid-Sweden University

Evangelia Petridou is a doctoral candidate in Political Science. Her research interests include theories of the policy process, political entrepreneurship, and urban governance. Her substantive policy area interests include economic development and territorial cohesion with a special interest in European peripheral areas.

Pircher, Brigitte – Linnaeus University, Sweden

Brigitte Pircher is Postdoctoral Researcher at the Department of Political Science and was former Lecturer at the University of Vienna, Austria. Her research includes European integration, EU institutions, EU decision-making processes, and the implementation of EU law in the various member states.

Silander, Charlotte – Linnaeus University, Sweden

Charlotte Silander is Senior Lecturer of Political Science at Linnaeus University. She works at the Department of Education at Linnaeus University. Her research focuses on European Union educational policy, gender equality in higher education, systems of higher education and university research policies.

Silander, Daniel – Linnaeus University, Sweden

Daniel Silander is Associate Professor of Political Science at Linnaeus University. His main areas of interest are the European Union, political entrepreneurship on a domestic and international level, international politics, democracy and state and human security.

Strömblad, Per – Linnaeus University, Sweden

Per Strömblad is Associate Professor of Political Science at Linnaeus University. He has conducted research on citizenship, integration and political participation with a focus on immigrants' democratic influence in Swedish society.

Tavassoli, Sam

Sam Tavassoli is a Research Fellow at CIRCLE, Sweden and an Assistant Professor at Royal Melbourne Institute of Technology (RMIT), Australia. Tavassoli's research areas are economics of innovation and technological change, the innovation strategies of firms, entrepreneurial firms and geography of innovation.

von Bergmann-Winberg, Marie-Louise – Mid-Sweden University, Sweden

Marie-Louise von Bergmann-Winberg is Professor of Political Science at Mid-Sweden University. She has conducted research on social and political entrepreneurship, multilevel governance, regionalisation and regional reforms in Sweden and plural economy and socio-economic regulation.

Wihlborg, Elin – Linköping University, Sweden

Elin Wihlborg is Professor of Political Science and Public Administration at Linköping University. Her research interests focus on theoretical and empirical analysis of regional and local public policy issues and public administration, especially regarding policies in the information society and sustainable development issues.

PART I

Framework of the study

1. European governance and political entrepreneurship in times of economic crisis

Daniel Silander

One major challenge for the member states of the European Union (EU) over the last two decades has been the economic crisis that began in 2007–2008. The global economic crisis (Amadeo, 2016; Nier and Forte, 2016; Suter and Herkenrath, 2012) has been assessed by economists and politicians as the worst crisis since the Great Depression of the 1930s (Dullien et al., 2010: 1). The crisis began in the United States (US) in 2007 (Nier and Forte, 2016) with indebtedness among homeowners, overvalued house prices and optimistic estimates of house price increases. While the financial system was overexposed to real estate, the major decline in real estate prices led to a system crisis in the US banking sector. In September 2008, the American investment bank Lehman Brothers collapsed, leading to immediate and desperate political actions to bail out other financial institutions. Bear Stearns and Merrill Lynch were sold for a bargain and Goldman Sachs and Morgan Stanley transformed into commercial banks with tougher regulations. All four major financial companies received government economic support (*The Economist*, 17 October 2007; RealtyTrac, January 2008; *The State of the Nation's Housing*, 2008; Dullien et al., 2010). In January 2011, the Financial Crisis Inquiry Commission (FCIC), appointed by the US government to investigate all causes of the economic crisis, listed the following factors:

> Widespread failures in financial regulation, including the federal reserve's failure to stem the tide of toxic mortgages; Dramatic breakdowns in corporate governance including too many financial firms acting recklessly and taking on too much risk; An explosive mix of excessive borrowing and risk by households and Wall Street that put the financial system on a collision course with crisis; Key policy makers ill prepared for the crisis, lacking a full

> understanding of the financial system they oversaw; and systematic breaches in accountability and ethics at all levels. (FCIC, 2011)

The global economic crisis also hit hard on the European economies. Despite EU and member state countermeasures to limit the economic recession, stock markets continued to drop, house markets destabilised, unemployment rates increased and economic growth halted significantly throughout Europe. In 2009, the overall EU gross domestic product (GDP) had fallen by 4 per cent, industrial production slowed to early 1990s levels, 23 million people (about 10 per cent of the active population) had become unemployed and average deficits were 7 per cent of GDP with several national debts of 80 per cent or more of GDP (European Commission, 2010; Dullien et al., 2010; *Financial Times*, 2016). The European Commission pointed out causes of the crisis similar to those stated by the FCIC:

> The crisis was preceded by a long term period of rapid credit growth, low risk premiums, abundant availability of liquidity, strong leveraging, soaring asset prices and the development of bubbles in the real estate sector. Over-stretched leveraging positions rendered financial institutions extremely vulnerable to corrections in asset markets. As a result a turn-around in a relatively small corner of the financial system (the US subprime market) was sufficient to topple the whole structure. (European Commission, 2009: 1)

The European economic crisis had different impacts in the north and south of Europe, where the latter was hit the hardest. While many European states, such as Germany and Sweden, could handle the economic recession and limit its negative impact, other states, such as Greece, Portugal and Spain, among others, were challenged by economic bankruptcy and political turmoil. The economic recession was visualised in many ways: economic crisis in real estate, construction and service sectors (Spain, Greece); economic diversification (Italy, Sweden); social stress in homelessness, curtailing of welfare benefits, poverty and social marginalisation (Spain, France, Italy, Greece, UK) and in spatial crises in the development of ghost towns (Spain) and limited infrastructure development (Greece, France).

Although the euro was largely protected, the long-term effects of the crisis in declining growth, rising unemployment and social tension led to political instability, disintegration, nationalism, protectionism and mistrust towards governments and the EU. In numerous European elections—in the Netherlands, France, Italy and Germany, among many states—and in the European Parliament, Eurosceptic candidates gained greater popular support. The economic crisis embedded social and political tension in many European states with demonstrations, rioting and rising social movements (Turcu et al., 2015). In 2009, the European Commission declared the crisis as "without precedent in post-war economic history" (European Commission, 2009: 1) and called for actions "to be bold and ambitious" (European Commission, 2010: 2). In 2010, the European Commission visualised a new European political and economic start in the wake of the global crisis. The former president (2004–2014) of the Commission, José Manuel Barroso, called for coordinated, innovative and immediate European reactions to the crisis to build a better Europe. The EU responses had to be based on "real ownership by European leaders and institutions", "a coordinated European response" to "act together" and with "new tools and the new ambition" (see European Commission, 2010: 2–3).

In 2015, five years later, the EU Commission stated in its report on *European Financial Stability and Integration* how Europe was perhaps on a slow path towards economic recovery. The Commission foresaw a slow and winding road of economic progress based on monetary stimulus initiatives and structural and regulatory reforms. It stated that, "For the first time since 2007, the economies of all EU Member States are expected to grow in 2015 … Over the course of 2015, economic activity is expected to pick up moderately in the EU and in the euro area, before growing further in 2016" (European Commission, April 2015: 10). It also stated, however, that European economic recovery remained slow with the remaining economic crisis impacting Europe due to structural weaknesses, a slow path of investment recovery and limited impact of exports on economic growth, leaving private sector consumption as the main driving engine for European economic recovery (European Commission, April 2015: 10–11).

In early 2017, the EU Commission forecasted an economic turning point in Europe. The Commission expected an important economic recovery in 2016–2018 and declared that a decade of economic recession now seemed to be met by economic growth in all 28 EU member states, although challenges and uncertainties remained. It was argued that this was at least partly due to the reforms the EU initiated and promoted to prevent, mitigate and resolve the economic crisis. First, crisis prevention involved identifying causes of the crisis and the necessary macroeconomic regulatory and supervisory mechanisms to be implemented. Second, crisis mitigation included limiting negative social and economic consequences of the recession, and third, crisis resolutions were adopted to halt the economic recession to the lowest possible economic and social costs for European citizens (European Commission, 2009: 1–2). The implemented policy reforms included governmental financial rescue policies to ensure a financial system of banks with liquidity: that is, raised deposit guarantees, low interest rents and state guaranteed liquidity facilities for institutions. The primary objectives were to develop financial policies that would restore the banking sector to being financially dynamic and to promote economic progress of productivity, but also to set up a functional regulative and supervisory framework for the financial market (European Commission, 2009: 2–5).

During a decade of European economic crisis, there have been numerous calls for European leadership with new, innovative and bold measures, that is, political entrepreneurship to counter the economic crisis. It was argued that European political entrepreneurship should be the cornerstone in a redeveloped, prosperous and highly modern European economy (Com, 2008, 394 final 2). Scholars in the social sciences and economics have also stated that European economic progress needs new political initiatives and collaboration within networks of different types of entrepreneurship and that it is within these networks that political entrepreneurship must thrive so as to set up institutional arrangements for a dynamic and prosperous Europe. In this study, to explore political entrepreneurship is to explore how European politicians, public servants, bureaucrats and institutions have acted to establish favourable conditions for economic growth and entrepreneurship in Europe. This book particularly explores if there exists, from a governance perspective, political entrepreneurship from the EU—member state authorities, politicians and public servants—to promote institutions favourable to growth and entrepreneurship in Europe in times of a long-lasting economic crisis. By political entrepreneurship, this study includes an actor and a structure perspective by focusing on politicians/public servants/bureaucrats/institutions within the publicly funded sector that, with innovative approaches, encourage entrepreneurship/business and where the goals are growth and employment (Karlsson et al., 2016). By governance, we refer to the multilevel authorities that together constitute European political steering and where EU institutions, member state governments and local and regional authorities are core actors (Wallace et al., 2010; Hix, 1998; Rhodes, 1996). It is argued that contemporary EU multilevel governance provides new opportunities for political entrepreneurship to identify and develop policies on various levels of authority, from the local and subregional to state and European levels, and that a European economic crisis may provide a window of opportunity (Kingdon, 1984) for political entrepreneurial measures.

POLITICAL ENTREPRENEURSHIP AND EUROPEAN GOVERNANCE

Political entrepreneurship has been frequently called for in European political discussions and especially so in times of social and economic challenges. The European debate has called for European leadership; innovative, bold and ambitious initiatives and new cohesive policies on the economic crisis. However, scholarly attention to political entrepreneurship and political entrepreneurs has been far more limited. Research on political entrepreneurship originally developed from an economics perspective on entrepreneurship and entrepreneurs as important aspects of a growing and dynamic economy (see Schumpeter, 1943). In traditional scholarly work in economics, entrepreneurs have been portrayed as economic driving engines and go-getters striving against the status quo for new ventures and windows of opportunity. In the 1990s, research on entrepreneurship and the entrepreneur slowly became multidisciplinary with new academic perspectives from behaviour science, sociology and anthropology, focusing on entrepreneurial characteristics, entrepreneurial behaviour, entrepreneurial networks and organisations (Grant, 1998). Such research perspectives led to a focus on entrepreneurs and entrepreneurship beyond the economic sector. Research shed light on entrepreneurship beyond the profit-seeking economic entrepreneur: social entrepreneurs were revealed as innovative leaders in cooperative associations, interest organisations, aid branches, infrastructure development, sustainable development, climate change, union issues, youth leisure, fair trade, animal protection and human rights (Westlund, 2010; Gawell et al., 2009; Borzaga et al., 2008; Brickerhoff, 2000). In more recent years, the multidisciplinary approach to entrepreneurship has also included political entrepreneurs (Scheingate, 2003). A political science perspective on entrepreneurship was introduced by Robert Dahl, who focused on resourceful and masterful leaders in the political sphere. He argued that a political entrepreneur was "the epitome of the self-made man" (1974: 25, 223–7, 282). While *Homo civicus* were active citizens trying to influence politicians to seek favourable policies, *Homo politicus* were citizens formally engaged in politics to shape politics. Based on this study, political entrepreneurship was about politically oriented individual capacity and ability to supply collective benefits to the many, but could also include seeking profit politically. The main objective for the political entrepreneur could be to provide goods/services to the many or a group of people to receive campaign contributions and/or political support (for elected politicians) and for public servants to receive political/administrative support/status (Simmons et al., 2011).

Despite the growing bulk of studies on political entrepreneurship, scholarly work has been criticised on some assumptions. First, most studies have focused on the political entrepreneur from an actor-oriented perspective by exploring the political/public motives behind the political entrepreneurship. It has been assumed that there is an individual profit-seeking objective for the political entrepreneur to act entrepreneurially in the political/public sector. Second, it has also been unclear what actually distinguishes political entrepreneurship from regular political/public activities in the public sector. Many studies have shown that politicians and bureaucrats may alter tax distribution, regulations and implementation procedures, but it is hard to explore how such day-to-day activities actually constitute political entrepreneurship in relation to ordinary political/public actions. The new institutionalism on entrepreneurship has, for example, explored how state authorities, both politicians and bureaucrats, may use coercively collected resources to promote economic activities (e.g. production, channelling tax money into different sectors, welfare distribution) that without state interference would not have happened (McCaffrey and Salerno, 2011: 556–8; see also Jones, 1978; Salerno, 2008; Holcombe, 2002; Schneider and Teske, 1992). Third, there are also questions about whether political entrepreneurship is about providing for change or providing for the status quo. Many studies have implied that political entrepreneurship could be about doing nothing—to seek no changes and to consolidate what is already established.

This study departs from the understanding that political entrepreneurship is about the public sector of public actors and structures (politicians, public servants, bureaucrats, institutions) that seek to create favourable conditions for other entrepreneurs (Silander and Silander, 2015; Karlsson et al., 2016; see also Schneider and Teske, 1992). It is about promoting favourable formal and informal institutions (North, 1990) for economic entrepreneurial activities and shaping and co-ordinating new procedures (McCaffrey and Salerno, 2011: 553) by making use of windows of opportunity (Kingdon, 1984). There is limited research on what political entrepreneurship should consist of to be successful. It must be stated that there is no single political entrepreneurial policy that is to be found as a universal solution to ongoing entrepreneurship, growth and employment. On the contrary, different geographical regions and economic sectors have different conditions. There is, therefore, no clear-cut policy to be implemented, but rather different policies according to the settings in which entrepreneurial activities are to be boosted. The existing research points out that different macroregions (e.g. Europe), nations, subregions and municipalities have different conditions that may be better or worse for economic growth. The role of the political entrepreneur is to interpret and understand the existing conditions and set out innovative measures to promote economic prosperity. It may be to act in new, innovative ways on education, infrastructure, health care, rule of law, bureaucracy or taxation, but the bottom line is to address such conditions with new, bold path-breaking reforms. Political entrepreneurship is about challenging traditional formal institutions in political steering, leadership, strategies, policies, rules, regulations, laws and budgets for entrepreneurial activities and/or to challenge traditional informal institutions in ideas, attitudes, values, perceptions, images and symbols that structure public day-to-day activities and culture around entrepreneurship (North, 1990; Hofstede, 1991; Morgan, 1986; Putnam, 1993; Casson, 1995; Aldrich, 1990; Aldrich and Fiol, 1994). Political entrepreneurship is about challenging existing institutions (Finnemore and Sikkink, 1998: 891) regarding how to promote entrepreneurship and growth. Political entrepreneurship takes place when traditional institutions are challenged and altered and when new institutions, formal and/or informal, are promoted to better serve the interests of entrepreneurial activities and economic growth (Silander, 2016).

Decades of research on European politics and integration have implicitly touched upon what this study explores as European political entrepreneurship in times of economic crisis. The large bulk of research on European studies and EU studies has explicitly and convincingly identified how European and EU politics are changed by new, innovative political ideas and how such progress must be understood from a governance perspective by identifying how contemporary politics is conducted on local, regional, national and European levels (Aberbach and Rockman, 1994; Aberbach et al., 1981; Mintrom and Norman, 2009). Scholarly research on European studies began in the 1950s. The functionalist/neo-functionalist perspective (see Haas, 1958) analysed societal non-state actors as driving forces of integration that impacted political actors within European states in how they conducted politics in a European setting. It was argued that European integration was a "process whereby political actors in several distinct national settings are persuaded to shift their loyalties, expectations, and political activities toward a new centre, whose institutions possess or demand jurisdiction over the pre-existing national states" (Haas, 1958: 16). European integration was the result of societal elites persuading political domestic elites to seek new ventures beyond territorial barriers to fulfil social and economic wants. Political and economic collaboration between elites within one sector was stated to spill over to others, providing for transnational and supranational integration.

Neo-functionalism was debated from an intergovernmentalism perspective (Moravcsik, 1998, 1993) where scholars argued in favour of a viable and powerful sovereign state with entrepreneurial political elites. It was argued that decades of European integration were a result of national governments' decisions to seek collaboration with other governments to solve common social, economic and political challenges. Based on national preferences, governments had for decades initiated negotiations with other European governments by acting politically entrepreneurially to deal with European policy issues and challenges. This led to widened cooperation among more and more member states in an increasing number of policy areas, but also deepened collaboration within such areas based on national interests. It was argued that European integration was a result of commercial interests within major European powers and that the transfer of sovereignty to EU institutions had been based on national strategies to preserve and promote domestic economic interests.[1] As expressed by Moravcsik,

> In a world in which governments are, broadly speaking, rational and instrumental, integration can be seen as a process in which they define a series of underlying objectives or preferences, bargain to substantive agreements concerning cooperation and finally select appropriate international institutions in which to embed them. (1998: 5)

In the 1990s, Europeanisation was conceptually introduced and debated (Radaelli, 2000: 2; Olsen, 2002: 921). Europeanisation referred to a transformative political change in how politics is organised in Europe, but also in political content (Quaglia et al., 2007; Olsen, 2002; Dyson and Goetz, 2002; Börzel, 1999). Europeanisation has developed into a theoretical perspective embedding a top-down and bottom-up approach to political entrepreneurship and European politics. First, scholars have argued that Europeanisation is a top-down transformation of European politics where Europeanisation embeds the political impact from the EU in member states with regional and local authorities (see also Ladrech, 1994; Börzel and Risse, 2000; Hix and Goetz, 2000). Europeanisation refers to decisions taken on a European level, within the EU, and how such decision-making promotes political change within member states (Hix and Goetz, 2000). Top-down Europeanisation includes formal and informal aspects of politics and political entrepreneurship. The formal

---

[1] For ideas on new intergovernmentalism, see Bickerton et al. (2015).

aspects refer to pressure from the EU level on member states to change formal institutions in laws, regulations and policymaking procedures, but also informal institutions in norms, values, political ideas, attitudes and standards of behaviour for how member states conduct politics as part of a European community (Radaelli, 2000).

Europeanisation of member states has come easier in some states compared to others. The closer domestic politics has been to the European "standard", the easier Europeanisation has been in domestic politics. Scholars have talked in terms of domestic fit or misfit to European policies, regulations, norms and values. The more formal and informal EU institutions fit domestic policies and regulations, the smoother the process of Europeanisation. However, a greater misfit includes European pressure on domestic politicians and authorities to adjust to European political expectations (Börzel and Risse, 2000; Olsen, 2002). The scholarly discussion on fit and misfit between EU and individual member states has resulted in analysis of variations of Europeanisation from one state to another. The level of harmonisation between EU and domestic policies, regulations, norms and values may of course vary from one policy area to another, providing a complex system of Europeanisation between the EU level of politics and individual member states. Europeanisation in one policy area may have a high impact on individual states, while in others the misfit may be greater with higher pressure from the EU level but also greater resistance from the domestic level (Cowles et al., 2001; Wallace, 2000).

Second, scholars have also argued against a top-down definition of Europeanisation by describing the two-way process where the EU influences domestic politics, but also vice versa, where politics and political entrepreneurship within member state politics influence politics on a European level and within the EU. This bottom-up approach to Europeanisation (see Börzel, 2002; Risse et al., 2001) stresses the importance of member states and their impact on European politics and on EU institutions (Börzel, 2002). Scholars of bottom-up Europeanisation stress that Europeanisation is a dual process of uploading and downloading and that European states are in no way passive entities, but rather are engaged in forming domestic and European politics in an interactive and interdependent pattern (Risse et al., 2001; Börzel, 2002: 193). Europeanisation as a dual process has gained increasing interest and impact in scholarly studies. Theories on intergovernmentalism have stated that European politics and the EU are a result of individual member states' seeking collaboration through political entrepreneurship in areas where they may be better off from a rational perspective. Europeanisation also comprises, therefore, bottom-up changes where member states individually and together are influencing and shaping EU institutions by uploading domestic agendas, policies, norms and values to a European level (Ladrech, 2010; Quaglia et al., 2007; Börzel and Panke, 2009; Börzel, 2002, 1999).[2] As stated by Olsen,

> Some scholars portray Europeanization as the institutionalization at the European level of a distinct system of governance with common institutions and the authority to make, implement and enforce European-wide binding policies ... Europeanization here includes both the strengthening of an organizational capacity for collective action and the development of common ideas, such as new norms and collective action and the development of common ideas, such as new forms and collective understandings regarding citizenship and membership ... A possible frame for understanding the dynamics and outcomes of European-level institutional development is purposeful choice. Within this frame, which is used by intergovernmentalists in particular, a group of actors have a choice between alternative forms of organization and governance ... They choose the one that, according to its inherent properties or expected effects, is assessed as being most valuable. Institutional developments, then, are seen as reflecting the will, power and understanding of identifiable actors. (2002: 929)

The scholarly literature on top-down and bottom-up Europeanisation and political entrepreneurship is strongly linked to the scholarly debate on governance (Héritier et al., 2001). Europeanisation has implied a transformation of European politics in terms of organisational structure and authoritative institutions, decision-making procedures and norms and values. It has been argued that European politics has come to be conducted on different levels of authority and in new networks of political relations with possibilities for political entrepreneurship from multiple formal actors within European governance. The most obvious political symbols of Europeanisation have been the development of the EU, the transfer of sovereignty to the EU level and the new myriad relations and networks of local, regional, national, transnational and European actors that are today engaged in European politics. Over time, the EU has widened and deepened and become a significant political power in European politics (Quaglia et al., 2007; Hix and Goetz, 2000). It has been most obvious in those policy areas where the EU has supreme authority, but the EU has, through political entrepreneurship, expanded its competence to new policy areas, which has resulted in direct

[2] A third, final approach to Europeanisation has emphasised a mid-approach, a horizontal transfer of politics from one EU member state to another. Horizontal Europeanisation refers to how individual member states influence other member states through cooperation within or outside the EU.

Europeanisation of member states. However, Europeanisation may also come as a consequence of spillover effects from one policy area to another. Therefore, although the member states formally have authority over a policy area, Europeanisation may influence member states and non-member states due to deepened cooperation in one area that leads to cooperation in others (Ladrech, 2010; Wallace, 2000). This has led to a European institutional fuzziness with changed patterns of authority in the multilevel EU governance in national, transnational and EU institutions. Political entrepreneurship, new policy ideas, policy formulation and policymaking and implementation are taking place in contemporary Europe on different levels. Although EU member states and EU institutions are core actors in European politics, there are also transnational, regional and local actors involved in shaping policies in the European system of governance (Marks and Hooghe, 2001). These multilevel authorities are also involved in networks across territories (Castells, 1996; Keohane and Nye, 1977), engaging companies, industries, unions and civil society organisations within education, economics, culture, the environment and social rights with their activities of lobbying and campaigning to impact authorities domestically and on a European level through double-edged diplomacy. As stated by Risse et al.:

> We define Europeanization as the emergence and development at the European level of distinct structures of governance, that is, of political, legal, and social institutions associated with political problem-solving that formalize interactions among the actors, and of policy networks specializing in the creation of authoritative rules. (2001: 3)

It was already argued in the globalisation literature of the 1990s that "political communities are in the process of being transformed" (Held, 2000: 17). In Europe, Europeanisation embeds changes of external European boundaries where Europe as geographical and political space becomes one; Europeanisation embeds the development of European institutions, formal and informal ones, that become a new political structure of coordination, coherence and capacities; Europeanisation implies how such European institutions penetrate national and subnational political space and together construct a multilevel system of European authorities; Europeanisation finally includes how Europe as a political entity and space relates to and promotes European political structures, norms and values regionally and globally beyond European frontiers (Olsen, 2002: 923–4).

The deepening and widening of the EU over the last decades (Avery and Cameron, 1999) has led to a bulk of studies on European transformations and EU governance. The deepening process has included the transfer of sovereignty from member states to the EU in an expanding number of policy areas. The widening process has referred to the increasing number of member states. The EU has become an organisational hybrid of international and supranational cooperation. While most politics is formally organised in terms of state politics, discussions and decisions have increasingly been transferred to the EU level of politics. While some studies on European governance have stressed the EU as sui generis, a unique political phenomenon that needs its own theoretical and empirical studies, EU governance should rather be understood as a regional political entity with advanced levels of regional deepening and widening. EU governance is on one hand about politics and political entrepreneurship in Brussels, Luxembourg and Strasbourg and on the other hand national, regional and local authorities. European governance should, therefore, be understood as a multilevel system of local, regional, state and European authorities engaged in a complex system of politics and political entrepreneurship with top-down and bottom-up processes of Europeanisation (Wallace et al., 2010).

Today, the EU and its member states have a division of competences. This division is referred to in the Treaties and more specifically the Treaty of Lisbon (Lisbon Treaty, 2009). The fundamental division of authority is that the EU has only the competences set out in the Lisbon Treaty. Competences not referred to in the Treaty remain at the state level. The Treaty of Lisbon sets out the division of competences between the EU and its member states in three main categories: exclusive competences, shared competences and supporting competences. First, *exclusive competences* are stated in Article 3 of the Treaty of Lisbon on the Functioning of the European Union; TFEU) and identify areas where the EU as political entity is the main authority to legislate and adopt binding acts. In these areas, individual member states have transferred sovereignty to the collective will of the EU and are only able to implement policies when they are empowered by the EU. It is the EU, through the Commission, that initiates and implements laws and regulations based on the mandate set out in the Treaty. It is the role of the Council, the Parliament and the European Court to assess the rights of the union in relation to what the Treaty says. The EU possesses exclusive competence in the following areas:

—customs union;—the establishing of competition rules necessary for the functioning of the internal market;—monetary policy for euro area

> countries;—conservation of marine biological resources under the common fisheries policy;—common commercial policy;—conclusion of international agreements under certain conditions. (EUR-Lex, 2017: Division of competences within the EU)

Second, *shared competences* are set out in Article 4 of the Treaty of Lisbon and refer to where the EU and member states are mutually able to legislate and adopt legally binding acts. In these areas individual member states are sovereign to decide and legislate as long as the EU has not exercised authority or expressed intention to exercise authority. If an individual member state already has laws and regulations, the EU is not authorised to decide on new laws and regulations that could harm or jeopardise national regulations. Shared competence between the EU and member states is exercised in the following areas:

> —internal market;—social policy, but only for aspects specifically defined in the Treaty;—economic, social and territorial cohesion (regional policy);—agriculture and fisheries (except conservation of marine biological resources);—environment;—consumer protection;—transport;—trans-European networks; —energy;—area of freedom, security and justice;—shared safety concerns in public health matters, limited to the aspects defined in the TFEU;—research, technological development, space;—development cooperation and humanitarian aid. (EUR-Lex, 2017: Division of competences within the EU)

Third and finally, *supporting competences* are listed in Article 6 of the Treaty of Lisbon that state the main authority is the individual member states and the EU may only support, coordinate or complement actions taken by states. The EU has no authority to call for harmonisation of state policies, laws and regulation, and can only have an assisting role in the implementation of decisions taken by states. Supporting competences concern the following:

> —protection and improvement of human health;—industry;—culture;—tourism;—education, vocational training, youth and sport;—civil protection; —administrative cooperation. (EUR-Lex, 2017: Division of competences within the EU)

Traditional policymaking patterns in the EU have been complemented by the use of "soft" governance tools such as benchmarking—recommendations on best practices and guidelines through the *Open Method of Co-ordination process* (OMC). The OMC was launched as part of the package from the Lisbon meeting in 2000 together with the *European Employment Strategy* as a way for the EU to act in areas where national situations differ substantially or where only limited competences exist on the EU level. OMC can be seen as a compromise to retain member state responsibility in an area while at the same time providing the EU with a coordinating and policy-shaping role (Warleigh-Lack and Drachenberg, 2013: 207). New modes of governance, including benchmarking and exchange of best practices, allow member states to co-ordinate policies at the same time as being executives because the member states are responsible for their compliance with the measures they have agreed on at the EU level. The OMC represents a voluntary and intergovernmental mode of cooperation.

In the OMC process, the Commission plays an important monitoring and agenda-setting role. The Council of Ministers is also central as it sets the policy goals and guidelines by unanimity. Member states submit annual reports on their progress and these reports are commented on and evaluated by the Commission. There is not one uniform OMC process; instead, it works differently depending on area. There are, however, a few common steps in the process. Step one is fixing the guidelines for the union combined with a timetable (what is to be completed in the short, medium and long term). Step two is to establish quantitative and qualitative indicators and benchmarks. Step three consists of translating the European guidelines into national and regional policies by setting specific targets and adopting measures for reaching such targets. Step four involves periodic monitoring and evaluations organised as mutual learning processes (see EUR-Lex, OMC, 2017).

The EU competences, in exclusive competences, shared competences and supporting competences, are all based on two fundamental principles of the EU as set out in Article 5 of the Treaty. The first principle is proportionality and refers to how all EU actions should be proportional to the objective to be met; that is, EU actions should not be more than necessary. The second principle is about subsidiarity and how the EU, on issues of non-exclusive competence, should refer decision-making to appropriate levels of authority. The EU is not to act upon issues in areas of non-EU competence, and could only intervene if EU member states are for some reason unable to fulfil the target goals and when such goals can be fulfilled on an EU level. It is important to acknowledge that, where the Treaty does not say anything about authority over policy areas, it is the individual state that has full sovereignty. Policy areas that are not explicitly regulated in the Treaty are formally for member states only to decide. For such policy areas to be included in EU competences requires approval by all member states and thereby a new ratification of a Treaty. It is only Article 352 that provides flexibility on these issues by referring decision-making power to the EU in non-EU policy areas if a measure is required to meet the overall objective of the policy area as set out in the

Treaty. It does, however, require full approval from all member states in the Council of Ministers and approval from the European Parliament. The different kinds of competences leave the EU as a political hybrid of authorities where EU institutions represent union interests (Commission), member states' interests (Council of Ministers) and citizens' interests (Parliament) (see Lisbon Treaty). It should, however, also be stated that the three categories of competences only portray the official way politics is handled. In the daily life of politics these competences are challenged by practical hindrances and possibilities. Although the EU has exclusive competence in certain areas, it consists of member states in the Council of Ministers and national politicians in the Parliament who influence and decide on political issues that are thereafter to be implemented by national politicians and public servants at home. It should also be stated that in those areas where member states have full authority, often the decisions made and the laws implemented are influenced by the EU system, as national and European politics is interwoven in a network of official and unofficial ties.

EUROPE 2020 AND THE STRUCTURE OF THIS STUDY

In the famous and strategically important European Commission Communication of 2010, *Europe 2020—A strategy for smart, sustainable and inclusive growth*, the Commission called for European political entrepreneurship throughout the governance system of European authorities to act as a countermeasure to the existing economic crisis. The Commission argued that fundamental efforts beyond day-to-day activities had to be implemented by multiple formal actors: "The crisis is a wake-up call, the moment where we recognise that 'business as usual' would consign us to a gradual decline, to the second rank of the new global order. This is Europe's moment of truth. It is the time to be bold and ambitious" (European Commission, 2010: preface).

Europe 2020 embedded numerous initiatives with a focus on more jobs, research and innovation, climate change policies and energy, education and poverty reduction. Major and immediate reforms in these areas were portrayed by the Commission as urgent, necessary transformations to serve as countermeasures to the devastating economic and social impact the crisis had had on Europe. In the Communication, three main innovative objectives were identified in smart, sustainable and inclusive growth. It referred to smart growth in promoting an economy based on knowledge and innovation, sustainable growth based on resource efficiency and a greener economy and inclusive growth providing for social integration (European Commission, 2010: 5). To meet these goals, the Commission developed seven flagship initiatives and guidelines for how such flagships had to be launched and implemented through a shared European partnership from a multilevel governance perspective, including political, economic and social actors from local to European levels:

> The European Council will have full ownership and be the focal point of the new strategy. The Commission will monitor progress towards the targets, facilitate policy exchange and make the necessary proposals to steer action and advance the EU flagship initiatives. The European Parliament will be a driving force to mobilise citizens and act as co-legislator on key initiatives. This partnership approach should extend to EU committees, to national parliaments and national, local and regional authorities, to social partners and to stakeholders and civil society so that everyone is involved in delivering on the vision. (European Commission, 2010: 6)

Europe 2020 proposed that the European Council would steer the project and consolidate the integration of policies and initiatives between the EU and member states through political guidance and direction. The Council of Ministers would implement flagship initiatives and discuss good practices. The Commission would annually monitor the progress made on each goal towards a smart, green and inclusive economy, assess member states' reports and provide policy recommendations. The European Parliament would engage citizens and civil society organisations and finally national, regional and local authorities individually and through the Committee of Regions to implement Europe 2020 by developing necessary and appropriate reforms in collaboration with citizens, civil society organisations and local businesses and entrepreneurs. European governance had to overcome different business structures, low levels of investment in research and enterprise, limited use of communication technologies and reluctance to see opportunities and innovations through shared new, bold commitments (European Commission, 2010: 28–30). Agenda 2020 should be perceived as an overall framework for European governance on the European economic crisis of 2007–2008 and onwards. The Agenda stressed the importance of both multilevel governance and political entrepreneurship in the economic crisis to see a future European economy of growth, entrepreneurship, employment and social integration. This chapter has addressed the notions of European governance and European political entrepreneurship in times of European economic crisis. It has been argued that Europeanisation is a transformative change of Europe and includes top-down and bottom-up dimensions. These dimensions of Europeanisation have influenced the organisation and content of European politics. The scholarly studies on governance have stressed how contemporary Europe is politically organised in a multilevel system. The many political authorities on different political levels are essential ingredients in what European governance looks like today. In a time of economic stress, the EU Commission and European governments have called for new, innovative political initiatives within the system of multilevel European governance to set out a new European path towards economic growth and prosperity.

Based on the above introduction, this study on European governance and political entrepreneurship in times of economic crisis is structured into four themes and a final concluding part. First, the theme of *Framework of Study*, including Chapters 1, 2 and 3, introduces a theoretical and conceptual discussion on political entrepreneurship. It is argued that, in times of economic stress, political entrepreneurship is essential to find new ways of promoting growth, employment and welfare. This combines an actor-structure approach by discussing political entrepreneurs as the actors that are creative and innovative and develop, consolidate and coordinate networks. Second, the theme on *European Institutions on Entrepreneurship and Regional Growth*, covered in Chapters 4 to 6, explores the three main bodies of the EU—the Commission, the Council of Ministers and the European Parliament—and their visions, programmes, strategies and debates on how to push for entrepreneurial development and growth in Europe. There are multiple models and theories on how policies could be developed and implemented and what the institutional framework for entrepreneurship may look like. These chapters explore how the three EU institutions reacted to the emerging economic crisis and acted to limit its negative consequences on the EU by forming new initiatives and policies to promote entrepreneurship and growth. They further identify internal debates and divisions on possible decisions and strategies to be taken and search for signs of political entrepreneurship by scrutinising official documents, action plans, debates and speeches.

Third, the theme of *EU Embedded Policies on Entrepreneurship and Regional Growth*, in Chapters 7 to 10, focuses on the role of political entrepreneurship within important EU policy areas. In its efforts to increase economic growth and employment, the EU has been interested in promoting entrepreneurship and growth through support from other policy areas. European politicians have often emphasised how the European economy needs to be supported by all policy areas and groups of society. EU policies often refer future economic growth to new industrial smart policies, policies on higher education, agriculture and migration etc., but also through entrepreneurial diversity in the importance of including women, immigrants and young adults in established economic and social networks for political and economic entrepreneurship.

Fourth, the theme of *Case Studies on Local Political Entrepreneurship*, in Chapters 11 and 12, addresses local/regional political entrepreneurship in times of Europeanisation, glocalisation (globalisation and localisation) and urbanisation and how local/regional actors in cities and municipalities may address ongoing economic structural transformations based on political entrepreneurship to see local growth, employment and social welfare. Both cities and municipalities are actors often addressed in the European debate as core entities for local and regional growth, employment and sustainable welfare. In a time of glocalisation, political entrepreneurship must not only be initiated from a top-down perspective, but more importantly be addressed by local initiatives to mitigate and adjust to major structural changes in Europe.

The fifth and final part, *Concluding Remarks*, Chapter 13, summarises the main findings or lessons learned on European governance and political entrepreneurship. This concluding part sheds light on how the political entrepreneur and political entrepreneurship are particularly important in times of economic crisis where normal work routines and everyday work do not necessarily solve European economic and societal challenges. In a time of profound socioeconomic challenges, it is particularly important to see political entrepreneurship that challenges traditional formal and informal institutions. The study on political entrepreneurship is thus to study what alternative approaches European politicians, bureaucrats, officials and institutions may take to provide better conditions for entrepreneurship and growth in Europe.

REFERENCES

Aberbach, J.D. and B.A. Rockman (1994). "Civil servants and policymakers: neutral or responsive competence?", *Governance*, 7(4): 461–9.

Aberbach, J.D., R.D. Putnam and B.A. Rockman (1981). *Bureaucrats and Politicians in Western Democracies*. Cambridge, MA: Harvard University Press.

Aldrich, H.E. (1990). "Using an ecological perspective to study organization founding rates", *Entrepreneurship Theory and Practise*, 19(4): 7–24.

Aldrich, H.E. and M.C. Fiol (1994). "Fools rush in? – The institutional context of industry creation", *Academy of Management Review*, 19(4): 645–70.

Amadeo, K. (2016). "11 Causes of the Economic Recession", *The Balance*. 28 December, accessed 21 March 2017 at https://www.thebalance.com/causes-of-economic-recession-3306010.

Avery, G. and F. Cameron (1999). *The Enlargement of the European Union*. Sheffield: Sheffield Academic Press.

Bickerton, C., D. Hodson and U. Puetter (2015). "The new intergovernmentalism: European integration in the post-Maastricht era", *Journal of Common Market Studies*, 53(4): 703–22.

Borzaga, C., G. Galera and R. Nogales (eds) (2008). *Social Enterprise: A New Model for Poverty Reduction and Employment Generation – An Examination of the Concept and Practice in Europe and the Commonwealth of Independent States*. UNDP Regional Bureau for Europe and the Commonwealth of Independent States.

Börzel, T. (1999). "Towards convergence in Europe? Institutional adaption to Europeanization in Germany and Spain", *Journal of Common Market Studies*, 39(4): 573–96.

Börzel, T. (2002). "Pace-setting, foot-dragging, and fence-sitting: Member State responses to Europeanization", *Journal of Common Market Studies*, 40(2): 193–214.

Börzel, T. and D. Panke (2009). "Europeanization", in M. Cini and N. Pérez-Solórzano Borragán (eds), *European Union Politics*. Oxford and New York: Oxford University Press.

Börzel, T. and T. Risse (2000). *When Europe Hits Home: Europeanization and Domestic Change*. Florence: European University Institute, No. 2000/56.

Brickerhoff, P.C. (2000). *Social Entrepreneurship – The Art of Mission-Based Venture Development*. New York: John Wiley and Sons.

Casson, M.C. (1995). *Entrepreneurship and Business Culture*. Aldershot and Brookfield, VT: Edward Elgar.

Castells, M. (1996). *The Rise of the Network Society: The Information Age: Economy, Society and Culture*, Vol. 1. Oxford: Blackwells.

Com (2008). "'Think Small First' – A 'Small Business Act' for Europe", 394 final. Brussels: European Commission.

Cowles, M.G., J.A. Caporaso and T. Risse (2001). *Transforming Europe: Europeanization and Domestic Change*. Ithaca, NY: Cornell University Press.

Dahl, R.A. (1974). *Who Governs? Democracy and Power in an American City*. New Haven, CT: Yale University Press.

Dullien, S., J. Detlef, J. Kotte, A. Márquez and J. Priewe (2010). "Introduction", in S. Dullien, J. Detlef, J. Kotte, A. Márquez and J. Priewe (eds), *The Financial and Economic Crisis of 2008–2009 and Developing Countries*. United Nations: New York and Geneva.

Dyson, K. and K. Goetz (2002). Conference Paper (unpublished) – *Germany and Europe: Beyond Congruence*. 11 March 2002 at Conference British Academy.

EUR-Lex, OMC (2017). *Open Method of Coordination*, accessed 17 October 2017 at http://eur-lex.europa.eu/summary/glossary/open_method_coordination.html.

European Commission (2009). *Economic Crisis in Europe: Causes, Consequences and Responses – European Economy 7*. Brussels: DG Economic and Financial Affairs.

European Commission (2010). *Europe 2020 – A Strategy for Smart, Sustainable and Inclusive Growth*. COM (2010) 2020 final. Brussels: European Commission.

European Commission (April 2015). *European Financial Stability and Integration – Commission Staff Working Document on European Financial Stability and Integration Review*. SWD 98 final. Brussels: European Commission.

FCIC – The Financial Crisis Inquiry Commission (2011). *The Financial Crisis Inquiry Report – Final Report of the National Commission on the Causes of the Financial and Economic Crisis in the United States*. Washington DC: U.S. Government Printing Office.

Financial Times (2016). *The 2008 to 2009 Global Financial Crisis Unfolds*, accessed 11 May 2017 at http://lexicon.ft.com/Term?term=global-financial-crisis.

Finnemore, M. and K. Sikkink (1998). "International norm dynamics and political change", *International Organizations*, 52(4): 887–917.

Gawell, M., B. Johannisson and M. Lundqvist (2009). *Samhällets entreprenörer – En forskarantologi om samhällsentreprenörskap* (Social Entrepreneurs – A Research Anthology on Social Entrepreneurship). Stockholm: KK-stiftelsen.

Grant, A. (1998). "Entrepreneurship – the major academic discipline for the business economic curriculum for the 21st century", in M.G. Scott, P. Rosa and H. Klandt (eds), *Educating Entrepreneurs for Wealth Education*. Burlington, VT: Ashgate.

Haas, E.B. (1958). *The Uniting of Europe*. Stanford, CA: Stanford University Press.

Held, D. (2000). "The changing contours of political community – rethinking democracy in the context of globalization", in B. Holden (ed.), *Global Democracy: Key Debates*. London and New York: Routledge.

Héritier, A., D. Kerwer, C. Knill, D. Lehmkuhl, M. Teutsch and A.C. Douillet (2001). *Differential Europe: The European Union Impact on National Policymaking*. Lanham, MD: Rowman & Littlefield.

Hix, S. (1998). "The study of the European Union 11: the new governance agenda and its rivals", *Journal of European Public Policy*, 5(1): 38–65.

Hix, S. and K. Goetz (2000). "Introduction: European integration and national political systems", *West European Politics*, 23(4): 1–26.

Hofstede, G. (1991). *Organisationer och kulturer – om interkulturell förståelse* (Organizations and Cultures – Intercultural Understanding). Lund: Studentlitteratur.

Holcombe, R.G. (2002). "Political entrepreneurship and the democratic allocation of economic resources", *The Review of Austrian Economics*, 15(2/3): 143–59.

Jones, P. (1978). "The appeal of the political entrepreneur", *British Journal of Political Science*, 8(4): 498–504.

Karlsson, C., D. Silander and C. Silander (2016). *Political Entrepreneurship – Regional Growth and Entrepreneurial Diversity in Sweden*. Cheltenham: Edward Elgar.

Keohane, R.O. and J.S. Nye Jr. (1977). *Power and Interdependence: World Politics in Transition*. Boston, MA: Little, Brown.

Kingdon, J.W. (1984). *Agendas, Alternatives and Public Policies*. New York: HarperCollins.

Ladrech, R. (1994). "Europeanization of domestic politics and institutions: the case of France", *Journal of Common Market Studies*, 32(1): 69–88.

Ladrech, R. (2010). *Europeanization and National Politics*. Basingstoke: Palgrave Macmillan.
Lisbon Treaty (2009). *The Lisbon Treaty*, accessed 17 October 2017 at http://www.lisbon-treaty.org/wcm/the-lisbon-treaty/treaty-on-european-union-and-comments/title-1-common-provisions/9-article-5.html.
Marks, G. and L. Hooghe (2001). *Multilevel Governance and European Integration*. Lanham, MD: Rowman & Littlefield.
McCaffrey, M. and J.T. Salerno (2011). "A theory of political entrepreneurship", *Modern Economy*, 2(4): 552–60.
Mintrom, M. and P. Norman (2009). "Policy entrepreneurship and policy change", *The Policy Studies Journal*, 37(4): 649–67.
Moravcsik, A. (1993). "Preferences and power in the European community: a liberal intergovernmentalist approach", *Journal of Common Market Studies*, 31(4): 473–524.
Moravcsik, A. (1998). *The Choice of Europe – Social Purpose and State Power from Messina to Maastricht*. London and New York: Routledge.
Morgan, G. (1986). *Images of Organizations*. Los Angeles, CA: Sage Publications.
Nier, E. and G. Forte (2016). *Preventing the Next Financial Crisis*. Washington, DC: International Monetary Fund.
North, D.C. (1990). *Institutions, Institutional Change and Economic Performance*. Cambridge: Cambridge University Press.
Olsen, J.P. (2002). "The many faces of Europeanization", *Journal of Common Market Studies*, 40(5): 921–52.
Putnam, R. (1993). *Making Democracy Work – Civic Traditions in Modern Italy*. Princeton, NJ: Princeton University Press.
Quaglia, L., M. Miyakoshi and M. Cini (2007). "Europeanization", in M. Cini (ed.), *European Union Politics*, 2nd edition. Oxford: Oxford University Press.
Radaelli, C. (2000). "Whither Europeanization? Concept stretching and substantive change", *European Integration*, online papers, 4/8.
RealtyTrac (2008). *U.S. Foreclosure Activity Increase 75 percent in 2007*. 30 January, accessed 25 April 2017 at http://www.realtytrac.com/content/press-releases/us-foreclosure-activity-increases-75-percent-in-2007-3604.
Rhodes, R.A.W. (1996). "The new governance: governing without government", *Political Studies*, 44(3): 652–67.
Risse, T., M.G. Cowles and J. Caporaso (2001). "Europeanization and domestic change: introduction", in T. Risse, M.G. Cowles and J. Caporaso (eds), *Transforming Europe: Europeanization and Domestic Change*. Ithaca, NY: Cornell University Press.
Salerno, J.T. (2008). "The entrepreneur: real and imagined", *Quarterly Journal of Austrian Economics*, 11(3): 188–207.
Scheingate, A.D. (2003). "Political entrepreneurship, institutional change and American political development", *Studies in American Political Development*, 17(2): 185–203.
Schneider, M. and P. Teske (1992). "Toward a theory of the political entrepreneur: evidence from local government", *American Political Science Review*, 86(3): 737–47.

Schumpeter, J.A. (1943). *Capitalism, Socialism and Democracy*. London: Unwin.
Silander, D. (2016). "The political entrepreneur", in C. Karlsson, D. Silander and C. Silander (eds), *Political Entrepreneurship – Regional Growth and Entrepreneurial Diversity in Sweden*. Cheltenham and Northampton: Edward Elgar.
Silander, D. and C. Silander (2015). *Politiskt Entreprenörskap – den offentliga sektorns sätt att skapa bättre förutsättningar för entreprenörskap lokalt, regional och nationellt (Political Entrepreneurship)* – (Public Sector Ways to Create Better Conditions for Entrepreneurship Locally, Regionally and Nationally), Stockholm: Santérus förlag.
Simmons, R.T., R.M. Yonk and D.W. Thomas (2011). "Bootleggers, baptists, and political entrepreneurs – key players in the rational game and morality play of regulatory politics", *The Independent Review*, 15(3): 367–81.
Suter, C. and M. Herkenrath (2012). *World Society in the Global Economic Crisis*. Zurich/Berlin: LIT Verlag Dr W Hopf.
The Economist (2007). *CSI: Credit Crunch*. 17 October, accessed 21 March 2017 at http://www.economist.com/node/9972489.
The Economist (2017). *Economist – A Helping Hand to Homeowners*, accessed 25 April 2017 at http://www.economist.com/node/12470547.
The State of the Nation's Housing (2008). *Joint Center for Housing Studies of Harvard University*. Harvard: 2008 President and Fellows of Harvard College.
Turcu, C., N. Karadimitriou and S. Chaytor (2015). *The Impact of the Global Financial and Economic Crisis on European Cities*. London: University College London, accessed 3 April 2017 at https://www.ucl.ac.uk/public-policy/for-policy-professionals/research-insights/Crisis_briefing.pdf.
Wallace, H. (2000). "Europeanisation and globalisation: complementary or contradictory trends?", *New Political Economy*, 5(3): 369–82.
Wallace, H., M.A. Pollack and A.R. Young (2010). "An overview" in H. Wallace, M.A. Pollack and A.R. Young (eds), *Policy-Making the European Union*. Oxford: Oxford University Press.
Warleigh-Lack, A. and R. Drachenberg (2013). "Policymaking in the European Union", in M. Cini and N. Pérez-Solórzano Borragán (eds), *European Union Politics*, 4th edition. Oxford: Oxford University Press, pp. 199–212.
Westlund, H. (2010). *Multidimensional Entrepreneurship: Theoretical Considerations and Swedish Empirics: Conference Paper*, 19–23 August 2010. Jönköping: European Regional Science Association, Sweden.

2. Political entrepreneurs as actors in governance networks: conceptualising political entrepreneurs through the actor-network approach

Elin Wihlborg

INTRODUCTION

Political entrepreneurs play a crucial role in the networked governance structure of contemporary policymaking (c.f. von Bergmann-Winberg and Wihlborg, 2011; Narbutaité, et al. 2015; Karlsson et al., 2016). In times of economic stress and crisis policymaking, delivery relies even more on new innovative and creative methods of promoting growth in different ways that provide sustainable welfare to society. In this context, there is an increased need for political entrepreneurs. Political entrepreneurs can be regarded as the actors knitting governance networks together (Wihlborg, 2015). Still, political science analyses lack a focus on actors and their networks.

Political entrepreneurs need to be understood in the processes of change that they are making. They have ambitions to change and form new networks to get issues addressed and managed (Mintrom and Norman, 2009). The process-oriented approach of policymaking is a way of including temporal aspects into the analysis of policymaking and governance networks (Pollitt and Bouckaert, 2011). These processes are not just happening; rather, they are being facilitated by what Kingdon (1995) calls the policy entrepreneurs. They identify and use the policy window to make innovative changes.

Political entrepreneurs can be identified at almost all levels of multi-level governance systems and in different policy areas, as we show throughout this edited volume. But who can be a political entrepreneur? What are their roles in relation to the networks, and how (and why) can they gain and express power to make changes? These are critical issues and basic preconditions for our understanding of political entrepreneurs.

In this chapter, I will address these issues by focusing on political entrepreneurs as actors, as well as on their networks. Because the actor is mostly hidden in the networked governance literature, I will use the sociological literature of actor-network theory (ANT) (Law and Callon, 1989; Latour, 2005) to enhance our actor-oriented analysis. A basic constituent of the ANT approach is that both human and non-human actors are included as actors in the network.[1] The ANT analysis focuses on social changes and translations by considering all actors included in the network and their asymmetric power relations. This approach helps to explore how networks are built or assembled and maintained to achieve a specific objective (Latour, 2005). It also has the potential to extend our understanding and interpretations of political entrepreneurs.

The aim of this chapter is to increase and extend our political scientific understanding of political entrepreneurs and policy networks. I posit that the sociological approach of the ANT can make an important contribution to our understanding of political entrepreneurs. Academic disciplines discipline us as scholars in different ways. The discipline of political science focuses mainly on politics as that which takes place in formal political institutions. Thereby, political science-based analyses most often delimit the political actors to those who participate in political institutions and related organisations. On the other hand, sociology in general and ANT in particular take a more open approach to what can be regarded as political. A sociological interpretation of politics includes all everyday activities in which power and meanings are interpreted and negotiated among actors.

This chapter will contribute to setting the scene for the discussions of political entrepreneurs in a networked governance perspective. By combining the political scientific discourse on policy networks and political entrepreneurs with the sociological ANT, I will show the potential of adding an actor–network perspective to the analysis of how political entrepreneurs form policy networks.

---

[1] For example, in the European Parliament, networks can be formed including actors such as single human members of parliament, party groups, interest organisations, the institutional arrangements of decision-making and policy processes in the parliament, and the proposals and counter proposals. All of these actors can provide meanings, both in material and semiotic ways, through the network they form, and thereby, they circumscribe the outcomes of the policy process.

The final discussion of this chapter will focus on three questions about how the ANT approach can enrich the research field of political entrepreneurship.

1. Who can be an actor in an actor network, and how can the broader interpretation of actors enhance our understanding of political entrepreneurs?
2. What can we learn by seeing how political entrepreneurs are embedded in, and at the same time forming, their networks?
3. What interpretations of power can we add to the policy analysis by seeing the political entrepreneur in the context of the ANT?

Before these questions are addressed, I will make a short note on the research design and methods. In the second section, I will study the political entrepreneur literature in relation to networked governance from a political science perspective. Then the approach of the ANT will be introduced, with a focus on how to relate to political entrepreneurs and policy networks. Based on these two perspectives, the three questions above will be discussed before some final implications are set out.

Political Entrepreneurs in Policy Networks and Governance Structures

The research field on entrepreneurship is interdisciplinary. It is addressed in fields such as organisation studies, sociology, business administration, organisation theory and innovation studies (c.f. Ács and Audretsch, 2006). The focus is on how human actors work in an entrepreneurial manner to be innovative regarding the content of policies, the ways politics manoeuvre and the problems that are addressed. Hereby, the entrepreneurial approach is related to theories and models in fields such as political science, public administration and politics.

In the introduction of this volume, the author presented a definition of political entrepreneurs including both actor and structure perspectives by focusing on a politician/bureaucrat/officer/institution within the publicly funded sector that, with innovative approaches, encourages entrepreneurship/business and where the goal is growth and employment as counter-measures to economic crisis. This definition also points to the wide impact of political entrepreneurs and political entrepreneurship because it influences the conditions for entrepreneurship and business. The political entrepreneur can be seen as a single human individual acting in entrepreneurial terms on a personal interest. However, the concept can also be used to visualise and analyse structural settings and institutional arrangements that support such behaviours. In between such individual and structural ways of political entrepreneurship, there are also organisations on a meso-level that both support the individual actor and connect the institutional framing to the daily setting of the individual. This is the networked governance setting.

Networked governance as the context of political entrepreneurs

The interactive forms of networked governance work both within and as a complementary structure for traditional governance within hierarchical government structures (Sørensen and Torfing, 2007; Torfing and Triantafillou, 2011). Networked governance is an open and collaborative form of governance (Kooiman, 2003), but it relies on the structures of government (Pierre and Peters, 2000). The improved collaboration of private and public partnerships is a core aspect of networked governance, focusing on complex policymaking through horizontal interaction among actors and organisations, which can be public, private or somewhere in between.

In the field of political science, networked governance has been considered not only a growing empirical phenomenon, but also an analytical lens through which policymaking processes can be understood (Carlsson, 2000; Rhodes and Marsh, 1992). In this light, the actors who form networks around specific policy problems become a relevant analytical unit to analyse in the study of policymaking, but before deconstructing the meanings of such actor networks, I will further elaborate on the conceptualisation of networked governance.

Policy networks can also include integrative and collaborative policymaking processes formed in governance settings that cross over sectoral borders, including both private and public actors, and not least crossing the borders that have formed our multi-level governance systems (Agranoff, 2006; Carlsson, 2000; Klijn et al., 2010). Networks are not formed by themselves; activities and projects within the networks do not just happen. So even if the networked governance approach is mainly a structural approach to analyse new forms of policymaking, there is an obvious actor-level impact of actors making these structural changes come through.

The actors of the governance networks, representing different societal sectors, also have various and maybe even opposing beliefs and values. The complexity of values and beliefs in contemporary policy problems has caused the formation of collaboration structures where networks function as sense-making arenas for policymaking (Persson, 2014) or as vertical levels of governance (Koppenjan and Klijn, 2004). Networked governance often entails a cross-sectoral collaborative approach that promotes sustainable and innovative management structures, public–private partnerships as triple-helix structures (Elg et al., 2015).

The networks are based on a complex web of values, resources and interests that are exchanged and negotiated through the networked governance processes (Rhodes and Marsh, 1992; Sandström and Carlsson, 2008). The networks are formed in relation to the specific policy issues and the available scarce resources, various uncertainties regarding the strategic choices, and the locations where the issues are to be solved (Newell, 2017).

Public policies are becoming more networked and there are new forms of quasi-markets, such as public–private partnerships, so there is growing potential (and possibly even a need) for different types of (policy) entrepreneurial activities. The increased use of public–private partnership demands policy entrepreneurial activities to build partnerships and form entrepreneurial regions (von Bergmann-Winberg and Wihlborg, 2011). Policy entrepreneurs, as argued above, play a key role in the context of networked governance.

Kingdon's (1995) focus on policy processes included the coordination of three streams: the problem stream, the political stream and the policy stream. The problem stream is formed when there is a common agreement on what has to be changed. The political stream is formed in the institutional arrangements of how decision-making takes place and finally, policies are the potential outcomes and solutions to the specific problem as it has been addressed in the political setting. When these three streams are coordinated and related, they can open a window of opportunity, a policy window. Through such a policy window, the policy entrepreneur can make creative connections. Kingdon (1995) used the concept of policy entrepreneur because he focused on policies as the outputs of the processes. When we use the concept of political entrepreneurship here, there is a slightly different focus, as presented by Silander in the first chapter, because we explicitly focus on innovations and contributions to growth and market developments. Based on Kingdon's argumentation, one can, however, distinguish the *policy entrepreneur* as the one focusing on the policy outputs and the content of the policy. This is in contrast to the *political entrepreneur* as the one focusing on the political game and innovative ways of finding coalitions and muddling through the political system (Assmo and Wihlborg, 2016). This conceptualisation builds on Kingdon's (1995) classical focus on the three streams of problems, politics and policy. The political entrepreneur is, according to this definition, taking off from the political stream and the structure to determine how, by whom and when problems can be solved. The policy entrepreneur on the other hand, in this perspective, takes off in the problem stream, focusing on possible policy solutions that can be identified even outside the political structures and the agenda, such as innovations and development in other contexts.

Political entrepreneurs are building the policy networks

Kingdon's original definition described policy entrepreneurs as being "willing to invest their resources – time, energy, reputation, money – to promote a position in return for anticipated future gain in the form of material, purposive, solidary benefits" (Kingdon, 1995: 179). This broad conceptualisation of policy entrepreneurs focuses on what they do and why, but not where, when and how in relation to the political arena and the structures.

Policy entrepreneurs do not necessarily act from one single organisational base, but rather show flexibility and rearrange networks for each policy issue (Mintrom and Norman, 2009). Political entrepreneurs are the ones building the policy networks that are the basis of the networked governance setting. Hereby, they manage through the specific institutional arrangements of the policy issues. Because it is obvious how they manage through and even develop institutional settings, political entrepreneurs are similar to what are sometimes seen as institutional entrepreneurs (see Chapter 3 in this volume). Institutional entrepreneurs are those who are entrepreneurial, not only in relation to a single issue, but also aim to reset the institution as such by transforming existing institutions or even forming new institutions (Garud et al., 2007). The approach to institutional entrepreneurship emerged through new institutionalism, which also shows how institutions as state authorities and institutional arrangements as such can promote economic activities.

To sum up, policy entrepreneurs expend considerable time, energy and resources to initiate policies because of the potential policy and political benefits engendered by redesigning the policy arena (Kingdon, 1995; Mintrom, 1997). There has to be a policy window giving the political entrepreneur opportunities to combine problems by building networks in the political context and mobilising resources for a policy. Political entrepreneurs coordinate and form the governance practice by building governance networks. Thus, there is a need to further elaborate on how and why they can contribute to network formation by relating the framework of political entrepreneurs in governance networks to the literature on ANT.

The Actor-Network Theory (ANT) Approach – The Networked Context

It is obvious that political entrepreneurs form, and at the same time are formed, by the policy networks they are working through. Thus, there is a close connection between the analytical perspectives on political entrepreneurs and the extensive research on networks in contemporary social sciences (c.f. Sandström and Carlsson, 2008). To grasp the constructive approach of networks and their relations to the complex interplay of different actors and structures, as highlighted above, I will relate the political entrepreneurship concept to the specific theories and analytical approaches of ANT (Law and Hassard, 1999; Latour, 2005). This sociological approach is extending the meanings of actors as well as of networks as such.

ANT as a network approach to translation of social change

In ANT, a basic notion is that social changes take place when actors actively translate meanings and resources from one setting into another. Thereby, they are knitting their network together. The network gives the actors a role and function, and the actors make the network sustaining and meaningful. Through the process of translation, the actors bring resources together and form a network to enact the changes they strive for. Translation takes place through networks and thus, a network can either stabilise or hamper such social changes (Czarniawska and Sevon, 2005; Latour, 2005).

Translation, as an analytical focus in the ANT approach, enables visualising and deconstructing how and why meanings are formed, developed and changed in the network. Translation, in the ANT approach, is analysed as an empirically based, bottom-up process. A core expression of this analytical perspective is to follow the actor through his or her network. By following the actor, the process of translation is uncovered (Law and Callon, 1989). The processes of forming and reforming actor networks are processes of translation (Latour, 2005; Harman, 2014). Translation focuses on how humans and artefacts and their meanings are translated among contexts and actors over time.

The translation in a network is not made on an equal basis; the actors in the network have different resources and capacities to influence and form the translation. In a study of how digitalisation was translated into local public administration, Gustafsson (2017) showed the roles of different actors in the translation process and how they established networks to reassemble the common meanings and ideas that they could translate into the new digitalisation practices. A translation process includes an active and motivated adoption to the receiving setting, in contrast to the passive transferring process (Latour, 2005). The key actors managing the translation and forming the networks are called mediators.

Mediators – the actors forming the network

The goal of the ANT approach is to be inclusive and to consider actors for what they perform. Power is here seen as an outcome of relations rather than deriving from the actor's general status or position (Latour, 2005). However, not all actors contribute to network building in the same way. Among the actors, the mediator has been identified as the critical actor facilitating networking (Law and Callon, 1989; Latour, 2005). A mediator has much in common with a political entrepreneur. Mediators translate rather than transfer information and knowledge to make a new network emerge (Wihlborg, 2015). By considering policy entrepreneurs as mediators in processes of change, other attributes and functions in the innovative practices may be identified (Wihlborg and Söderholm, 2013).

The focus on mediators is set in ANT's focus on translation processes. Translation has also been used in broader organisational analyses beyond ANT (c.f. Rövik, 2000; Czarniawska and Sevon, 2005). In such processes of translation, the critical actor is the mediator. The mediator is the key actor mediating ideas, values and resources by promoting and sometimes conducting the translation. In the translation process, the mediator, any type of actor, facilitates processes but does not always have to be active or present in the process. A traditional mediator as an arbitrator can facilitate a discussion and make the parties meet without actively getting involved in the discussion. However, the mediator can also translate meaning from one actor to another. The mediator's translation of meanings forms the network and holds it together (Czarniawska and Sevon, 2005). Mediators are actors that have power to enhance translation, as well as invite and involve other actors in the network; thus, they are similar to political entrepreneurs (Wihlborg, 2015). However, in contrast to the concept of political entrepreneurs, the ANT approach also extends the meaning of actors and thereby who can be an actor in the actor network.

The extensive meanings of actors in ANT

The ANT builds on a broad notion of who, or even what, can be an actor (Law and Hassard, 1999; Latour, 2005). For most social scientists, it may be complicated to see actors as something other than single human individuals, or maybe organisations. On an ontological level, ANT does not separate properties such as "technology" and "the social" (Law, 1992). Based on this integrative understanding of how networks embed actors and how actors are given meanings by their networks, some key analytical concepts are developed to describe and analyse processes of social change (Harman, 2014). Through the network, the human and non-human actors associate in different ways. They shape the virtue of their relations with one another through the network. In ANT, it is assumed that nothing lies outside the network of relations. As soon as actors are associated, they make up the network and can contribute to change in a new way, completely different from what they can do on their own.

The power to form and keep the network together

Power is indeed a disputed concept in ANT (Harman, 2014). It is based on the notion that translation is a political process. Translation includes political dimensions in terms of struggles for power, alliance building and representation of interests among actors in networks (Callon and Law, 1995). Through the network, actors are associated and the association defines the role of the actor in the specific setting and translates the meanings of the actors and the meanings they want to give power in the relations. In Latour's writing (1999: 165), "an event is created at the occasion of each of those associations", which indicates that networks are sets of occasions when actors are given meanings. The actor has the power to define and select which association he or she makes. This is how translations continue to go on and how the occasions are linked together in a chain of translation.

Power is relational, and in the ANT approach power thus becomes a basic notion because it is all about relations in networks. It is the relations in the network that form the meanings of an actor and thereby the power of the actor. The actor is giving, and given, meanings through his or her relations in the network. Thereby, power is always based in the network. Or, as Harman (2014) puts it, the actors are formed by their networks and the networks are formed by their actors.

Political Entrepreneurs in an Actor Network – Analysis and Discussion

This chapter elaborates on the meanings of political entrepreneurs in relation to ANT. The main contribution, grounded in letting the political entrepreneurs be seen through the lenses of the ANT (Latour, 2005), is that political entrepreneurs are nothing without their networks and the networks are nothing without the political entrepreneurs. The network needs to be a fruitful soil nurturing the growth of the political entrepreneur and contributing to policy changes. This general standpoint – on the co-construction of the political entrepreneur and his or her network – has implications for how we approach the political entrepreneur. This will be further discussed in this section. Three main points will be highlighted. First, I extend the meanings of who, and even what, can be regarded as an actor in a network. Second, the political entrepreneur and his or her network will be regarded as co-constructed. Finally, I discuss how the political entrepreneur can gain and sustain power in networks.

The first implication: extending the meanings of the actor

Starting from the overall contribution of this chapter, ANT extends the meanings of actors in a way that is indeed relevant for the interpretations of political entrepreneurs. When the political entrepreneur is seen in relation to his or her actor network, it allows for a more elaborative understanding of whom and what can be an actor in such a network. In this perspective, everything included in the network can be regarded as an actor. ANT opens up a broader and more flexible meaning of actors and thereby it extends the understanding of political entrepreneurs.

This combines an actor-structure approach by discussing political entrepreneurs as the actors that are creative and innovative and develop, consolidate and coordinate the governance networks. The analytical approach of considering even "non-humans" as actors is one of the most basic, but also (the most) complicated dimensions of the ANT approach. By including even non-human actors as components of the network, several "bonus" dimensions are added to the analysis and the power analysis is shown in a new light. Thereby it can be revealed how and why actors form a network (Latour, 2005; Harman, 2009). This also extends the meaning of what can be seen as political because it enables inclusion of actors other than human actors in the processes of making politics. The politics of artefacts, institutions and even non-humans can hereby be included in the analysis of how and why a political entrepreneur is successful.

In relation to networked governance, and not least the analysis of political entrepreneurs, there is great potential if we could come to see what we regard as an actor. A broader and more open approach to the concept of actors in relation to political entrepreneurs will show how governance networks are formed by many actors associated with the translation process. This is not completely unfamiliar in the governance network literature. In the early conceptualisation of the "issue network" (Rhodes and Marsh, 1992), it was shown that the issue as such can play a crucial role in the formation of a network and associate other actors in the network. In the issue network, other actors are associated with the issue to support it and make political changes come through. In a study of broadband infrastructure, I showed how actors in rural communities associated with the issues of improved tele- and data-communication through networks came together to fulfil completely different demands. There were strong issue networks promoting investments in broadband even before the breakthrough of the Internet, when there was not really any use for broadband (Wihlborg, 2000). The issue as such was such a powerful actor that it could form policy networks, promote political changes and decisions and even create a new infrastructure.

It is even more common to see the involvement of institutions and organisations in policy networks (Sørensen and Torfing, 2007; Torfing and Triantafillou, 2011; Kooiman, 2003). However, most often, the institutions are regarded as the structural setting or context for the networking among the human actors. One or two human actors may speak for the institution, and the institution becomes something in the network that the other actors relate to. For example, the institution of the European Parliament is a setting for many networks. However, the institution of the Parliament as such is an actor addressing new issues in a common European perspective that would never happen without the involvement of the Parliament. In the networks formed in the Council, the member states take their national stake and in the Commission, the issues, evidence and knowledge as such are at the core of the networks. Thus, the European Parliament can be considered an actor speaking for the common European agenda and building networks that otherwise would not have been formed. There is potential to include institutions and organisations in policy networks and thereby also open up the possibility that they can act as political entrepreneurs with innovative approaches that encourage other actors in the network to make policy changes. In the policy network analysis, it is not uncommon to see the issue as a driving actor forming networks (Sandström and Carlsson, 2008). Thus, we may have to be open to issues and ideas functioning as political entrepreneurs forming networks and contributing to changes.

Second implication: political entrepreneurs are nothing without their networks, and vice versa

The second implication of the combination of political entrepreneurs and ANT points at the mutual co-construction of the political entrepreneur and his or her network. This is based on the overall contribution of this chapter, that the political entrepreneur has to be considered and understood in relation to his or her network and that they form each other. This argument is based on Harman's (2014) main conclusion that the ANT approach shows us that the network is nothing without its actors and the actor is nothing without his or her network.

Based on this notion, it also becomes obvious just how embedded political entrepreneurs are in their policy networks. This means that we have to describe and analyse political entrepreneurs through the networks they form. Such an analysis will also uncover how they combine other actors (humans as well as non-humans) and recourses in the networks to fulfil their aims. The networking activities of political entrepreneurs expose their relations to other actors enrolled in the network and those in turn facilitate the success of the political entrepreneurs. The political entrepreneur uses networking as a social process to reassemble other actors to facilitate the entrepreneur's aims and ambitions, to paraphrase the title by Latour (2005), it is "Reassembling the social". Political entrepreneurs are the ones pointing out the assembly point and reassembling other actors to make changes happen.

The social process of networks includes elements of social, natural and material origin, and the translation processes create meanings that are both material and semiotic in constant making. These are processes through which translation is promoted by mediators in the same way as political entrepreneurs; there are always political interpretations of what is translated and brought into the network and what is left outside. The network is kept together as long as the translation goes on and the relations are repeatedly "performed". When this ceases, the network will dissolve (Woolgar and Neyland, 2015). The continuing translation is the glue of the network that keeps the actors together.

In the networked governance setting, political entrepreneurs translate meanings and policy aims among actors and structures. Political entrepreneurs can also constrain and structure the formation of networks. As the mediator, in the ANT vocabulary, the policy entrepreneur aims to "translate" and knit together the networks through mediating competences and activities. Even if this is not the vocabulary of the more structural policy entrepreneurial approach, there would be value added to our understanding of the political entrepreneurs if we could see them as the ones translating, reassembling and building the networks for change. Through this combined perspective, we will open up a more constructive and reflexive understanding of the political entrepreneur.

Third implication: the power of political entrepreneurs

Based on the overall contribution of this chapter – that the political entrepreneur has to be considered and understood in relation to his or her networks – the analysis of power has to be seen through such a networked perspective. Here, ANT opens up a more complex interpretation of power, in particular, how non-human actors can facilitate or constrain other actors and thereby have power to influence the consequences of the policy processes. Policy networks are formed through translation. The political entrepreneur is the one who has the power to define what is translated or not, who is included or not and how the network is developed or not. Translation takes place through networks and thus can also stabilise and hamper changes; translation processes have the power to define the outcomes of the networks (Czarniawska and Sevon, 2005).

Kingdon (1995) identified the function of political entrepreneurs as actors combining and coordinating the streams of problems, politics and policymaking. Thereby, political entrepreneurs have the power to set the agenda and frame the issue through the policy window they open. This points to their power to set the agenda. Agenda-setting is the second face of power in the classical theory of power presented by Lukes (2005). He defined the second face of power as the power to determine what we talk about and how. By deciding when, where and what others will be discussing, the political entrepreneur has the power to focus the network's activities and enrol the actors that contribute to the activities the political entrepreneur aims to enhance.

What is translated is an outcome of the power relations within the networks. In line with the second implication above, the network is formed by the included actors. The political entrepreneur has the power to determine what actors are included in the network and thereby participate in the translation. In line with the first implication regarding actors, these can also be institutions, artefacts and knowledge. Thus, political entrepreneurs, in this view, have the power to determine the knowledge, institutions, artefacts and human actors that are involved in the translation towards policy change.

There is often a positive connotation to (political) entrepreneurs that they are doing good. Also, the overall definition here of a political entrepreneur (see Chapter 1 in this volume) carries the same meaning when defined as *a politician/bureaucrat/officer/institution within the publicly funded sector that with innovative approaches encourages entrepreneurship/business and where the goal is growth and employment.* This indicates that the political entrepreneur is seeking to promote growth, but the political entrepreneur can be innovative in various ways and contribute to policy areas other than economic growth. The ANT approach starts in the networks and follows the actor in his or her formation of networks. Political entrepreneurs assemble the network and thereby have power to define who is included and construct meanings. Hereby, the ANT approach can provide a more nuanced understanding of the function of political entrepreneurs, their networks and the power they express in processes of social change.

CONCLUSION

This extension of the conceptualisation of political entrepreneurs, by adding the basics of ANT (Law and Callon, 1989; Latour, 2005), opens up several approaches that can be further expanded and illustrated through practical case studies. The basic ANT argument, that the political entrepreneur is nothing without his or her network and that the network cannot be formed without its actors – including the political entrepreneurs – indicates that we need to include political entrepreneurs in the analysis of policy networks and that an analysis of political entrepreneurs needs to include a network analysis. There is a need to open up more process-focused analyses and highlight the practices and processes when political entrepreneurs are building, forming and sustaining policy networks using ANT (Law, 1992; Latour, 2005).

Through this contribution, I have shown the more general need to combine the analyses of political processes with the ANT that extends our understanding of actors and how power is framed in relations within networks, as summarised in the Table 2.1 below.

Table 2.1 Summarising the implications on analysis of political entrepreneurs with inspiration from ANT

	Value added by ANT	**Usability in the analysis of Political Entrepreneurs (PE)**
Actors	More than human actors	Non-humans can also function as PEs and facilitate innovative processes
Networks	The networks are built by the actor	The PE can build his or her network and decide on the limits of the network
Power	Power is what is performed in the network	No actor, nor the PE, has power without his or her performed relations in the network
Methodological approach	Follow the actor	The analysis of PEs has to focus on the formation of the network around the PEs, which do not have to be human actors

In spite of the partly contradictory approaches of ANT and the more structural approach of political entrepreneurship, there is a need to strive to overcome these challenges to extend the understanding of political entrepreneurship. We have to include more actors and see how the actors are both made by, and making, their networks. Hereby, we also get a new and broader way to see and analyse the power of political entrepreneurs. We have to contextualise the political entrepreneurs in their networks, and we have to see power as formed through these networks.

REFERENCES

Ács, Z. J. and Audretsch, D. B. (eds) (2006). *Handbook of Entrepreneurship Research: An Interdisciplinary Survey and Introduction* (Vol. 1). New York: Springer Science & Business Media.

Agranoff, R. (2006). "Inside collaborative networks: ten lessons for public managers". *Public Administration Review*, 66, 56–65.

Assmo, P. and Wihlborg, E. (2016). "Political entrepreneurship and sustainable growth in rural areas". In: C. Karlsson, C. Silander and D. Silander (eds) *Political Entrepreneurship: Regional Growth and Entrepreneurial Diversity in Sweden*. Cheltenham: Edward Elgar Publishing.

Callon, M. and Law, J. (1995). "Agency and the hybrid collectif". *South Atlantic Quarterly*, 94, 481–507.

Carlsson, L. (2000). "Policy networks as collective action". *Policy Studies Journal*, 28(3), 502–520.

Czarniawska, B. and Sevon, G. (eds) (2005). *Global Ideas: How Ideas, Objects and Practices Travel in the Global Economy*. Copenhagen Business School. Malmö: Liber.

Elg, M., Ellström, P. E., Klofsten, M. and Tillmar, M. (eds) (2015). *Sustainable Development in Organizations: Studies on Innovative Practices*. Cheltenham: Edward Elgar Publishing.

Garud, R., Hardy, C. and Maguire, S. (2007). "Institutional entrepreneurship as embedded agency: an introduction to the special issue". *Organization Studies*, 28(7), 957–969.

Gustafsson, M. S. (2017). *Reassembling Local e-Government: A Study of Actors' Translations of Digitalisation in Public Administration*. PhD-thesis, Linköping: Linköping University Electronic Press.

Harman, G. (2009). *Prince of Networks. Bruno Latour and Metaphysics*. Melbourne: Re-Press.

Harman, G. (2014). *Bruno Latour: Reassembling the Political*. London: Pluto Press.

Karlsson, C., Silander, C. and Silander, D. (eds) (2016). *Political Entrepreneurship: Regional Growth and Entrepreneurial Diversity in Sweden*. Cheltenham: Edward Elgar Publishing.

Kingdon, J. W. (1995). *Agendas, Alternatives and Public Policies*. New York: Longman.

Klijn, E.-H., Steijn, B. and Edelenbos, J. (2010). "The impact of network management on outcomes in governance networks". *Public Administration*, 88(4), 1063–1082.
Kooiman, J. (2003). *Governing as Governance*. London: Sage.
Koppenjan, J. and Klijn, E. H. (2004). *Making Uncertainties in Networks: Public Private Controversies*. London: Routledge.
Latour, B. (1999). *Pandora's Hope: Essays on the Reality of Science Studies*. Harvard: Harvard University Press.
Latour, B. (2005). *Reassembling the Social: An Introduction to Actor-Network Theory*. Oxford: Oxford University Press.
Law, J. (1992). "Notes on the theory of the actor-network: ordering, strategy, and heterogeneity". *Systems Practice*, 5(4), 379–393.
Law, J. and Callon, M. (1989). "On the construction of sociotechnical networks: content and context revisited". *Knowledge and Society*, 9, 57–83.
Law, J. and Hassard, J. (1999). *Actor Network Theory and After*. Oxford: Blackwell.
Lukes, S. (2005 [1975]). *Power: A Radical View*. 2nd edition. Basingstoke: Palgrave Macmillan.
Mintrom, M. (1997). "Policy entrepreneurs and the diffusion of innovation". *American Journal of Political Science*, 41(3), 738–770.
Mintrom, M. and Norman, P. (2009). "Policy entrepreneurship and policy change". *Policy Studies Journal*, 37(4), 649–667.
Narbutaité Aflaki, I., Petridou, E. and Miles, L. (2015). *Entrepreneurship in the Polis: Understanding Political Entrepreneurship*. London: Ashgate.
Newell, D. (2017). *Locating Wind Power Policy: The Mechanics of Policy Subsystem Interactions*. PhD-thesis. Luleå: Luleå University of Technology.
Persson, M. (2014). *The Dynamics of Policy Formation. Making Sense of Public Unsafety*. PhD-thesis. Örebro: Örebro University Press.
Pierre, J. and Peters, G. (2000). *Governance, Politics, and the State*. New York: St. Martin's Press.
Pollitt, C. and Bouckaert, G. (2011). *Continuity and Change in Public Policy and Management*. Cheltenham: Edward Elgar Publishing.
Rhodes, R. A. W. and Marsh, D. (1992). "New directions in the study of policy networks". *European Journal of Political Research*, 21, 181–205.
Rövik, K.A., (2000). *Moderna organisationer – trender inom organisationstan kandet vid millennieskiftet*. Malmö: Liber förlag.
Sandström, A. and Carlsson, L. (2008). "The performance of policy networks: the relation between network structure and network performance". *Policy Studies Journal*, 36(4), 497–524.
Sørensen, E. and Torfing, J. (eds) (2007). *Theories of Democratic Network Governance*. New York: Palgrave Macmillan.
Torfing, J. and Triantafillou, P. (eds) (2011). *Interactive Policy Making, Meta-governance and Democracy*. Colchester: ECPR Press.
von Bergmann-Winberg, M. L. and Wihlborg, E. (2011). *Politikens entreprenörskap: kreativ problemlösning och förändring*. Malmö: Liber förlag.
Wihlborg, E. (2000). *En lösning som söker problem: hur och varför lokala IT-policyer utvecklas i landsbygdskommuner*. PhD-thesis, Linköping: Linköping University Press.

Wihlborg, E. (2015). "Policy entrepreneurs meeting mediators – a conceptual extension". In: I. Narbutaitė Aflaki, E. Petridou and L. Miles (eds) *Entrepreneurship in the Polis: Understanding Political Entrepreneurship.* London: Ashgate.

Wihlborg, E. and Söderholm, K. (2013). "Mediators in action: organizing sociotechnical system change". *Technology in Society*, 35(4), 267–275.

Woolgar, S. and Neyland, D. (2015). *Mundane Governance: Ontology and Accountability*. Oxford: Oxford University Press.

3. Institutional entrepreneurship: a different perspective on political entrepreneurs?

Birgit Leick and Susanne Gretzinger

INTRODUCTION

From a theoretical perspective, the concept of institutional entrepreneurship offers persuasive answers to the question of how change in established and persistently stable, institutionalised practices can be achieved. As the proponents of the concept would argue, it is through the actions of skilled and powerful actors who promote collective action and use resources in order to achieve this change (Sotarauta and Pulkkinen, 2011; Hung and Whittington, 2011; Battilana et al., 2009; Wijen and Ansari, 2007). Indeed, rooted in institutionalism, institutional entrepreneurship has been proposed as a conceptual approach that can explain how individuals overcome the so-called *paradox of embedded agency* by changing the institutional structures that govern their strategies and interaction (Hardy and Maguire, 2008; Henrekson and Sanandaji, 2011).

In a similar vein, agency in terms of the behaviour or activities of individuals, groups of individuals, or organisations who work in the policy area and have such an agenda for change, is central to the contemporary debate on political entrepreneurship (Silander, 2016; Christopoulos and Ingold, 2011; Ireland and Webb, 2007; Björkman and Sundgren, 2005). Therefore, both institutional and political entrepreneurship have common roots in the underlying Schumpeterian understanding of entrepreneurship as the result of combinations of existing material and structure, on the one hand, and perceptiveness regarding opportunities, on the other (Hwang and Powell, 2005: 202; Henrekson and Sanandaji, 2011: 49). This joint understanding assumes that an actor's ability to recombine existing resources in order to exploit opportunities is not restricted to corporate entrepreneurs and new business ventures alone (Hederer, 2007; Henrekson and Sanandaji, 2011; Klein et al., 2010). Instead, it opens the door for conceptualising non-corporate entrepreneurial activities outside the business organisation. Against the backdrop of the obvious inter-relatedness of the two concepts, the question is whether and, if so, how institutional entrepreneurship differs from political entrepreneurship. In this chapter, we aim to give, at least, a partial answer to this question by placing emphasis on institutional entrepreneurship from a process perspective (see Battilana et al., 2009). Based upon a literature review, we highlight the triggers that activate such agents and the effects that they might have on the institutionalised practices of economic actors. Moreover, the chapter describes the main behavioural features associated with institutional entrepreneurship, and concludes by putting institutional and political entrepreneurship in relation to one another.

THE ORIGINS OF INSTITUTIONAL ENTREPRENEURSHIP: EMBEDDING AGENCY IN INSTITUTIONALISM

Institutionalist Accounts and "Change Agents"

Institutions represent various mechanisms that structure agents and their interaction (see Chapter 1 in this volume). These "rules of the game" (North, 1990: 3) incorporate both formalised rules, such as laws, and written regulations, and informal, but socially accepted and legitimised, behavioural patterns (tradition, norms, moral viewpoints, etc.). Institutions are also commonly understood as the physical or organisational representations of the social patterns of behaviour and formal rules in a society (North, 1990; Langlois and Robertson, 1995). These carriers or bearers of institutions include all sorts of groups or networks of individuals that incorporate and formally legitimate institutions, for example, business organisations (Langlois and Robertson, 1995), or political, economic and educational bodies.

With regard to the functions of institutions, two different claims co-exist in social and economic theory (North, 1990; Powell and DiMaggio, 1991). According to neo-institutional accounts, institutions govern and structure the behaviour of economic agents such as key actors in business organisations. As rational actors (Simon, 1957), they are both guided and constrained by a complex framework of institutions, which influences their economic decisions. By structuring and channelling the interaction between economic actors, institutions reduce the uncertainties that arise from market and business environments, provide incentives for actors to opt for specific strategies according to cost and efficiency motives, and impose sanctions on them (Ménard and Shirley, 2008). Based upon this rationale, institutions facilitate the search for relevant information, lower the transaction costs and raise the efficiency of interactions. In this line of thought, Amin (1999: 367) concludes that "institutions provide stability in the real economic context of information asymmetry, market uncertainty and knowledge soundness, by restricting the field of possibilities available, garnering consensus and common understandings and guiding individual action". Therefore, neo-institutionalism considers institutions as stabilising mechanisms in contexts of uncertainty in the market and business environments.

Therefore, it is claimed that institutions remain relatively stable over time and tend to evoke path-dependency (David, 1994). This view emphasises the static and rigid nature of many formal and informal institutions. Given the path-dependent institutions, firms develop corporate strategies in compliance with the existing institutional setting and change their strategies in reaction to external stimuli or shocks (Hancké et al., 2007), for example, to take advantage of the institutional support available (see also Hall and Thelen, 2009). Hence, change in institutions appears to constitute a technical mechanism in which modifications of existing institutional features trigger a change in firm behaviour through a re-setting of incentives and feedbacks from the firms in reaction to the incentives (North, 1990).

By contrast, the second theoretical account – sociological institutionalism – puts more emphasis on the interdependence between institutions and individual firm strategies, notably in contexts of change (Wilkens et al., 2003; Hodgson, 2007; Oliver, 1991). Institutions are considered to be socially constructed and are, therefore, subject to societal, economic and political developments (Hodgson, 2007: 96). In line with this thinking, institutions not only restrict the range of options for economic actors, but also offer opportunities to them, either within the existing institutional settings, or for those who seek to change them (Garud et al., 2007). Compared to neo-institutional accounts, organisational sociology conceptualises individuals or economic actors (for example, business organisations and corporations) not primarily as the recipients of incentives and the reactors to triggers from the institutional framework; instead, institutional change can be explained because of powerful agents that work to change the existing or newly established institutional fields (Beckert, 1999).

This perspective actually corresponds to the observation that, in reality, institutions have always been modified, amended and renewed in response to changes in both the global and regional market environments, which often happens through the involvement and commitment of large corporations, powerful political alliances or scale-crossing coalitions in specific areas (Martin, 2000). At the local level, this is described by Gertler (2010: 6) as "the process by which new institutional forms come to be 'layered' upon older, pre-existing institutions, thereby setting in train a dynamic of path-dependent, locally distinctive institutional evolution". Such "change agents" (Battilana and Casciaro, 2012; Cels et al., 2012) can be firms and other economic or non-economic actors which turn into proactive facilitators of institutional change (Kalantaridis and Fletcher, 2012) and steer its overall direction (Amin, 2001: 1238).

INTRODUCING THE CONCEPT OF INSTITUTIONAL ENTREPRENEURSHIP

In particular, contexts of change or crisis in markets, industries or, more generally, business environments may induce such agents to seek a supportive institutional setting for their own agendas and strategies (Battilana and Casciaro, 2012); such actors or groups of actors have the potential to overcome the inertia of the existing institutions by using and establishing powerful networks and pushing an agenda for change against the established structures and frameworks. DiMaggio (1988: 14) calls them "institutional entrepreneurs", describing them as "organized actors with sufficient resources" who "see … an opportunity to realize interests they value highly". Reflecting DiMaggio (1988), Beckert (1999: 781) emphasises that institutional entrepreneurs raise and command resources in order to influence the institutional setting according to their interests.

In conceptual terms, institutional entrepreneurship offers two points of departure to describe the behaviour and actions of such change agents (Kalantaridis and Fletcher, 2012; Bruton et al., 2010): First, the concept reflects the characteristics of an entrepreneurial person in terms of forward-looking and opportunity-seeking behaviour, but rests on a broader understanding of entrepreneurship as innovative capacities beyond corporate entrepreneurship and new firm creation only (Hwang and Powell, 2005). Second, the concept focuses on power and legitimacy as two important elements associated with agents of change in established institutional settings (Maguire, 2008; Garud et al., 2007; Hardy and Maguire, 2008). Hence, institutional entrepreneurship is associated with the behaviour of agents and their mechanisms to break with the prevailing institutionalised practices, on the one hand, whilst using resources, power and legitimacy to promote and enact this break, on the other. The reaping of opportunities and legitimisation of new, and potentially diverging, practices are other important features associated with institutional entrepreneurs (Sotarauta and Pulkkinen, 2011; Battilana et al., 2009).

However, who and what are institutional entrepreneurs? Given that the concept can be applied to the actions of all kinds of individuals, organisations, networks, associations, social movements "or even (policy) networks" (Perkmann, 2002: 124), the question is what kind of characteristics and activities qualify as institutional entrepreneurship. As Sotarauta and Pulkkinen (2011: 100) rightly state, it is important to acknowledge that, obviously, "not all actors working for change are institutional entrepreneurs". Based upon a literature review (Leick, 2017), Table 3.1 summarises some of the key activities associated with institutional entrepreneurship (see, also, McCarthy, 2012; Lounsbury and Crumley, 2007).

Table 3.1 Key characteristics of institutional entrepreneurs

Strategic outset	– Having self-interest as motivation to establish a specific institutional arrangement – Pursuing their strategy by using collaborative arrangements – Mobilising resources to achieve their goals – Recognising opportunities arising from the field they are working in or are familiar with – Being endowed with a vision about a specific institutional setting – Using uncertainty or crisis in the field as stimulus to design problem-solving
Interpretation and network power	– Having the ability to convince others to collaborate and build networks – Being endowed with the power to forge alliances and create collective action – Giving others reason to join collaboration by creating meaning and offering alternative ways of problem-solving – Gaining legitimacy for the practices they wish to introduce
Political agenda	– Accompanying and directing learning processes – Championing their own interests or the interests of the parties they are involved in – Exerting power through social skills, negotiation and communication – Building powerful coalitions to promote desired institutional features

Source: Based upon Leick (2017).

1. With regard to *strategic outset*, institutional entrepreneurs are supposed to be driven by strategies which are in line with their self-interests and that aim to establish or change a specific institutional practice (Battilana et al., 2009; Maguire et al., 2004: 657). Institutional entrepreneurs envision change and recognise the opportunities arising from the institutional fields to which they are aligned (Phillips and Tracey, 2007; Beckert, 2010). From a social constructivist understanding, they advance their own interests and fight for power positions in these areas by taking intentional actions (Sotarauta and Pulkkinen, 2011: 101; Maguire et al., 2004). As Sotarauta and Pulkkinen (2011: 101) note, much in line with Mintzberg and Waters (1985: 257), institutional entrepreneurship may, however, also unfold through emergent, subconscious patterns of behaviour, instead of fully-fledged intentional actions. As entrepreneurial agents, these agents are able to take on a reflective stance with regard to the established institutions (Beckert, 1999: 786). Moreover, the mobilisation of resources (both tangible and intangible, see Battilana et al., 2009) belongs to the strategy of institutional entrepreneurs because they expect rewards from their commitment to institutional change (Maguire et al., 2004).
2. Through the legitimisation and institutionalisation of novel practices in reward-promising fields, institutional entrepreneurs build common ground among the groups in the field that they want to influence (Maguire et al., 2004). With regard to the *interpretation and network power*, it is argued that institutional entrepreneurs are capable of building alliances among various stakeholders to promote change according to their interests. An important characteristic is their capacity to convince others to collaborate and help establish a specific institutional practice (Dorado, 2005). To this aim, institutional entrepreneurs forge inter-actor relationships and networks and encourage collective action, using these networks (Hardy and Maguire, 2008). The power of interpretation refers to the fact that such agents are convincing in that they provide others with reasons to co-operate; in addition, they create meaning about the institutional change that they favour (Weik, 2011: 486; Garud et al., 2007: 962 f.; Wijen and Ansari, 2007). Therefore, the interpretative capacity of institutional entrepreneurship is associated with the influence of such agents on the behaviour of others – individuals, groups and organisations – through network relationships. By using this power, institutional entrepreneurs gain legitimacy for the new practices that they wish to introduce, especially if these practices are divergent from the existing ones (Sotarauta and

Pulkkinen, 2011: 102; Garud et al., 2007: 961). To this aim, institutional entrepreneurs offer alternative meanings, explanations and interpretations (Battilana et al., 2009; Battilana and Casciaro, 2012).

3. In addition, institutional entrepreneurs are described as having a *political agenda* (Hwang and Powell, 2005; Perkmann, 2002). This refers to their capacity to apply political strategies by "choreographing and directing learning processes" (Sotarauta and Pulkkinen, 2011: 103). The political agenda-building capacity is associated with the social skills of institutional entrepreneurs who promote their own interests or the interests of parties to whom they are aligned. Whereas established coalitions or actors with powerful positions in a specific field are often unable or unwilling to change the existing institutional practices and prefer their stability, instead (Hardy and Maguire, 2008: 1999) institutional entrepreneurs consciously break with the dominant institutional logic in that field (Garud et al., 2007: 962). Through the power of networking and communication, and the introduction of new discourses as well as negotiation of their position, institutional entrepreneurs follow a political agenda to introduce change within and outside their networks (Hardy and Maguire, 2008; Battilana and Casciaro, 2012).

THE PROCESS OF INSTITUTIONAL ENTREPRENEURSHIP

Bruton et al. (2010) emphasise that institutional entrepreneurship takes place as a genuinely social process of interaction, communication, negotiation and consensus building. In this process, institutional entrepreneurs establish and communicate alternative ways of looking at and solving problems within the established institutional structures. Moreover, they work to get these novel ideas legitimised and therefore institutionalised. This capacity or activity is associated with resource mobilisation and the production of – what Perkmann (2002: 125) calls – "the knowledge and narrative frameworks for institutional innovations", that is, templates that amend or modify the dominant institutionalised practice. Therefore, we argue in this chapter, institutional entrepreneurship can be understood as a process in which the activities conducted by institutional entrepreneurs influence firms with their established (and therefore, institutionalised) practices towards adopting different, and new, ones.

A first point of departure for understanding this process lies in the factors that trigger institutional entrepreneurship. From the process perspective, the *triggers* can activate institutional entrepreneurs. An important trigger is the uncertainty associated with market/business environments that acts as a stimulus for institutional entrepreneurship (Hardy and Maguire, 2008). More generally, DiMaggio (1988) also points to the problems, tensions and contradictions associated with established institutionalised practices as triggers. Triggers can be found both in emerging and mature, that is, structured and organised, contexts (Maguire et al., 2004).

Because emerging fields with a low degree of structure are associated with high levels of uncertainty with the institutional settings, they provide considerable scope for rewards to the agents who work to structure the field (Maguire et al., 2004). Often, no fixed scripts exist that give orientation to economic actors (for example, companies and employers) in such a scenario; thus, uncertainty arises because firms cannot assess the probable outcomes of their choices and establish appropriate strategies for coping with uncertainty (Beckert, 1999: 779). More generally, Maguire (2008: 674) notes that "(i)n emerging fields, … , relationships are fluid, meanings are heterogeneous, understandings are not widely shared, and multiple possible scripts for action exist". In such a context, insiders from established organisations or outsiders may be motivated to work to introduce structure into the field (Hardy and Maguire, 2008). With their wish to stabilise the fluid relationships by creating new meanings, institutional entrepreneurs would not come into conflict with the prevailing, and therefore dominating, views (Maguire, 2008). Hence, the fact that there are often no established, collectively legitimised, practices with regard to certain aspects of social or economic problems or challenges in the market/business environments can be regarded as another trigger for institutional entrepreneurship.

In the parlance of organisational sociology, tensions and contradictions in association with established, yet changing, markets or business environments are, therefore, triggers that can activate institutional entrepreneurs. Because such structured and mature fields are "populated by diverse organizations, many of whom are invested in, committed to, and advantaged by existing structural arrangements" (Garud et al., 2007: 962), the crisis or transformation of these fields can give rise to contradictions and tensions between dominant organisations that work in the fields, thereby opening up opportunities for new players (Hardy and Maguire, 2008: 204). Institutional entrepreneurs can be actors who are disadvantaged by the prevailing institutional practice and thus have a strong incentive to break with it (Maguire, 2008). Change in mature fields can also occur through entrepreneurial actions of established players, for instance, in reaction to exogenous shocks (ibid.).

A second point of departure in the process of institutional entrepreneurship can be the *impact* of institutional entrepreneurs on the established, institutionalised, practices. Several authors point out that sense-making is an important impact (Dorado, 2005; Zilber, 2007). Sense-making is associated with the creation of meaning through narratives, discourses and frameworks (see Sandberg and Tsoukas, 2015); it is also related to the raising of awareness and persuasion (Zilber, 2007; Maguire, 2008). Sense-making is an important mechanism for institutional entrepreneurs to identify and frame these tensions, problems or challenges, and thereby create meaning about them (Greenwood et al., 2002). Moreover, it has been acknowledged that institutional entrepreneurs can facilitate the diffusion of novel ideas and information about alternative practices (Greenwood et al., 2002). The dissemination of knowledge can result in new specifications of an existing practice or the introduction of a standard (Garud et al., 2002; Casile and Davis-Blake, 2002), which implies, for example, certification (Battilana et al., 2009) or the generation of local innovations (Sotarauta and Pulkkinen, 2011). However, the effects or outcomes of the institutionalisation efforts of institutional entrepreneurs are often less clear than the activities or triggers (Leick, 2017).

CONCLUSION

What can be learnt about the relationship between institutional and political entrepreneurship? First, the two concepts are clearly related and have common ground because they are not only rooted in economic theory, but they have also been influenced by, and are linked to, institutionalism (see, for example, McCaffrey and Salerno, 2011). Therefore, both concepts stress the capacity and power of change agents. Two characteristics are central to the behaviour of both institutional and political entrepreneurs: (a) the will to identify and exploit opportunities that arise from the institutional structures, which is much in line with the Schumpeterian concept of the entrepreneur (Henrekson and Sanandaji, 2011); and (b) the ambition to step into a powerful position or use power as a means to change formal and informal institutions (Silander, 2016; Björkman and Sundgren, 2005), a feature that is rooted in organisational sociology.

Second, another commonality of institutional and political entrepreneurship is that much emphasis is placed on the characteristics of change agents rather than explaining their economic impact in terms of the generation of innovative products, services and processes. Altogether, the two approaches – institutional and political entrepreneurship – contribute to shed light on the contemporary directions in entrepreneurship research in business and management research, in the political sciences and related disciplines because they stress the importance of entrepreneurial actions and behaviour outside the corporation.

It is also important to mention differences between the concepts. First, the political entrepreneur is defined as an actor or structure in the public sector that is working for institutional change to, through innovative measures, promote new formal and informal institutional settings (Silander, 2016). Political entrepreneurs are found in the public sector and are not defined as leaders in companies, societal influential groups, movements or corporations etc. Political entrepreneurship is also more about promoting public interests or the common good – in this study entrepreneurship for growth and employment. In addition, political entrepreneurship is about bold and innovative measures beyond day-to-day activities. In DiMaggio's (1988) original conceptualisation, institutional entrepreneurs appear to be driven by a desire to follow their interests and own agendas in order to achieve goals that are in line with said agendas. In addition, more recent contributions (for example, Battilana et al., 2009) have developed the concept into a more consistent explanation of the behaviour, actions and effects of change agents in all kinds of arenas and fields, and not necessarily those of politics and policy exclusively. Examples such as Ritvala and Kleymann (2012) or Perkmann (2002) stress both the institutionalisation efforts and the influence of institutional entrepreneurs on groups or coalitions of followers. Hence, to conclude, our claim is that institutional entrepreneurship represents the broader concept and complements conceptual explanations of the political entrepreneur in the policy arena.

REFERENCES

Amin, A. (1999). "An institutionalist perspective in regional economic development". *International Journal of Urban and Regional Research* 23(2): 365–378.

Amin, A. (2001). "Moving on: institutionalism in economic geography". *Environment and Planning A* 33(7): 1237–1241.

Battilana, J. and Casciaro, T. (2012). "Change agents, networks, and institutions: a contingency theory of organizational change". *Academy of Management Journal* 55(2): 381–398.

Battilana, J., Leca, B. and Boxenbaum E. (2009). "How actors change institutions: towards a theory of institutional entrepreneurship". *The Academy of Management Annals* 3(1): 65–107.

Beckert, J. (1999). "Agency, entrepreneurs, and institutional change. The role of strategic choice and institutionalized practices in organizations". *Organization Studies* 20(5): 777–799.

Beckert, J. (2010). "How do fields change? The interrelations of institutions, networks, and cognition in the dynamics of markets". *Organization Studies* 31(5): 605–627.

Björkman, H. and Sundgren, M. (2005). "Political entrepreneurship in action research: learning from two cases". *Journal of Organizational Change Management* 18(5): 399–415.

Bruton, G. D., Ahlstrom, D. and Li, H. L. (2010). "Institutional theory and entrepreneurship: where are we now and where do we need to move in the future". *Entrepreneurship Theory and Practice* 34(3): 421–440.

Casile, M. and Davis-Blake, A. (2002). "When accreditation standards change: factors affecting differential responsiveness of public and private organizations". *The Academy of Management Journal* 45(1): 180–195.

Cels, S., de Jong, J. and Nauta, F. (2012). *Agents of Change. Strategy and Tactics for Social Innovation.* Washington, DC: Brookings Institution Press.

Christopoulos, D. and Ingold, K. (2011). "Distinguishing between political brokerage and political entrepreneurship". *Procedia Social and Behavioral Sciences* 10: 36–42.

David, P. A. (1994). "Why are institutions the 'carriers of history'? Path dependence and the evolution of conventions, organizations and institutions". *Structural Change and Economic Dynamics* 5(2): 205–220.

DiMaggio, P. (1988). "Interest and agency in institutional theory". In Zucker, L. (ed.). *Institutional Patterns and Culture.* Cambridge: Ballinger.

Dorado, S. (2005). "Institutional entrepreneurship, partaking, and convening". *Organization Studies* 26(3): 385–414.

Garud, R., Hardy, C. and Maguire, S. (2007). "Institutional entrepreneurship as embedded agency: an introduction to the special issue". *Organization Studies* 28(7): 957–969.

Garud, R., Jain, S. and Kumaraswamy, A. (2002). "Institutional entrepreneurship in the sponsorship of common technological standards: the case of Sun Microsystems and Java". *The Academy of Management Journal* 45(1): 196–214.

Gertler, M. S. (2010). "Rules of the game: the place of institutions in regional economic change". *Regional Studies* 44(1): 1–15.

Greenwood, R., Suddaby, R. and Hinings, C. R. (2002). "Theorizing change: the role of professional associations in the transformation of institutionalized fields". *The Academy of Management Journal* 45(1): 58–80.

Hall, P. A. and Thelen, K. (2009). "Institutional change in varieties of capitalism". *Socio-Economic Review* 7(1): 7–34.

Hancké, B., Rhodes, M. and Thatcher, M. (2007). *Beyond Varieties of Capitalism: Conflict, Contradictions and Complementarities in the European Economy*. Oxford: Oxford University Press.

Hardy, C. and Maguire, S. (2008). "Institutional entrepreneurship". In: Greenwood, R. et al. (eds). *The SAGE Handbook of Organizational Institutionalism*. London: Sage.

Hederer, C. (2007). "Political Entrepreneurship and Institutional Change: An Evolutionary Approach". MPRA Paper No. 8249, accessed 6 October 2017 at http://mpra.ub.uni-muenchen.de/8249/.

Henrekson, M. and Sanandaji, T. (2011). "The interaction of entrepreneurship and institutions". *Journal of Institutional Economics* 7(1): 47–75.

Hodgson, G. M. (2007). "Institutions and individuals: interaction and evolution". *Organization Studies* 28(1): 95–116.

Hung, S.-C. and Whittington, R. (2011). "Agency in national innovation systems: institutional entrepreneurship and the professionalization of Taiwanese IT". *Research Policy* 40(4): 526–538.

Hwang, H. and Powell, W. W. (2005). "Institutions and entrepreneurship". In: Alvarez, S. A., Agarwal, R., and Sorensen, O. (eds). *Handbook of Entrepreneurship Research: Interdisciplinary Perspectives*. New York: Springer.

Ireland, R. D. and Webb, J. W. (2007). "A cross-disciplinary exploration of entrepreneurship research". *Journal of Management* 33(6): 891–927.

Kalantaridis, C. and Fletcher, D. (2012). "Entrepreneurship and institutional change: a research agenda". *Entrepreneurship & Regional Development* 24(3–4): 199–214.

Klein, P. G., Mahoney, J. T., McGahan, A. M., and Pitelis, C. N. (2010). "Toward a theory of public entrepreneurship". *European Management Review* 7: 1–15 (doi: 10.1057/emr.2010).

Langlois, R. N. and Robertson, P. L. (1995). *Firms, Markets and Economic Change: A Dynamic Theory of Business Institutions*. London: Routledge.

Leick, B. (2017). "Institutional entrepreneurs and small firms: how firm practices are being shaped in the context of demographic transformations". *Journal of Small Business & Entrepreneurship* 29(1): 1–24.

Lounsbury, M. and Crumley, E. T. (2007). "New practice creation: an institutional perspective on innovation". *Organization Science* 28(7): 993–1012.

Maguire, S. (2008). "Institutional entrepreneurship". In: Clegg, S. R., and Bailey, J. R. (eds). *International Encyclopedia of Organization Studies*. Thousand Oaks, CA: Sage.

Maguire, S., Hardy, C. and Lawrence. T. B. (2004). "Institutional entrepreneurship in emerging fields: HIV/Aids treatment advocacy in Canada". *The Academy of Management Journal* 47(5): 657–679.

Martin, R. (2000). "Institutional approaches in economic geography". In: Sheppard, E. (ed.). *A Companion to Economic Geography*. Oxford: Blackwell.

McCaffrey, M. and Salerno, J. T. (2011). "A theory of political entrepreneurship". *Modern Economy* 2: 552–560.

McCarthy, B. (2012). "From fishing and factories to cultural tourism: the role of social entrepreneurs in the construction of a new institutional field". *Entrepreneurship & Regional Development* 24(3–4): 259–282.

Ménard, C. and Shirley, M. M. (2008). *Handbook of New Institutional Economics*. New York: Springer.

Mintzberg, H. and Waters, J. A. (1985). "Of strategies, deliberate and emergent". *Strategic Management Journal* 6(3): 257–272.

North, D. C. (1990). *Institutions, Institutional Change and Economic Performance*. Cambridge: Cambridge University Press.

Oliver, C. (1991). "Strategic responses to institutional processes". *The Academy of Management Review* 16(1): 145–179.

Perkmann, M. (2002). "Euroregions: institutional entrepreneurship in the European Union". In: Perkmann, M., and Sum, N. L. (eds). *Globalization, Regionalization, and Cross-Border Regions*. Basingstoke: Palgrave.

Phillips, N. and Tracey, P. (2007). "Opportunity recognition, entrepreneurial capabilities and bricolage: connecting institutional theory and entrepreneurship in strategic organization". *Strategic Organization* 5(3): 313–320.

Powell, W. and DiMaggio, P. (1991). *The New Institutionalism in Organizational Analysis*. Chicago, IL and London: The University of Chicago Press.

Ritvala, T. and Kleymann, B. (2012). "Scientists as midwives to cluster emergence: an institutional work framework". *Industry and Innovation* 19(6): 477–497.

Sandberg, J. and Tsoukas, H. (2015). "Making sense of the sensemaking perspective: its constituents, limitations, and opportunities for further development". *Journal of Organizational Behavior* 36(51): S6–S32.

Silander, D. (2016). "The political entrepreneur". In: Karlsson, C., Silander, C. and Silander, D. (eds). *Political Entrepreneurship: Regional Growth and Entrepreneurial Diversity in Sweden*. Cheltenham: Edward Elgar.

Simon, H. A. (1957). *Models of Man – Social and Rational*. Oxford: Wiley.

Sotarauta, M. and Pulkkinen, R. (2011). "Institutional entrepreneurship for knowledge regions: in search of a fresh set of questions for regional innovation studies". *Environment and Planning* 29(1): 96–112.

Weik, E. (2011). "Institutional entrepreneurship and agency". *Journal for the Theory of Social Behaviour* 41(4): 466–481.

Wijen, F. and Ansari, S. (2007). "Overcoming inaction through collective institutional entrepreneurship: insights from regime theory". *Organization Studies* 28(7): 1079–1100.

Wilkens, U., Lang, R. and Winkler, I. (2003). "Institutionensoziologische ansätze". In: Weik, E. and Lang, R. (eds). *Moderne Organisationstheorien 2: Strukturorientierte Ansätze*. Wiesbaden: SpringerGabler.

Zilber, T. B. (2007). "Stories and the discursive dynamics of institutional entrepreneurship: the case of Israeli high-tech after the bubble". *Organization Studies* 28(7): 1035–1054.

PART II

EU institutions on entrepreneurship and regional growth

4. The European Commission: the EU as agenda-setter for economic growth and entrepreneurship

Daniel Silander and Charlotte Silander

The European Commission has a significant role as a driving engine and agenda-setter for entrepreneurship. Most important for entrepreneurship is the Directorate General (DG) for Growth (for the Internal Market, Industry, Entrepreneurship and SMEs). The DG for Growth has explicitly and repeatedly stated how Europe's economic growth and job creation depend on the development of entrepreneurship and SMEs. Entrepreneurship is necessary to create companies and job opportunities, to identify and enter new markets and to promote new technologies and skills. It is therefore vital for Europe's economy that more Europeans become entrepreneurs and develop new businesses and enterprises. In 2016, 30.6 million people aged 15 to 64 were self-employed in the European Union (EU), accounting for 14 per cent of total employment (Eurostat, 2016). In comparison, 37 per cent of Europeans (declining from 45 per cent in 2009), versus 51 per cent in the US and 56 per cent in China, state that they are willing to be self-employed (European Commission, 2012b: 4). The low number of self-employed in Europe is explained by different existing challenges for European entrepreneurs, such as limited know-how for developing an entrepreneurial career, limited access to finance and markets, obstacles in transferring businesses, overload of administrative procedures and a culture of fear of punitive measures in case of entrepreneurial mistakes. The Commission has declared a need for more European citizens to engage in entrepreneurial activities based on skills, creativity, innovation and risk-taking. The Commission further stressed the important role of education in promoting more entrepreneurial attitudes, as attitudes are related to actual self-employment (European Commission, 2012c).

This chapter will focus on entrepreneurship policy and the economic crises. In a time of long-term economic crisis, the Commission has approached entrepreneurship and the promotion of entrepreneurial activities through different initiatives. For example, *the Agenda 2020* (see Chapter 1 in this volume) stresses the importance of reigniting an entrepreneurial spirit in Europe. As argued, the economic recession has provided an opportunity for the Commission to expand its influence as an agenda-setter by promoting entrepreneurship education as an important tool for structural change of the European economy (see Chapter 8 in this volume). From a broader perspective, exogenous events outside the control of policymakers are often a triggering factor for policy change (Baumgartner and Jones, 2002). Studies on policy reform and organizational change have shown that it is common to think of crises as opportunities for desired change (Keeler, 1993) and as ways to break old patterns of thought and behaviour and open up possibilities for new approaches and ideas (Luebbert, 1991: 312; see also Kingdon, 1984). People experience crises as threat and uncertainty, which might turn into situations that call for urgent actions (Rosenthal et al., 2001; Stone, 1989; Keeler, 1993). Crises have historically played an important role for understanding European integration (Schmitter, 1970).

This chapter explores the Commission's role in entrepreneurship and growth. The main objective is to scrutinize how the Commission has approached European challenges to economic growth and entrepreneurship as the expected institutional political entrepreneur within the EU system. The main question is: in what ways has the Commission tried to act as a political entrepreneur in times of economic crisis? The introduction to this chapter discusses the Commission as an expected political entrepreneur and agenda-setter for European economic growth and entrepreneurship. This section is followed by a discussion on the general role and organization of the Commission within the EU's multilevel governance system. The third section focuses on the ways in which the European Commission has acted as a political entrepreneur to promote entrepreneurship in times of crisis, which is followed by concluding remarks that highlight the main findings.

THE COMMISSION, AGENDA-SETTING AND EMBEDDED POLITICAL ENTREPRENEURSHIP

The Commission, located in Brussels, is one of three EU institutions with executive duties, the other two being the Council of Ministers and the European Parliament. The Commission is a unique EU body in that it represents the overall interests of the EU rather than those of member states. Article 17 of the Treaty states that the Commission "shall promote the general interest of the Union and take appropriate initiatives to that end". In addition, the structure of the Commission is quite unique. The college of the Commission consists of 27 members and a president and is the highest decision-making body. The president represents the Commission as the public face of the European Union and meets with world leaders. The president and commissionaires are obliged not to take any instructions from any member state or other actor and to only seek and take initiatives that are in the interest of the union. The Commission must stand on its own in promoting general European interests by identifying, proposing, preparing, coordinating, managing and implementing EU policies. The Commission consists of 40 DGs, each focusing on a specific policy area and each run by a general director (McCormick, 2011: 167–179; Lelieveldt and Princen, 2011: 62–66).

Political actors are often expected to be entrepreneurial (Christopoulos, 2006: 757) to identify societal problems, promote solutions to problems and implement decisions. As stated in Chapter 1 of this volume, political entrepreneurship is, in this study, defined as something extraordinary compared to day-to-day political activities. Political entrepreneurship is about being bold and innovative and seeking new political solutions; it is about seeing windows of opportunity and making use of them by promoting and protecting growth and entrepreneurship in times of economic crisis. Previous research has identified the Commission as being active in a wide range of policy areas. This has been argued to be a consequence of the Commission's unique role as the main think tank, driving engine or political entrepreneur for the European project at large. The Commission is expected to set out shared European ideas, strive for collective solutions and "propose packages that will carry the majority of the member-states" (Laffan, 1997: 424). It can also provide valuable support to the member states' national and regional strategies (European Commission, 2004: 16). First, the Commission is expected to be an agenda-setter for European collective politics. To set the agenda is to initiate a European policy process by identifying needs for decision-making and making sure that relevant actors act upon the identified needs. The Commission must push for interests and attention among various European actors to mobilize interest and participation. When the Commission successfully mobilizes support for its ideas, the Commission might become an agenda-setter (Princen, 2011: 927–931). Second, making the Commission an agenda-setter also demands credibility to be built that certain issues should be handled within the EU and that the Commission should play a pivotal role. It is important that the Commission be portrayed as an expert in the area and have a track record of being an efficient and successful agenda-setter. Without such expertise and track record, it is questionable if the Commission has the credibility to push for certain agendas. An obvious hindrance to the Commission becoming an agenda-setter is of course the legal framework, including the judicial system of competences and the fundamental EU principle of subsidiarity, leaving issues to be dealt with at the most appropriate level of governance (Princen, 2011: 927–931).

It has been argued that the agenda-setting process is dependent on the correct kinds of venues and how the issue is framed by engaged actors. It is therefore up to the potential agenda-setter to identify the correct institutional platform for an agenda to be promoted and how to define the issue to attract as many supporters as possible. The main role of the potential agenda-setter is to raise an issue in the most favourable and relevant institutional setting to reach out to supporters and to frame the issue as well as possible to attract attention and receive credibility (Princen, 2011: 929). Research has pointed out four strategies in EU agenda-setting, as illustrated in Table 4.1 below:

Table 4.1 Four strategies in EU agenda-setting

	Venues	***Frames***
Gaining attention	Mobilizing supporters	Arousing interest
Building credibility	Capacity-building	Claiming authority

Source: Princen, 2011: 931.

First, *mobilizing supporters* is about promoting participation through institutional venues within the EU or the broader institutional setting of European governance to push for an issue to be placed on the agenda. Second, participation requires a process of framing the issue by *arousing interest* to attract active participants and supporters. This may occur by using big words linking the specific issue to broader norms, values and commitments within the European political system. Another way may be the opposite: to use small steps and attract growing interest to the issue step by step, and then initiate a debate or a conference to try to promote participation gradually (Princen, 2011: 931–935). Third, *capacity-building* refers to building organizational strength and having enough resources to promote an issue to formally enter the agenda. Such capacity-building must take place within EU institutions, but it is also important that EU institutions develop networks of interest groups, companies, experts and think tanks outside formal institutions to provide for capacity. Fourth, *claiming authority* is strongly related to building capacity in the sense that capacity provides the legitimacy to deal with issues. For EU institutions, claiming authority is therefore about promoting issues as European issues by linking the issue to EU policies or stressing the importance of a common European approach to an issue (Princen, 2011: 935–938).

The Big Five: Functions of the EU Commission

The Commission sets the agenda for the general interests of the European Union. It has five foremost functions (see Lelieveldt and Princen, 2011; McCormick, 2011). The Commission pursues its *powers of initiation* of legislation to the Council of Ministers and the European Parliament in all areas except the Common Foreign and Security Policy (CFSP) and police collaboration. A core duty of the Commission is therefore to gather information about and evaluate existing policies, initiate new legislative measures and manage the legislative process through consultations and negotiate potential amendments with the other two institutions. It may also propose new policy areas, as happened with the Single European Act. It is fair to argue that the Commission may provide political entrepreneurship by holding the right of initiative on new legislation and proposing new ideas for policy areas. The *power of implementation* refers to managing policies and programmes within EU policy areas and makes executive decisions to ensure the implementation of EU legislation. Each individual member state must collect and provide to the Commission information on how EU law is being embedded into national laws, but the Commission also monitors member states' progress by gathering information from individuals, interest groups, experts, companies and media sources, for example. *Powers of financial management* refers to administering the EU budget by collecting revenues and overseeing EU spending. It also includes assessing whether EU finances are being spent wisely to ensure efficiency and transparency and to avoid financial mismanagement within EU institutions or member states in relation to rights and obligations to the EU. *Power to guard the treaties* refers to the supervision of member states for adherence to mandatory EU laws and the implementation of policies by both member states and private actors. The Commission's role is to monitor EU laws and regulations and, if not followed by individual parties, send out warnings, decide on fines or bring the case to the European Court of Justice. Finally, *the power of external relations* includes overseeing applications to become an EU member state and also being the EU's representative body in EU policy areas when negotiating with third parties internationally.

Perhaps the Commission's most important role is to propose, monitor and implement new EU laws. Although the Commission seeks negotiations with individual member states, the Commission consistently gathers information from citizens, organizations, businesses and public authorities to be able to propose, monitor and implement new laws. The Commission may use different legal tools to promote the EU's general interests, monitor the application of treaties by member states and other actors and oversee the implementation of EU law. These legal tools, illustrated in Table 4.2 below, are regulations, directives, decisions, recommendations and opinions.

Table 4.2 The EU's legal tools

Regulations	The most powerful of the EU's laws. Directly and immediately binding in their entirety on all member states. Often designed to establish rules of procedure or technical standards, or to amend or adjust an existing law. Used where the intention is to ensure uniformity across all member states in dealing with a particular problem.
Directives	Binding on all member states in terms of goals, but member states are left to decide how best to achieve the goals and must make changes to national law within a specified period. Most focus on outlining general policy objectives, while some are aimed at harmonization (bringing different national laws into line).
Decisions	Although also binding, decisions are targeted at specific member states, individuals or institutions, with usually narrow objectives and administrative rather than legislative goals.
Recommendations	No binding force. The EU can choose to develop a regulation, directive or decision if the recommendations are ignored.
Opinions	No binding force. The loosest of all legal tools.

Source: McCormick, 2011: 179.

New Modes of Governance

Traditional policymaking patterns in the EU are increasingly being complemented by the use of "soft" governance tools such as benchmarking, recommendations on best practices and guidelines through the open method of coordination (OMC). New modes of governance, including benchmarking and exchanges of best practices, allow member states to coordinate and carry out policy, since the member states are responsible for their compliancy with the measures they have agreed on at the EU level. In the OMC process, the Commission plays an important monitoring and agenda-setting role. Member states submit annual reports on their progress, and the Commission reports on and evaluates these reports.

The OMC is applied in areas where the national situation differs substantially or where only limited competences exist at the EU level. This is the case for the areas relevant to entrepreneurship, such as education, industrial policy, employment policy and social policy. OMC is a compromise, as it retains member state responsibility while providing the EU with a coordinating and policy-shaping role (Warleigh-Lack and Drachenberg, 2011: 207). The OMC was launched as part of the action and development plan for the EU economy at the Lisbon meeting in 2000, together with the European Employment Strategy. The OMC represents a voluntary and intergovernmental mode of cooperation. The process does not allow for imposing policy solutions on member states, and there is no single uniform OMC process; instead, the OMC works differently depending on the policy area, but with a few common steps taken.

The first step is to set guidelines for the union combined with a timetable for what is to be completed in the short, medium and long term. This step is driven by the Commission; for entrepreneurship, it has been done through action plans. The targets set by the member states, in cooperation with the Commission, and member states' performance are periodically assessed. Step two is to establish quantitative and qualitative indicators and benchmarks, and step three is to translate the European guidelines into national and regional policies by setting specific targets and adopting measures for reaching the targets. The actions taken in the context of the action plan need to show results in terms of their impact on entrepreneurial performance in the EU. The Commission draws up a report on progress towards the targets set within the action plan, both at the EU level and within the member states (European Commission, 2004: 18). The progress and fulfilment of the established targets are evaluated in national reports for "naming and shaming" that point out lagging member states. The reports also form the basis for mutual learning processes, in which officials and stakeholder representatives can meet at conferences and workshops to represent and discuss important issues and progress.

The European Commission on Economic Growth and Entrepreneurship

One area of particular importance for economic growth and employability is the Single Market. The European Single Market is one of the EU's most important and successful accomplishments. The Commission has supreme authority to initiate legislation to promote a dynamic and competitive European market with free trade and mobility of goods, services, capital and people. It is of utmost importance that the Commission safeguard the fundamental principle of free competition in the Single Market. Such responsibility embeds assessing and monitoring political, economic, judicial and administrative hindrances for entrepreneurship, innovations, industries and SMEs in Europe. It is also the Commission's role to identify and counter any challenges to free trade and competition in the Single Market in terms of protectionism, state aid and cartels, for example. The Commission's Single Market Strategy includes reforms to improve the full potential of the European Single Market by promoting the mobility of goods, services, business innovations and know-how within the EU. Today, the Single Market includes about 500 million consumers and about 21 million SMEs, and a huge potential Digital Single Market exists that could provide hundreds of billions of euros and hundreds of thousands of new jobs to the EU economy (European Commission, 2015).

The Commission highly prioritizes the role of SMEs in the Single Market. The Commission has estimated that SMEs constitute about 99 per cent of all businesses within the EU and provide about 85 per cent of all new jobs and about two-thirds of employment in the private sector. Therefore, promoting improved conditions for SMEs is essential for a dynamic economy, wealth and social integration (European Commission, 2017a). It is about providing a business-friendly environment (see below on the Small Business Act), boosting the transformation of existing industrial structures (see below on Industrial Policy), promoting entrepreneurship and improving access to finances and markets (see below on Entrepreneurship Action Plan) and relations to SMEs based on clean, smart and sustainable industrial production (European Commission, 2017b).

Years before the economic crisis hit EU member states hard, the Lisbon Strategy of 2000 stressed the importance of structural changes to European economies to deal with economic slowdowns, as symbolized by limited job creation in the service sector, regional imbalances between old and new member states, long-term unemployment, misfit between labour supply and demands, the economic marginalization of certain social groups (women, immigrant, young people) and demographic challenges causing economic stress on the welfare system. The Lisbon Strategy highlighted the importance of adapting to ongoing technological changes and challenges, pushing for a knowledge-based society, promoting an improved business climate to make Europe more competitive, fostering a European entrepreneurial spiritual culture and favouring reforms to improve the social inclusion of marginalized groups by strengthening the social model. The overall goal with the Lisbon Strategy was to see a Europe of 2010 as the most competitive and dynamic know-how-based economy in the world (Lisbon Special European Council, 2000).

Major challenges in fulfilling the Lisbon Strategy, the failure to make Europe the most competitive economy in the world and the economic crisis of 2008 and forward, led the Commission to launch *Agenda 2020* in 2010 (see Chapter 1 in this volume). *Agenda 2020* was a 10-year strategy to promote a smart, sustainable and socially inclusive European economy and resulted in many important initiations by the Commission to protect Europe from the economic crisis and build a more competitive, smarter and more sustainable economic and social model for the future. In late November 2008, the Commission addressed the economic crisis in its communication to the European Council, *A European Economic Recovery Plan* (European Commission, 2008b). The Commission argued that "A Europe ready to take swift, bold, ambitious and well-targeted action will be a Europe able to put the brakes on the downturn and begin to turn the tide" (European Commission, 2008b: 2). The Commission called for political entrepreneurship and added the importance of strengthened governance to the economic crisis by stating, "The particular contribution of the European Union is its ability to help partners work together. Harnessing Member States' and Community action will add up to a powerful lever for change. It will open the door to using the strengths of each part of Europe to best effect" (European Commission, 2008b: 2). The European Economic Recovery Plan embedded two pillars. The first is the injection to push for increased demand on the European market. The Commission proposed a EUR 200 billion injection to the EU and member states to promote growth. The second is short-term actions to stimulate smart investments into the right skills for tomorrow's economy, sustainable development, energy efficiency, clean technologies, a transformation into low-carbon markets and infrastructure development (European Commission, 2008b: 23).

Small Business Act

In June 2008, the Commission presented the communication *"Think Small First" – A "Small Business Act" for Europe* (SBA), which stressed the importance of Europe adapting to globalization by becoming a knowledge-based economy (European Commission, 2008a: 2). Dynamic entrepreneurs were stated as being crucial for the growth and development of SMEs, and SMEs were highly important for employment opportunities and for local and regional development. The act emphasized the importance of SMEs in a prosperous European economy and argued: entrepreneurship and the associated willingness to take risks will therefore have to change: entrepreneurship and the associated willingness to take risks should be applauded by political leaders and the media, and supported by administrations (European Commission, 2008a: 3).

The SBA identified 10 principles to be implemented at the EU and member state levels targeting legal and administrative barriers to promote SMEs (European Commission, 2008a: 5–18). *The first principle* targeted entrepreneurs and the promotion of individual entrepreneurial talent and willingness to become entrepreneurs. The Commission aimed to promote an entrepreneurial culture and exchanges of best-practice enterprise education; implement the Erasmus for Young Entrepreneurs to exchange information and know-how between entrepreneurs; as well as an EU network for female entrepreneurship. The member states were encouraged to embed entrepreneurship into their school curricula, reform tax systems, provide mentoring and support for business transfers and entrepreneurship among underrepresented groups (the young, women, the elderly, migrants). *The second principle* stressed the importance of providing entrepreneurs with honoured bankruptcies a quick second chance to re-start, and thereby provide new opportunities for employment. The Commission emphasized the importance of fighting existing stigmas regarding bankruptcy. *The third principle* addressed judicial, regulatory and administrative reforms to promote small businesses and avoid unnecessary burdens and costs. The Commission stated that the goal was to fundamentally screen the business environment for small businesses and to promote necessary reforms to reduce administrative burdens. Modernizing public administration through new technology and e-government was raised as the *fourth principle* to better serve the interests and needs of SMEs. The Commission advised member states to reduce the administrative *requirements* (registration, licences, permits etc.) for businesses and to establish contact points and services to assist stakeholders by providing information on how necessary administration may be implemented online. *The fifth principle* addressed necessary public policy tools to assist SMEs with public procurement procedures. Statistics have shown that smaller businesses are unaware of, or discouraged from, participating in the public procurement market and discouraged from competing with larger enterprises. To reduce barriers for SMEs, the Commission would work to reduce bureaucracy and improve transparency and information as well as ask member states to provide more online information, subdivide contracts to better fit SMEs' capacities and support closer ties between SMEs and large buyers or products and services. *The sixth principle* concerned how to improve SMEs' access to finances through risk capital, microcredit and mezzanine finance and was addressed as a major hindrance for businesses beyond the previously mentioned administrative burdens. The Commission set out to improve European venture capital markets, support member states with establishing investment readiness programmes and financing programmes and advise member states with assessing regulatory and tax obstacles that might hinder investments and venture capital funds in the European Single Market. *The seventh principle* stressed the importance of the Commission and member states supporting SMEs by improving the governance of and information about market opportunities and existing policies; engaging SMEs with standards, access to patents and trademarks; and discussing how different national legal systems have a negative impact on SMEs' ability to enter new markets. *The eighth principle* addressed education, the importance of providing skills and competences for SMEs as well as know-how about new technologies and providing links between SMEs and research projects and universities. *The ninth principle* addressed how to turn environmental challenges into business opportunities in green markets with sustainable production and green products and services. The Commission and member states should support SMEs and provide them with incentives to adapt to climate change challenges and become energy efficient through eco-efficient activities. Finally, *principle 10* focused on external markets beyond EU territory and promoting SMEs in markets in, for example, EU candidate and neighbourhood states.

In 2011, a review of the SBA was presented, which included an assessment of the 10 principles presented in the 2008 Act (European Commission, 2011). Despite the full commitment of the Commission and

EU member states to promote an improved economic, legal and administrative environment for SMEs, the 2011 review listed several existing challenges. The review summarized remaining challenges in access to finances, administrative overload for SMEs and complex and time-consuming bankruptcy procedures. The Commission further stated the importance of strengthened governance of the SBA by collecting information on member states' actions and presenting annual reports on EU member states' policies and competitiveness to the Council of Ministers. The Commission also stated the importance of establishing an SBA advisory group consisting of government officials and business representatives to assess and inform about the SBA and taken policy actions (European Commission, 2011: 18). As stated in the review,

> Much has been achieved since the adoption of the SBA. The Commission has been faithful to commitments and implemented most of the measures promised. Member States, on the other hand, present a patchier record. For the SBA to achieve its objective of an SME friendly economic policy, it is important to ensure that the actions to which the EU and Member States committed themselves at the time of its adoption are fully implemented. (European Commission, 2011: 6)

Industrial Policy Communication

In late 2010, the European Commission presented the communication *An Integrated Industrial Policy for the Globalisation Era: Putting Competitiveness and Sustainability at Centre Stage* (European Commission, 2010). The communication stressed the importance of a competitive, industrial Europe in times of economic crisis and globalization. It was further stated that about one of four jobs in the EU's private sector came from the manufacturing industry; about one of four jobs involved related services based on industry, such as suppliers and customers; and about 80 per cent of private-sector research was conducted in industry (European Commission, 2010: 3). It was further argued that competitive European industrial production depended on the Single Market, with about 500 million consumers, 220 million workers and 20 million entrepreneurs. In addition, SMEs were estimated to account for about two-thirds of the total employment in European industries, making SMEs driving economic engines for European growth and employment crucial for a successful EU industrial policy. The communication's main objective was to set out a new approach to industrial policy aimed at dynamic economic growth and employment through increased EU competitiveness globally and the development of a low-carbon and resource-efficient economic base (European Commission, 2010: 5–23). European governance was stated to be essential for success. The improved European governance had to embed (1) a coordinated European vision between the Commission, the Council, the Parliament and relevant European institutions and (2) cooperation and coordination between EU institutions and member states in assessing competitiveness policies and the performance of EU and member state policies focusing on business environment, innovation structures, factors of competition, communication and transportation systems and regulatory and public administration (European Commission, 2010: 31). The Commission pointed at improved EU and member state legislation to push for competitiveness by looking for new judicial and regulatory opportunities, regulatory simplifications and lower administrative hindrances. The Commission also demanded improved access to finances for SMEs.

Lowered trade costs and increased competition needed to be promoted by harmonizing member state laws and regulations, standardizing systems that benefit both economic actors and public authorities, increasing access to some market sectors and improving the efficiency of energy, transport and communication infrastructure services. The communication pointed to using industrial innovations to meet global competitiveness and sustainable development based on improved coordination among higher education, research and innovations, training policies, investments, SMEs and industrial partners. The *final* objective set out in the communication was to promote trade liberalization with access to new markets and monitoring of potential state interventions and protectionism (European Commission, 2010: 17).

In late 2012, the European Commission presented an industrial policy communication to update the 2010 communication: *A Stronger European Industry for Growth and Economic Recovery* (European Commission, 2012a). It stated how "... the harsh impact of the economic crisis on several Member States, the subsequent economic stagnation in the EU and the deteriorating outlook for the global economy have given a new urgency to this Mid-term Review of the Industrial Policy" (European Commission, 2012a: 4–5). The communication stressed the importance of stronger European governance of Europe's economic crisis (European Commission, 2012a: 3) by proposing a partnership between the EU, member states, regional authorities and industry. The crisis had to be met by an industrial revolution targeting green energy, clean transport, improved communication and sustainable resources and materials. European governance for a new industrial revolution was to focus on new investments in technologies, innovation and resource efficiency; improving the Single Market to push for increased trade; assessing international markets for EU exports; public and private finances for innovations and

SMEs; and human capital and skills for an industrial revolution (European Commission, 2012a: 6).

Overall, the industrial revolution called for sustainable, green, clean production with resource efficiency and for promoting key enabling technologies. The industrial revolution was to be based on a stable Single Market with a simplified regulatory platform for new innovations, products and services; improved communication and transportation systems (from infrastructure to high-speed broadband); and coordination within the EU in research and development to foster new technologies. It was further stressed how the internal market had to be modernized by monitoring and updating existing rules and procedures to stay vital and avoid hindrances. The Commission pointed at full integration of certain sectors; the harmonization of products and of member state legislation to fully comply with mutual recognition clauses on products and services; a review of unitary patent and intellectual property rights in the internal market; assessing potential regulatory hindrances in policy areas decided by each member state; and improved access to finance and capital markets for European SMEs (European Commission, 2012a: 6–23). The final area was to foster entrepreneurship. As stated in the SBA, the Commission stressed the importance of supporting SMEs in the start-up phase through access to finances, easier regulations, lowered administrative burdens and networks with older entrepreneurs (European Commission, 2012a: 18).

In early 2014, the Commission presented the communication *For a European Industrial Renaissance*, which again stressed the importance of coordinated steering between the Commission, the Council and member states (governance) for a modernized industrial policy to foster growth and competitiveness. The main objectives were once again to develop the Single Market, invest in innovations and new technology to modernize industries, access new international markets and support SMEs and entrepreneurship (European Commission, 2014: 2–22). Based on previous hindrances in financial support, the Competitiveness and Innovation Programme (CIP) was launched in late 2013 to support financial institutions with about EUR 30 billion to financially support over 300,000 SMEs. In addition, Structural Funds added about EUR 70 billion in investments into enterprises, projects and start-ups, and the Commission improved the administration burdens on starting new businesses by lowering the costs and time required. From 2014 to 2020, a new financial instrument worth EUR 2.3 billion, COSME, is being launched to support SMEs, and another instrument – Horizon 2020 – will financially support research and innovations by SMEs (European Commission, 2014: 17–19).

In September 2017, the Commission promoted an updated industrial policy strategy by collecting previous horizontal and sector-specific initiatives into one strategy (see Chapter 7 in this volume). It further emphasized the importance of developing a smart, clean, innovative, empowered and sustainable industrial structure. On the reform agenda were measures to empower people through training, education and the recognition of qualifications across borders. The policy also stressed the importance of facilitating access to finances and innovations as well as to local and regional networks and clusters of collaboration between businesses, investors, universities and research centres. A final important reform was to unfold new technologies and a digital European Single Market through the support of a digital transformation in European industrial structures (European Commission, 2017b).

Entrepreneurship 2020 Action Plan

The *Entrepreneurship 2020 Action Plan* of 2012 is based on the *Small Business Act of 2008* and *2011* and of *the Industrial Policy Communication of 2012* (European Commission, 2012b: 3). The action plan identifies three pillars of entrepreneurship in Europe; improved entrepreneurial education and training, the framework conditions for entrepreneurs and a culture of entrepreneurship. *Action Pillar 1 on Entrepreneurial Education and Training to Support Growth and Business Creation* focuses on the role of education in fostering entrepreneurial learning about business know-how, entrepreneurial attitudes, ideas for innovations and the transfer of creative ideas into entrepreneurial actions. The European Commission stated the importance of promoting entrepreneurship education, to include entrepreneurial learning in course curricula, using practical experimental learning models, promoting volunteering and internships and promoting more entrepreneurship among universities and in higher education. The Commission also stated a willingness to see European practitioners and experts coming together to share knowledge, impact analysis and development of theories and methods, assess entrepreneurship education, encourage entrepreneurial schools and universities etc. The member states were invited to embed entrepreneurship into curricula throughout all levels of education, assist young people with obtaining practical entrepreneurial experience and promoting entrepreneurial training in relation to existing structural funds and with linkages to national job plans (European Commission, 2012b: 5–8).

Action Pillar 2 to Create an Environment Where Entrepreneurs Can Flourish and Grow addresses existing hindrances for entrepreneurship and growth by pointing out challenges concerning access to finance, support for entrepreneurs in strategic important business phases, new business opportunities, transfer of businesses, bankruptcy procedures and reductions in regulatory burdens. The European Commission identified problems with accessing adequate funding possibilities when setting up a business or aiming for growth and advised reduced tax-compliance costs to facilitate starting and growing small businesses. The limited financial support was especially obvious in the start-up phases of developing businesses, which has a negative impact on the possibility of seeing businesses grow. The Commission addressed the importance of venture capital funds and social entrepreneurship funds as alternative financial sources to the banking sector to support start-ups and existing businesses so they can afford to test innovations. An improved financial situation could also be accomplished through tax reductions and reformed tax legislation and tax-reporting systems to make it easier for smaller businesses to successfully handle their day-to-day activities. A third issue raised was the importance of improving the social security of self-employed persons to provide for welfare benefits for business owners comparable to social benefits designed for employed people. The Commission also addresses potentials in the digital age by promoting the idea of new business opportunities through new digital products and services. The Commission explicitly mentioned Web entrepreneurs and e-commerce providing digital products and services. The European Commission set out a wide range of reform proposals to EU member states. Among these were establishing an EU Entrepreneurship Day for students, appointing national entrepreneurship ambassadors as role models for entrepreneurship and assessing how existing domestic business models and legal structures support entrepreneurship. The Commission also called upon member states to amend financial legislations to improve funding schemes; make use of structural funds to promote microfinance support systems; reduce unnecessary and complex hindrances and taxation costs; scrutinize the risk of double taxation and limited tax deductions; support the commercialization of research, innovations and projects; improve national and regional assistance for Web entrepreneurship; offer information, services and platforms for business transfers; and modernize the labour market to allow for simplified employment (European Commission, 2012b: 8–22).

Action Pillar 3 on Role Models and Reaching Out to Specific Groups addresses the importance of both entrepreneurial success stories to attract new entrepreneurs and of reaching out and supporting new societal groups to become entrepreneurial and start businesses. The European

Commission stated the importance of promoting an improved entrepreneurial culture in Europe in which entrepreneurship is perceived as a positive career option.

An important element to change the entrepreneurial culture is thus a change in the perception of entrepreneurs through practical and positive communication about the achievements of entrepreneurs, their value to society and the opportunities of new business creation or acquisition as a career destination (European Commission, 2012b: 21).

Pillar 3 also declares the importance of reaching out to societal groups that have previously been underrepresented within entrepreneurship, such as women, young people, migrants, the elderly and disabled people. It was argued that these groups constitute marginalized human capital that could bring new entrepreneurial activities to society. The Commission stated how 52 per cent of the European population are women, but women are only one-third of the self-employed or business starters. The Commission also identified barriers to women's entrepreneurship in access to financial support, training and social and economic networks while handling the burdens of both running a business and family duties. The Commission also described a forgotten group of seniors who are healthier than ever and often highly experienced and educated but not politically and economically supported to be entrepreneurial. The unemployment among young Europeans is also stated to be high, and it was argued that engaging young people in entrepreneurial training and entrepreneurship is crucial for them to become self-employed. In addition, migrants were considered a growing group of citizens and a potential group to become entrepreneurs and self-employed. The challenges were considered to the migrant businesses to grow and engaging migrants to become entrepreneurs. The European Commission would like to see an EU Entrepreneurship Day for students in secondary education, with lectures, workshops and company invitations for students, entrepreneurs and other professionals. The Commission also declared a willingness to see an online networking platform for mentoring, advising and educating to support female entrepreneurship and to exchange best practices between member states. In addition, to help the elderly, the Commission wanted senior entrepreneurs to advise and mentor new younger entrepreneurs to exchange best practices. On migrant and entrepreneurship, the European Commission recommended new policy initiatives to attract migrants to become entrepreneurs based on best practices examples within European states. Finally, the Commission also addressed ideas about the unemployed and young people regarding entrepreneurship and self-employment by pointing out reforms for microfinance facilities; support schemes for young entrepreneurs; a forum for microfinance and social entrepreneurship stakeholders to push for a green economy; conditions for entrepreneurship among the unemployed; and policy recommendations for improvements.

The Commission called upon the member states to implement initiatives, policies and reforms to improve the conditions for entrepreneurship and start-ups among entrepreneurial marginalized groups. This ambition included setting up national strategies for female entrepreneurship, producing annual updates on women's entrepreneurship, expanding existing networks of ambassadors and mentors for women's entrepreneurship, implementing policies to empower women in the labour market through support via affordable child care and promoting senior entrepreneurs sharing knowledge with younger entrepreneurs by establishing teams and projects. The Commission also asked member states to remove legal barriers for migrants to start businesses and to establish information centres targeting migrant areas to provide strategic information and networking for potential and actual entrepreneurs and business operators. Finally, the Commission also addressed the need to link public employment, business support services and finance providers to empower the unemployed and provide business training programmes, entrepreneurship education schemes and labour market programmes (European Commission, 2012b: 22–28).

POLITICAL ENTREPRENEURSHIP AND ENTREPRENEURSHIP EDUCATION

Since the introduction of the Lisbon Strategy, entrepreneurship education has increasingly been stressed as a tool for European economic growth. With limited provisions in the treaty, the EU has no legal power over education or training systems in individual member states but instead needs to base policy measures on non-legal control practitioners (Lawn, 2011). The lack of formal provisions has made the EU increasingly adapt new modes of governance (NMGs), referring to a variety of policy-making instruments such as soft law, policy agreements and social partnerships introduced in the wake of the Maastricht Treaty (Borrás and Jacobsson, 2004). NMGs represent a form of pragmatic accommodation of emerging needs perceived by the EU and a lack of political will by the member states to maintain responsibility for an area while at the same time providing coordinating power to the EU.

Entrepreneurial competence is seen as an important policy issue for governments striving for economic growth. European policymakers have a common belief that entrepreneurship education is a way to influence culture and build enterprising economies (Martinez et al., 2010). Therefore, interest is growing in education as a tool to guarantee economic growth (see Chapter 8 in this volume). In the EU, education policy has increasingly changed from a focus on shaping a European identity and support for cohesion among the people of Europe to a competitive tool for strengthening the European economic market. Until the 2000s, there was no formal educational policy at the European level, only a series of specific programmes. This changed around the start of the new century, accentuated by the introduction of the Lisbon process in 2000, which set the objective for Europe to become the most competitive region in the world (European Council, 2000: 1). The Lisbon process stressed education as an important tool for employment and growth by focusing on the link between knowledge and economic growth. The way to become the most competitive knowledge-based economy in the world was to have the member states compete with each other, through the Lisbon process, to provide for national and European growth (European Council, 2000). At the same time, the OMC was launched with the European Employment Strategy as a way for the EU to act in areas where the national situation differed substantially or where only limited competences existed at the EU level, such as areas related to entrepreneurship education. This meant that traditional policymaking patterns in the EU were complemented by the use of "soft" governance tools.

By reviewing documents on entrepreneurship and education produced by the EU, the Commission has engaged, step by step, in educational issues to increase self-employment and promote entrepreneurship in the European economy. Before the economic crisis, Europe's future was painted in optimistic colours: "The union possesses a generally well-educated workforce as well as social protection systems able to provide, beyond their intrinsic value, the stable framework required for managing the structural changes involved in moving towards a knowledge-based society" (European Council, 2000: 2). However, this optimistic view changed, and the rhetoric of crises became more accentuated. A much-cited report presented in 2004 by a high-level group of politicians and representatives from trade unions and industry criticized the slow pace of the Lisbon process (Kok, 2004: 6). The OMC process was considered to be ineffective, and the member states were criticized for failing to commit to a common agenda (Kok, 2004: 6). The report argued that drastic measures needed to be taken to prevent a disaster: "At risk – in the medium to the long run – is nothing less than the sustainability of the society Europe has built" (Kok, 2004: 16). The Kok report was followed up in the mid-term report written by the Commission in 2005, which stated: "Europe's performance has diverged from that of our competitors in other parts of the world" (European Commission, 2005: 4).

In 2004, the same year as when the Kok report was published, the Commission launched its *Action Plan: The European Agenda for Entrepreneurship*. Europe was considered to need more entrepreneurship as a major driver of innovation, competitiveness and growth. Recurrent references were made to the positive correlation between entrepreneurship and economic performance in terms of growth (European Commission, 2004: 1). In order to fight the impact of the economic crisis, Europe needed more entrepreneurial individuals: "If Europe wants to successfully maintain its social model, it needs more economic growth, more new firms, more entrepreneurs willing to embark in innovative ventures, and more high-growth SMEs" (European Commission, 2006: 3). The offer from the Commission to Europeans who wished to keep their welfare system was therefore to engage in entrepreneurship. Much attention was paid to the lack of entrepreneurial spirit among Europeans, which hindered the EU from fully exploiting its entrepreneurial potential. Europeans were described as risk averse and not sufficiently entrepreneurial:

> The prevailing attitudes towards entrepreneurship and the current balance of the risks and rewards appear to make many Europeans less inclined to become entrepreneurs […] Entrepreneurship education was seen as an important way to create more entrepreneurial mindsets among young people. To alleviate the burden of risk, the severe consequences of failure and the need to accept a lower degree of social security should be addressed. (European Commission, 2004: 5)

The reference to "risk and rewards" indicated implicit problems caused by the tradition of a strong European welfare system and that entrepreneurship education would serve to teach Europeans to "accept a lower degree of social security", as stated in the quote above. Also, cultural aspects needed to be taken into account, as "Europeans are reluctant to take up opportunities for self-employment and entrepreneurial activities. Research suggests that cultural support (e.g. through education programmes, promotional campaigns, etc.) is positively linked with the amount of entrepreneurial activity in the EU" (European Commission, 2006: 3).

The Commission pointed to national educational systems as being responsible for the shortfalls in innovative and creative entrepreneurs who can handle the necessary adaptation to the knowledge society. Ever since its action plan was created (European Commission, 2004: 5), the Commission had called for changes in education to deal with the lack of an entrepreneurial spirit in Europe. As it stated:

> People in Europe need to be made more aware that self-employment is a potentially attractive career option and be provided with the necessary skills to turn their ambitions into successful ventures. The education system, and in particular the school curricula, do not focus enough on entrepreneurship and do not provide the basic skills which entrepreneurs need. (European Commission, 2008a: 5)

In 2008, the Council concluded that the pace of educational reforms needed to speed up. In order to achieve the goals of the Lisbon process, education needed to be linked to more areas, and standardization and monitoring of education needed to increase (European Council, 2008). It was argued:

> [the] concrete objective is to bring entrepreneurship into the mainstream of national educational policy and practice in every country in the EU, to enhance the understanding of education as growth-friendly investment and inspire long-term policy reform at the member state level. (Thematic Working Group on Entrepreneurship Education, 2013: 4)

Universities and technical institutes were expected to "integrate entrepreneurship as an important part of the curriculum, spread across different subjects, and require or encourage students to take entrepreneurship courses" (European Commission, 2006: 9). The desire to produce a greater impact on the national educational system was declared, and the instruments of governance and monitoring were sharpened. The Europe 2020 campaign launched a range of reforms for "smart and sustainable and inclusive growth" (European Commission, 2010) through which actions in the respective areas and in member states were to be closely followed up. Europe 2020 argued for a strong governance framework, resulting in the OMC process being improved. In 2013, by the release of the Entrepreneurship 2020 Action Plan, entrepreneurship education had reached the top of the list of ways to make Europeans more entrepreneurial and the European Commission stated that "to make entrepreneurship the growth engine of our economy Europe needs a thorough, far-reaching cultural change" (European Commission, 2013: 4).

The EU has called for educational reforms for Europe to maintain its position in the world, highlighting globalization and the knowledge-driven economy as the main drivers of radical reforms (Robertson, 2008; Alexiadou, 2014). The formulation at the Lisbon summit, as a new strategic goal for the next decade, for the EU to become the "most competitive and dynamic knowledge-based economy in the world, capable of sustainable economic growth with more and better jobs and greater social cohesion" (European Council, 2000), created a link between education policy and employment policy that connected the Single Market to education (Warleigh-Lack and Drachenberg, 2011: 1004). Education was considered an important tool to create a more entrepreneurial mindset among young people. Entrepreneurship thus became a key ingredient in the EU's educational policy, and education was now seen as an important part of promoting entrepreneurship.

CONCLUSION

The agenda-setting power of the Commission provides the potential for political entrepreneurship, and the Commission has indeed been active in promoting entrepreneurship in the European context. However, most of its measures can be considered traditional day-to-day activities expected to come from an agenda-setter. Political entrepreneurship by the Commission can also be viewed in the light of increasing cooperation, stronger EU influence on national policymaking and a wider use of policy-coordinating methods (Wallace et al., 2015). The push for reigniting the entrepreneurial spirit and reforming the educational system has been legitimated by a rhetoric of crises communicated through policy documents.

A new approach to education policy has been stressed as necessary to solve the European economic crises. The urgent need for Europe to deal with the lack of entrepreneurial spirit through education to address its economic crises and unemployment was presented in the Action Plan 2004 and has been strengthened ever since. The urgency mechanism was frequently used both to legitimize EU action in education and to emphasize the need to introduce entrepreneurship into higher education curricula. Education policy has come to be linked to EU policies on growth, entrepreneurship and SMEs. Today, the EU often deliberately discusses education policy in economic terms to provide the EU with competence and legitimacy to have a say as an agenda-setter (see Chapter 1 in this volume). The linking of education to the Single Market has proven crucial to legitimizing action at the EU level, and the link between employment and education established in the Lisbon process is an example of European integration advancing by linking areas in line with the early neofunctionalist ideas of integration (Haas, 1968). In this way, the economic crises of 2008 and forward served as a "window of opportunity" (Kingdon, 1984) for new EU political entrepreneurship by the Commission.

REFERENCES

Alexiadou, N. (2014). "Policy learning and europeanisation in education: the governance of a field and the transfer of knowledge". In: Nordin, A. and Sundberg, D. (eds). *Transnational Policy Flows in European Education: The Making and Governing of Knowledge in the Education Policy Field*. Oxford: Symposium Books.

Baumgartner, F. R. and Jones, B. D. (eds) (2002). *Policy Dynamics*. Chicago, IL: University of Chicago Press.

Borrás, S. and Jacobsson, K. (2004). "The open method of coordination and new governance patterns in the EU". *Journal of European Public Policy*, 11(2).

Christopoulos, D. (2006). "Relational attributes of political entrepreneurs: a network perspective". *Journal of European Public Policy*, 13(5): 757–778.

European Commission (2004). *Action Plan: The European Agenda for Entrepreneurship*, COM (2004) 70 final. Brussels: European Commission.

European Commission (2005). *Communication to the Spring European Council. Working Together for Growth and Jobs. A New Start for the Lisbon Strategy*. COM (2005) 24.

European Commission (2006). *Entrepreneurship Education in Europe: Fostering Entrepreneurial Mindsets through Education and Learning*. Brussels: European Commission.

European Commission (2008a). *Think Small First – A "Small Business Act" for Europe*. Brussels: European Commission.

European Commission (2008b). *A European Economic Recovery Plan*. Brussels: European Commission.

European Commission (2010). *An Integrated Industrial Policy for the Globalisation Era Putting Competitiveness and Sustainability at Centre Stage*. Brussels: European Commission.

European Commission (2011). *Review of the "Small Business Act" for Europe*. Brussels: European Commission.

European Commission (2012a). *A Stronger European Industry for Growth and Economic Recovery – Industrial Policy Communication Update*. Brussels: European Commission.

European Commission (2012b). *Entrepreneurship 2020 Action Plan – Reigniting the Entrepreneurial Spirit in Europe*. Brussels: European Commission.

European Commission (2012c). *Effects and Impact of Entrepreneurship Programmes in Higher Education*. Brussels: European Commission.

European Commission (2013). *Entrepreneurship 2020 Action Plan – Reigniting the Entrepreneurial Spirit in Europe*. Brussels: European Commission.

European Commission (2014). *For a European Industrial Renaissance*. Brussels: European Commission.

European Commission (2015). *Entrepreneurship and Small and Medium-sized Enterprises (SMEs)*, accessed 5 October 2017 at https://ec.europa.eu/growth/smes_en.

European Commission (2017a). *Promoting Entrepreneurship. Growth – Internal Market, Industry, Entrepreneurship and SMEs*, accessed 23 August 2017 at https://ec.europa.eu/growth/smes/promoting-entrepreneurship_en.

European Commission, Industry (2017b). *The European Single Market*, accessed 5 October 2017 at https://ec.europa.eu/growth/single-market_en.

European Council (2000). *Lisbon European Council 23 and 24 March 2000 – Presidency Conclusions.*

European Council (2008). Draft 2008 joint progress report of the Council and the Commission on the "Education & Training 2010" work programme "Delivering lifelong learning for knowledge, creativity and innovation". Joint Interim Report.

Eurostat (2016). *Eurostat Database on Employment and Unemployment*, accessed 30 October 2017 at http://ec.europa.eu/eurostat/web/products-eurostat-news/-/DDN-20170906-1.

Haas, E. (1968). *The Uniting of Europe: Political, Social and Economic Forces*, 2nd edition. Stanford, CA: Stanford University Press.

Keeler, J. T. S. (1993). "Opening the window for reform: mandates, crises and extraordinary policymaking". *Comparative Political Studies*, 25(4): 433–486.

Kingdon, J. W. (1984). *Agendas, Alternatives, and Public Policies.* Boston, MA: Little Brown.

Kok, W. (2004). *Facing the Challenge Ahead: The Lisbon Strategy for Growth and Employment.* Report from the high level group chaired by Wim Kok. Brussels: European Commission.

Laffan, B. (1997). "From policy entrepreneur to policy manager: the challenge facing the European Commission". *Journal of European Public Policy*, 4(3): 422–438.

Lawn, M. (2011). "Standardizing the European education policy space". *European Educational Research Journal*, 10(2): 259–272.

Lelieveldt, H. and Princen, S. (2011). *The Politics of the European Union.* Cambridge: Cambridge University Press.

Lisbon Special European Council (2000). *The Lisbon Special European Council (March 2000): Towards a Europe of Innovation and Knowledge*, accessed 5 October 2017 at http://eur-lex.europa.eu/legal-content/EN/TXT/HTML/?uri=LEGISSUM:c10241&from=SV.

Luebbert, G. M. (1991). *Liberalism, Fascism, or Social Democracy.* New York: Oxford University Press.

Martinez, A. C., Levie, J., Kelley, D. J., Saemundsson, R. J. and Schøtt, T. (2010). "Global Entrepreneurship Monitor Special Report: A Global Perspective on Entrepreneurship Education and Training". Strathclyde: Hunter Centre For Entrepreneurship.

McCormick, J. (2011). *European Union Politics.* Basingstoke: Palgrave Macmillan.

Princen, S. (2011). "Agenda-setting strategies in EU policy processes". *Journal of European Public Policy*, 18(7): 927–943.

Robertson, S. L. (2008). "Embracing the Global: Crisis and the Creation of a New Semiotic Order to Secure Europe's Knowledge-Based Economy". Bristol: Centre for Globalisation, Education and Societies. Centre for Globalisation, Education and Societies: University of Bristol.

Rosenthal, U., Boin, A. and Comfort, L. (2001). *Managing Crisis: Threats, Dilemmas, Opportunities.* Springfield, IL: Charles C. Thomas.

Schmitter, P. C. (1970). "A revised theory of regional integration". *International Organization*, 24(4): 836–868.

Stone, D. A. (1989). "Causal stories and the formation of policy agendas". *Political Science Quarterly*, 104(2): 281–300.

Thematic Working Group on Entrepreneurship Education (2013). Entrepreneurship Education and the Future of Learning. Thematic Report Vienna: 17–19 April.

Wallace, H., Pollack, M. A. and Young, A. R. (2015). *Policy-making in the European Union*. Oxford: Oxford University Press.

Warleigh-Lack, A. and Drachenberg, R. (2011). "Spillover in a soft policy era? Evidence from the open method of co-ordination in education and training". *Journal of European Public Policy*, 18(7): 999–1015.

5. Entrepreneurship policy in the Council of the EU: reaching consensus among member states?

Brigitte Pircher

INTRODUCTION

Why are institutions important to entrepreneurship? In principle, institutions determine the set of rules and possibilities for engaging in economic activities (Bruton et al., 2009; North, 1990, 1991; Djankov et al., 2002). They provide the regulatory framework and incentive structures of an economy, and organize the economic, social, and political interplay in a society (North, 1990, 1991). They impact the economic action not only by way of formal rules, but also by way of informal rules, such as culture, traditions, norms, and values (Bruton et al., 2009; North, 1991). Institutions may have constraining effects on the degree of economic activity by introducing restrictions for individuals or enterprises that enter into business. However, institutions also have favourable effects by creating opportunities for economic engagement (Roper, 2013: 1–4). They are therefore regarded as key in providing a solid foundation for economic involvement.

The potential of institutions to introduce favourable conditions for economic engagement tends to increase in times of economic crisis, and the crisis is used as a 'window of opportunity' to adopt policies conducive to entrepreneurs and economic growth. The European economic crisis is no exception. In responding to the crisis, the European Union (EU) has developed novel and innovative policies, instruments, and measures aimed at fostering economic growth, which are considered crucial for the creation of jobs, improving social welfare, and reducing unemployment (Ribeiro-Soriano and Galindo-Martín, 2012). Entrepreneurship has been discussed as a relevant factor in increasing economic growth (Acs et al., 2005; Audretsch et al., 2006). As a result, national governments assume that boosting entrepreneurship is decisive for a sound economy. This assumption has led the EU and national governments to promote entrepreneurship and the economic potential of businesses within the internal market. Moreover, studies demonstrating that good governance is a prerequisite for stimulating entrepreneurship (see, for example, Méndez-Picazo et al., 2012) have accelerated this development.

Even though several policies were adopted to promote economic recovery and growth, welfare, and entrepreneurship, little is known about how these novel entrepreneurial policies and measures were discussed within and introduced by the EU institutions in times of economic crisis. The following chapter therefore addresses the political dimension of entrepreneurship and sheds more light on these questions by dealing with the Council of the EU as the dominant legislator. To begin with, the chapter discusses the role of the Council after the onset of the financial crisis in 2008 and the EU regulatory framework for entrepreneurship. Then, on the basis of an analysis of the Council debates, there is an examination of how and under which circumstances EU institutions provide for enabling institutional structures and policies favourable to entrepreneurship and regional growth. This main section demonstrates the extent to which institutions may serve as political entrepreneurs. By analysing the contentious issues that arose during the Council's discussions, the chapter further illustrates the political limitations of an entrepreneurship-friendly policy in Europe.

ENTREPRENEURSHIP AS AN ANTI-CRISIS POLICY STRATEGY

The EU legal framework has the potential to constrain or to enable entrepreneurship and innovation. Over the past few decades, reforms in the EU regulatory framework and the jurisprudence of the Court of Justice of the EU have favoured the broadening of the EU internal market, and positively influenced the degree of entrepreneurship and innovation (Pelkmans and Renda, 2014; European Commission, 2007).

However, the financial crisis revealed weaknesses in the EU's institutional design with regard to economic affairs (Verdun, 2013: 53–59). Member states first responded individually to the crisis, but a joint EU response was inevitable, especially in view of the developments in Greece (Verdun, 2015: 223). The need for an immediate response to the crisis brought about new institutional changes favouring an intergovernmental approach and intergovernmental institutions, such as the Council of the EU or the European Council (Fabbrini, 2013; Puetter,

2012). The crisis has placed the EU's post-Maastricht institutional paradox at the forefront. Even though the Lisbon Treaty nowadays provides for greater integration of certain policies and enhances the role of the European Parliament as a co-legislator, several new financial and economic policies fall exclusively under the control of intergovernmental institutions, that is, national governments (Fabbrini, 2013: 1004). Rather than competencies being transferred to the Community level, policy coordination has become the common method of decision-making (Bickerton et al., 2015), leading to a new form of deliberative and consensus-seeking intergovernmentalism (Puetter, 2012). Since a range of new economic governance mechanisms was established via intergovernmental agreements, policymaking has become more informal, and the access to policy dialogue decisive (Bickerton et al., 2015; Puetter, 2012).

During the economic crisis, the promotion of entrepreneurship became a policy strategy for boosting economic growth. Between the onset of the financial crisis in October 2008 and March 2017, 38 binding legislative acts (19 regulations, 6 directives, and 13 decisions) were adopted, explicitly stating that one aim of the respective EU law was to promote, encourage, support, stimulate, enhance, or foster entrepreneurship. The Council adopted 12 recommendations pursuing the same objective.[1] This demonstrates the abundant use of the term 'entrepreneurship' in current EU legislation, and is in line with the argument that it has in fact become a buzzword at the EU level. Furthermore, the EU aimed to improve conditions for entrepreneurs in various areas by slashing administrative burdens, reducing business risk, making procedures or systems more flexible, abolishing obstacles for entrepreneurs, introducing favourable conditions for small and medium-sized enterprises (SMEs), and supporting innovative companies. Examples include legislation in the area of competition and company law; taxation; financial regulation; regulations for self-employment; and equal treatment of men and women *inter alia*. Over and above EU legislation, policy strategies and action plans have been discussed and adopted by various EU institutions. Even though extensive legislation in this area has been initiated in the past years, little is known about how the EU institutions discussed entrepreneurship in times of crisis or how they provided for favourable conditions for entrepreneurs.

---

1 Based on the source EUR-Lex, all regulations, directives, decisions and Council recommendations having 'entrepreneurship' in the title or in the text in the time period from 1/10/2008 until 22/03/2017 (date of document) have been analysed.

ENTREPRENEURSHIP POLICY: THE MULTIPLE STREAM APPROACH

How and why was entrepreneurship policy discussed in the Council? What solutions were formulated, and what were the factual outcomes? The first step in a policy process is the perception of a problem (problem stream), caused by certain systematic indicators signalling that a specific problem exists. Attention is drawn to a specific problem when there is a focus on events or a crisis to which pre-existing perceptions are attached (Kingdon, 2011: 94–115; Cohen, March and Olsen, 1972: 3). Even though problems are defined first and solutions subsequently elaborated, Cohen et al. (1972) argue in their garbage can model that solutions and programmes developed by actors within a political system are also made for the desk drawer or 'garbage can', waiting for a suitable problem; or as Kingdon (2011: 86) puts it, 'solutions search for problems'.

The next stage involves policy proposals being generated, debated, and narrowed down to common solutions (policy stream). In this phase, advocates – so-called policy entrepreneurs that are willing to invest their resources (time, energy, reputation, and money) – advocate their proposals in many ways (Kingdon, 2011: 116–144). At the agenda-setting level, decision makers have to narrow down their political attention to certain focus areas. Frequently, external events or crises that have a strong influence on the political system are seen as factors with the potential to set the political agenda and to introduce policy change (Baumgartner and Jones, 1993; Sabatier and Jenkins-Smith, 1999; Weible et al., 2008; Zahariadis, 2014). Ultimately, the politics stream reaches the decision-making stage, where the degree of consensus determines the policy outcome.

Kingdon (2011: 87) argues that when the three different streams couple at critical junctures, a window of opportunity opens and produces the greatest agenda change. This policy window is crucial for the success of policy entrepreneurs. They must be prepared, their pet solutions ready, and their problems formulated. A successful policy entrepreneur (an expert or leader, for example), should be taken seriously, should have a political network and negotiating skills, and should be persistently waiting for a window of opportunity (Capano, 2009: 19–25; Kingdon, 2011: 165). Entrepreneurs are made up of officials, politicians, lobbyists, academics, lawyers, bureaucrats, *inter alia*, who focus on the development of public goods rather than on individual profits (Kingdon 2011: 122–180). Normally, policy entrepreneurs are individuals, but can also be other types of actors (Bernhard and Wihlborg, 2014: 290). These characteristics may also refer to supranational institutions at the EU level (Pollack, 1999: 6).

Even though we use the term 'political entrepreneur' in our current book, there are various similar characteristics with Kingdon's definition of policy entrepreneur. Our definition of political entrepreneur as presented in Chapter 1 includes the definition of policy entrepreneur. However, the concept of political entrepreneur is broader as it also includes a structure perspective by focusing on institutions that understand and challenge existing formal and informal structures and conditions in order to set out new and innovative reforms for the promotion of entrepreneurship and economic prosperity or the common good. This may involve political strategies and programmes, policies, laws, rules, regulations, and budgets for entrepreneurial activities as well as informal structures, attitudes, norms and values, and perceptions that are cultivated in the daily work. In this respect, political entrepreneurship occurs if existing structures are challenged and altered in order to better serve the interests of entrepreneurial activities (see Chapter 1 in this volume and Silander, 2016).

With regard to entrepreneurship policy at the EU level, the question arises whether the economic crisis really provided a window of opportunity. Who were the political entrepreneurs, and how did the EU institutions behave? Was it possible to promote and foster entrepreneurship at the EU level?

TAKING STOCK OF COUNCIL DISCUSSIONS ON ENTREPRENEURSHIP

In order to answer the research questions above, this study draws upon the multiple stream approach of John Kingdon (2011), as it provides a potential way of analysing a policy process in a certain area. Further, it allows for an examination of the driving actors in such a policy process within a specific timeframe, and particularly in times of crisis.

As the EU regulatory framework on entrepreneurship is overarching and comprises a number of different policy fields and legislative acts that led to a host of long debates in the Council, the study narrows down the scope of the investigation to the two main entrepreneurial action plans, namely the Small Business Act for Europe and the Entrepreneurship 2020 Action Plan. This has several advantages. First, the action plans include both overarching policy strategies and concrete policy measures, including proposals for legislation. Second, focusing on these action plans requires a long period of time to be covered – from late 2008, directly after the onset of the financial crisis, until 2014. Third, the action plans were broadly discussed in the Council, and the Council adopted concrete policy measures on how to implement them. Fourth, the action plans are representative of EU entrepreneurship policy, as they specify future policy objectives in this area. In examining the Council debates on the action plans, the following sources were taken into account and evaluated via content analysis: the action plans and adopted policy measures, the debates during the decision-making process, official documents, the opinions of states, press releases, and, in particular, *Agence Europe* newspaper articles.

The Small Business Act for Europe

One of the measures adopted to promote entrepreneurship is the Small Business Act (SBA) for Europe. Even though it is a communication without legal effect, it nonetheless comprises a set of new legislative proposals (European Commission, 2008a; see also Chapter 3 in this volume). A communication is usually preceded by public consultations, when the Commission invites interested parties to contribute to a certain problem. On this basis, the Commission formulates the communication addressed to the Council and the European Parliament. Both institutions reply to the communication by proposing concrete policy measures. We can identify the economic crisis as one of the important reasons for entrepreneurship being discussed and placed on the highest political agenda in late 2008. Entrepreneurship was regarded as one of the decisive factors for economic growth in Europe. Therefore, when the severe effects of the economic crisis were felt by the EU and its member states, the fostering of entrepreneurship took centre stage.

In the case of the SBA, it appears that the garbage can model of Cohen et al. (1972) fits, as concrete measures for boosting SMEs in order to improve entrepreneurship in Europe had already been formulated by the Commission and discussed by the Council before the economic crisis (EUR-Lex, 2017). In May 2008, the Council stressed the need to create favourable conditions for SMEs, and highlighted that further efforts in this area were needed (Council of the EU, 2008c). The SBA measures were communicated to the Council in June 2008 (EUR-Lex, 2017) and initially discussed at an informal meeting of ministers in Versailles, France, in July 2008 (Council of the EU, 2008d). Even though proposals in this area had already been formulated, the plan was placed on the highest political agenda only after the onset of the financial crisis in September 2008, when swift action was needed to boost economic growth. This means that the problem was perceived and decision makers focused their political attention on this area. As Pollack (1999: 5) points out, in the EU the Commission's right to propose legislation 'is not sufficient to ensure agenda-setting power'. It is rather dependent on the legislators, in particular the Council, and the mechanisms at their disposal (specific voting procedures and applicable rules). A communication from the Commission can be regarded as a memorandum, and it is subsequently up to the legislators to undertake concrete policy measures for the decision-making stage. The economic crisis provided the momentum to take ready-made plans out of the drawer and bring them to the political level, the decision-making stage.

When the SBA was launched, there was a coupling of the problem and policy streams, which provided a window of opportunity to create a need to decide upon concrete actions and solutions to the crisis (politics stream). As will be seen in the following section, throughout the Council debates on the SBA, the EU ministers strongly emphasized the urgency for concrete short- and medium-term policy measures to improve the situation for SMEs as a result of the economic situation.

In September 2008, the competitiveness ministers reached broad consensus in prioritizing certain objectives in the light of the economic slowdown (Council of the EU, 2008d). Three main priorities were identified: first, expediting SMEs' access to funding; second, the simplification of legislation by reducing and simplifying administrative burdens; and third, promoting the access of SMEs to markets. Günter Verheugen, former Commissioner and Vice-President of the Barroso Commission – who played a crucial role in promoting the SBA – stressed the importance of strong measures with regard to the financial crisis that had severely affected SMEs. He highlighted that Germany's prioritized aim would be the revision of the directive on reduced value-added tax rates in order to foster entrepreneurship (*Agence Europe*, 2008b).

The Council took action with regard to the SBA objectives in December 2008. The ministers stressed the importance of introducing favourable conditions for enterprises in order to counteract the negative impacts of the economic crisis on competitiveness and to boost the creation of jobs in Europe (Conseil de l'UE, 2008). Prior to that, the European Investment Bank decided to mobilize 30 billion Euro in support of SMEs (Council of the EU, 2008a). At its meeting in December 2008, the Council adopted its conclusions on the SBA and announced an unambiguously named action plan, 'Translating Intentions into Actions', to be implemented jointly by the member states and the Commission (Council of the EU, 2009a). The conclusions and the action plan reflect the prioritized short- and medium-term measures already broadly announced in the Council meeting in September 2008. Acting president of the Competitiveness Council and former French Secretary of State for Trade, Crafts and SMEs, Hervé Novelli, viewed these measures as a rapid response to the economic downturn affecting the economies of all EU member states (*Agence Europe*, 2008a).

The first priority of the action plan is improved SME access to finance. This includes credit institutions and banks being encouraged not to restrict the availability of credit to SMEs, a reduction of the fragmentation in the current venture capital market, facilitation of cross-border investments, greater flexibility with regard to state aid rules, and the support and monitoring of the European Investment Bank (measures such as increasing the volume of financial lending to SMEs, simplifying money-lending procedures, and sharing risk with commercial banks) (Council of the EU, 2008b). The second priority is the creation of a regulatory environment that is supportive of SMEs, including the goal of a 25 per cent reduction in administrative burden. In formulating and implementing policies, the so-called 'think small first' principle, as well as tests that assess the impact of specific laws and measures on SMEs, should apply (Council of the EU, 2008b: 9–11). The third priority aims to enhance SMEs' market access by increased market and sector monitoring and by addressing remaining barriers. One aspect relates to the facilitation of SMEs' access to public procurement. By allowing public authorities to divide procurement contracts into lots, SMEs should enjoy a higher success rate with regard to their participation in procurement procedures. Additionally, e-procurement, which slashes administrative burden, should be broadly implemented. In 2014, a revised procurement regime that achieved these objectives was adopted at the EU level. Under the new procurement regime, public authorities are nowadays also able to include innovation or societal aspects as award criteria (European Commission, 2016). Moreover, the Council's plans stress the need for a timely implementation of the service directive, the adoption of the Private European Company (EPC) statute, SMEs' access to third-country markets, and easier regulations on patent questions (Council of the EU, 2008b: 8–9; *Agence Europe*, 2008a).

The European Association of Craft, Small and Medium-Sized Enterprises, UEAPME, welcomed the Council's measures and stated that they were a positive signal for European SMEs (UEAPME – The Voice of SMEs in Europe, 2008). The topic of entrepreneurship had already been explicitly addressed at this stage of the discussions. The Council highlighted its importance and included a chapter on 'encouraging entrepreneurship', in which the fostering of an 'entrepreneurial spirit' across Europe was seen as the main future objective (Council of the EU, 2008b).

It is significant that the strengthening of competition moved to centre stage, whereas possible negative impacts on other policies were not considered. As a result, the plan predominantly included measures that aimed to establish more businesses and companies in Europe by focusing on greater financial resources and support, and enhancing SMEs' market access. Whereas minor provisions on environmental challenges for SMEs were mentioned in the Council's conclusions, social and labour law considerations were totally left out of both the conclusions and the action plan, even though it could already be foreseen at this time that the crisis would also exacerbate the precariousness of employment.

However, the Council utilized the crisis as a window of opportunity to create innovative programmes, policies, and legislation aimed at promoting entrepreneurship and economic growth. Based on the common goal of overcoming the crisis situation, a general understanding that fostering entrepreneurship was decisive for economic recovery, and a broad consensus on crucial questions – which is decisive within the politics stream – the Council was able to act as a policy entrepreneur, as defined by Kingdon. When we go back to our definition of a political entrepreneur, we include both actor and structure perspectives by focusing, *inter alia*, on institutions within the publicly funded sector that adopt innovative approaches to encourage entrepreneurship with a view to achieving economic growth. This definition also applies to the Council's adoption of the SBA measures. From this perspective, therefore, the Council served as a political entrepreneur.

The European Private Company Statute and the SBA Review

Even though the Council acted as a political entrepreneur and agreed upon important measures relating to the SBA, the European Private Company (EPC) statute suggests that Council policy on promoting entrepreneurship has its limitations. Despite the positive steps made at the Council meeting in 2008, the EU ministers failed to agree upon the EPC statute, which had been set as a major goal in the SBA plan. The statute was aimed at facilitating the establishment and operation of businesses within the EU internal market, by providing legal status and a unified legal and management system for private companies when they wanted to conduct business in other EU countries. The idea behind this was to help companies to increase their competitiveness by cutting start-up and operating costs. Philippe de Buck, Director General of BusinessEurope, strongly criticized this failure and stated that the statute would have provided vigorous help for cross-border expansion of SMEs (Euractiv, 2008).

A study published in 2009 by UEAPME assessed that there was a huge discrepancy between the adopted policy provisions and their concrete effects on SMEs. Study unit director, Gerhard Huemer, explained that the beneficial effects of the improved regulations would not yet have reached SMEs. The study demonstrated that SMEs would continue to face administrative burdens and a significant lack of access to financing (*Agence Europe*, 2009a). BusinessEurope, Eurochambres, and UEAPME repeatedly emphasized that the SBA had so far had only a marginal impact on SMEs. It was argued that the 'think small first' principle and the SME tests, in particular, would not be sufficiently implemented and applied at the member state level (*Agence Europe*, 2009c). In May 2009, the Council held a policy debate on the progress of the SBA measures and their implementation, based on questions from the Czech presidency to the member states (Council of the EU, 2009a). In line with the critical UEAPME study, the main policy advice of the meeting was to strengthen the application of the 'think small first' principle at both the EU and the national level, and to follow up the implementation progress on a regular basis (Council of the EU, 2009b).

The EPC statute, as a key objective within the SBA plan, was again the subject of controversial discussions in May 2009. As a result of widely divergent political preferences on key elements of the statute – such as having a cross-border component or a threshold on the minimum capital needed for establishing future businesses – its implementation was stalled. The Czech presidency presented a new draft compromise that did not include a compulsory cross-border component, although several delegations and the European Parliament were in favour of such a compulsory component. Furthermore, the proposed compromise retained the Commission's idea of setting the minimum legal capital requirement at 1 Euro, which would have been of significant assistance to start-ups (European Commission, 2008b). However, eight member states (Austria, Belgium, Germany, Latvia, Lithuania, Luxembourg, Malta, and Spain) opposed this low requirement. As several member states raised further concerns in relation to the separation of the European private companies' legal headquarters from its management headquarters, or to the application of the Commission's proposed limited rights on employee participation, the Czech presidency tried to draft a revised framework taking these reservations into account. Nevertheless, the EU ministers once again failed to reach a consensus (*Agence Europe*, 2009b).

New attempts to reach a compromise on the EPC statute were undertaken by the Swedish presidency in the autumn of 2009 (Council of the EU, 2009c, 2009d, 2009e). Germany opposed the proposal by arguing that it would lead to the legal protection being watered down and wanted stricter legal protection for staff and lender to future private companies. Cognizant of the fact that a unanimous decision would not be possible, Sweden's former trade minister Ewa Björling did not hand the chair to Austria, Luxembourg, and Latvia, which also contested the compromise (*Agence Europe*, 2009c).

In view of the ongoing economic crisis – which had cost more than three million SME jobs up to 2011 – the Commission adopted a review of the SBA in 2011 and communicated it to the Council and the European Parliament (European Commission, 2011). The Council maintained its core priorities and again called upon the member states to fully implement the 'think small first' approach and the SME tests. Moreover, the Council's conclusions stressed the need to stimulate entrepreneurship by 'improving the skills and promoting the creativity and innovative potential for entrepreneurs' and to dismantle the remaining barriers for entrepreneurs (Council of the EU, 2011).

Another attempt towards a EPC was made by the Hungarian presidency in 2011. Yet again, the ministers failed to reach the necessary unanimity on the compromise. Germany and Sweden contested the agreement. Germany criticized the separation of management offices from head offices for private companies, and the low amount of company capital proposed in the rules. Sweden opposed the statute because of the proposed regulations in the field of worker participation. The Hungarian presidency proposed a compromise by establishing thresholds beyond which the worker participation measures must apply (a minimum of 500 workers in a member state where higher worker participation standards exist than in the country where the legal headquarters are located). In the case of the legal headquarters being moved to another EU member state, the worker participation rules would apply if at least one-third – and no less than 500 workers – were employed in the original country, if it had higher worker participation rules than the new country. Sweden argued that 'it must not be made possible for the draft regulation to be used to wriggle round national legislation and the suggested levels are unacceptable' (*Agence Europe*, 2011). Since a compromise was not reached, the EPC statute was ultimately never realized. The requirement of unanimity in the Council hindered the adoption of one important SBA target.

This case demonstrates that a lack of consensus-building in the political stream might block proposals favourable to entrepreneurship. As Kingdon (2011: 160) points out, 'In the political stream, if one does not pay sufficient attention to coalition-building through bargaining, one pays a major price …'.

Entrepreneurship 2020 Action Plan

The Entrepreneurship 2020 Action Plan is, like the SBA, an example of a case where the Council was able to act as a political entrepreneur. In this case, the high unemployment rate – especially among the youth in Europe – placed the action plan high on the political agenda. Prior to the official debates, the Council had held two previous informal exchanges of view in 2012 (Conseil de l'UE, 2013). Under the Cypriot presidency, the role of an entrepreneurial spirit for economic growth and employment was broadly discussed with the European Commissioner for Trade, Antonio Tajani. The presidency invited Constantinos Markides from the London School of Economics to give a speech on the promotion of entrepreneurship in Europe. The main policy objective included an enhanced spirit and culture for entrepreneurs. The outcomes formed the basis of the Commission's Entrepreneurship 2020 Action Plan communication, and its prior consultation of stakeholders (Council of the EU, 2013; *Agence Europe*, 2012).

As in the case of the SBA, the Council was able to utilize a window of opportunity in order to push its proposals through. Whereas the 2013 documents speak about the importance of creating jobs, and stress the decreasing percentage of 'Europeans preferring entrepreneurship to being an employee' (Council of the EU, 2013: 2), the Council referred to the 2014 situation as a major 'crisis' and stressed the urgent need to create concrete policy measures as 'the youth unemployment crisis has had a profound effect on young people and the societies in which they live' (Council of the EU, 2014c: 2). By calling it a major crisis and stressing the urgent need to adopt policy measures, the Council created a justification for placing the promotion of entrepreneurial mindsets high on the political agenda. The Council recommendations define entrepreneurship predominantly as self-employment and therefore the fostering of competition by bringing people to get self-employed was central.

Some attempts were made to include a social dimension in the action plan. Nevertheless, this social dimension was also subordinated to a neoliberal discourse, as it referred mainly to specific underrepresented groups that should enter labour markets and establish businesses. Moreover, it referred to the inculcation of entrepreneurial spirit, training, and education from an early stage; it did not refer, for example, to an improvement in labour law rights or social security.

In 2013, the ministers discussed various national strategies and reforms at member state level, with a view to the establishment of such an entrepreneurial culture (Council of the EU, 2013). With regard to the high level of youth unemployment in Europe, the focus of the Greek presidency in the first half of 2014 was on fostering an entrepreneurial spirit in young people and their social inclusion in labour markets (Council of the EU, 2014b). As a result, in 2014, the Youth Council adopted conclusions and recommendations on enhancing youth entrepreneurship, which for the first time provided marginal elements of a social dimension with regard to entrepreneurship. The existence of broad consensus at the decision-making stage (politics stream) triggered a swift adoption of the plan.

The conclusions referred to above included the promotion of social entrepreneurship, entrepreneurial culture and creativity, innovation, and green jobs. Social entrepreneurship seeks to provide young people with greater opportunities to respond innovatively to both the economic crisis and to social and environmental challenges (Council of the EU, 2014a). The Council recommendations followed this strategy by stressing the promotion of an educational culture, the development of entrepreneurial skills, the so-called 'freedom to fail', better access to financing, and the slashing of bureaucratic burdens (Council of the EU, 2014b). Young people should be encouraged to enter into businesses by helping them at the EU level with the assistance of European structural funds, particularly the European Social Fund and the Erasmus+ programme. The EU should further provide a platform for networking and exchange among young entrepreneurs.

CONCLUSION

This chapter demonstrates how entrepreneurship has been discussed in the Council of the EU in times of economic crisis. It demonstrates that the economic crisis created a window of opportunity, where the three main streams that flow through a policy process (problem stream, policy stream, and politics stream) combined, providing the Council with the opportunity to advocate a certain entrepreneurship policy.

The Council behaved as political entrepreneur by utilizing a crisis-induced policy window to place entrepreneurship on the political agenda and by taking ready-made plans out of the drawer and bring them to the decision-making stage as illustrated in the garbage can model by Cohen et al. (1972). According to our definition, political entrepreneurship takes place if existing structures are challenged and altered by new and innovative reforms that are conducive to entrepreneurial activities. When debating the SBA for Europe and the Entrepreneurship 2020 Action Plan, the Council acted as a political entrepreneur by initiating and adopting new and innovative programmes, policies, and legislation aimed at promoting entrepreneurship and economic growth. The main reason the Council was successful in this was the fact that a broad consensus was reached during the decision-making stage – based on a common understanding that entrepreneurship was crucial for economic growth and for lifting the EU out of the crisis. When debating the Entrepreneurship 2020 Action Plan, continuing financial pressures and the high level of youth unemployment in the EU member states were used as an argument for policy innovation leading to the promotion of entrepreneurial mindsets.

This demonstrates that over and above an actor-centric approach, the 'agent of change' may not be limited to the specific actor or entrepreneur, that is, the decision maker (North, 1990), but may in fact be entire institutions. An institution, as a whole, may serve as an entrepreneur by introducing entrepreneurial policies. This more structure-oriented perspective allows for the detection of certain stimuli that trigger the initiation of conditions favourable to entrepreneurship and institutional adjustments in the light of a specific crisis (see also Hardy and Maguire, 2008).

However, the failure to agree upon a EPC statute as a primary objective of the SBA action plan demonstrates that if member states' preferences strongly diverge, a decision-making gridlock might occur, thus hindering the promotion of entrepreneurship.

The debates and conclusions on the action plans bring the Council's logic with regard to entrepreneurship to the forefront. Entrepreneurship is regarded primarily as a way to provide opportunities for people to set up businesses and companies, and as a tool to boost the internal market, which is a core objective of the EU. Entrepreneurship was discussed from an economic perspective, providing limited scope for a social dimension, or indeed any other dimension; this despite the fact that entrepreneurship is conceptualized in a broader sense (Steyaert and Katz, 2004; Berglund and Johansson, 2007). The action plans therefore contain no reference to important aspects such as social issues or labour law. For example, the debates and policy documents failed to address measures to improve the working conditions of entrepreneurs, to strengthen the way entrepreneurs are protected, or to prevent entrepreneurial precarity. However, as the next chapter will demonstrate, policy-promoting entrepreneurship goes hand in hand with the consideration of other societally relevant policies, such as employment or social affairs.

REFERENCES

Acs, Z., D. Audretsch, P. Braunerhjelm and B. Carlsson (2005), 'Growth and Entrepreneurship: An Empirical Assessment', Papers on Entrepreneurship, Growth and Public Policy, Nr 3205, Jena, Max Planck Institute of Economics, November 2005.

Agence Europe (2008a), EU/Competitiveness Council: Action plan to implement Small Business Act for Europe, Brussels, 01/12/2008, AE 9794, 2.12.2008.

Agence Europe (2008b), EU/Competitiveness Council: Ministers prioritise Small Business Act measures in light of economic slowdown, Brussels, 26/09/2008, AE 9749, 27.9.2008.

Agence Europe (2009a), EU/Business: Small Business Act has only limited impact, Brussels, 06/05/2009, AE May 2009 (9893-9910).

Agence Europe (2009b), EU/Competitiveness Council: Ministers' agenda contains patents system, Small Business Act and Agreement on Eric, Brussels, 26/05/2009, AE May 2009 (9893-9910).

Agence Europe (2009c), EU/Competitiveness Council: Germany opposes deal on adoption of EU company statute, Brussels, 07/12/2009, AE 10035, 8.12.2009.

Agence Europe (2011), EU/Single Market: Agreement on European companies hoped in June, Brussels, 30/05/2011, AE 10389, 31.5.2011.

Agence Europe (2012), Competitiveness: Ministerial debate on stimulating spirit of enterprise, Brussels, 19/07/2012, AE 10659, 20.7.2012.

Audretsch, D., M. C. Keilbach and E. E. Lehmann (2006), *Entrepreneurship and Economic Growth*. Oxford: Oxford University Press.

Baumgartner, F. R. and B. D. Jones (1993), *Agendas and Instabilities in American Politics*. Chicago, IL: University of Chicago Press.

Berglund, K. and A. W. Johansson (2007), 'Entrepreneurship, discourses and conscientization in processes of regional development', *Entrepreneurship & Regional Development*, 19(6), 499–525.

Bernhard, I. and E. Wihlborg (2014), 'Policy entrepreneurs in networks: implementation of two Swedish municipal contact centres from an actor perspective', *International Journal of Entrepreneurship and Small Business*, 21(3), 288–302.

Bickerton, C. J., D. Hodson and U. Puetter (2015), 'The new intergovernmentalism: European integration in the post-Maastricht era', *Journal of Common Market Studies*, 53(4), 703–722.

Bruton, G. D., D. Ahlstrom and T. Puky (2009), 'Institutional differences and the development of entrepreneurial ventures: a comparison of the venture capital industries in Latin America and Asia', *Journal of International Business Studies*, 40(5), 762–778.

Capano, G. (2009), 'Understanding policy change as an epistemological and theoretical problem', *Journal of Comparative Policy Analysis Research and Practice*, 11(1), 7–31.

Cohen, M. D., J. G. March and J. P. Olsen (1972), 'A garbage can model of organizational choice', *Administrative Science Quarterly*, 17(1), 1–25.

Conseil de l'UE (2008), Projet de Procés-Verbal: 2910ème session du Conseil de l'Union européenne, Compétitivité (Marché intérieur, Industrie, Recherche), tenue à Bruxelles, les 1er et 2 décembre 2008, Bruxelles le 19 janvier 2009, 16580/08.
Conseil de l'UE (2013), Communiqué de Presse, 3223e session du Conseil, Compétitivité (Marché intérieur, Industrie, Recherche), Bruxelles, les 18 et 19 février 2013, 6399/13.
Council of the EU (2008a), Brussels European Council, 15 and 16 October 2008, Presidency Conclusions, Brussels, 16 October 2008, 14368/08.
Council of the EU (2008b), Competitiveness Council of 1–2 December 2008, Council Conclusions on 'Think Small First – A Small Business Act for Europe' – Adoption, Brussels, 4 December 2008, 16788/08.
Council of the EU (2008c), Competitiveness Council of 29 and 30 May 2008, Council Conclusions: A Fresh Impetus for Competitiveness and Innovation of the European Economy, Brussels, 3 June 2008, 10174/08.
Council of the EU (2008d), Press Release 2891st Council meeting, Competitiveness (Internal Market, Industry and Research), Brussels, 25 and 26 September 2008, Brussels, 4.10.2007, COM(2007) 592 final, 12959/1/08 REV 1 (Presse 251).
Council of the EU (2009a), Competitiveness Council, 28 May 2009, Small Business Act for Europe: State of play – Policy debate: Presidency questions, Brussels, 11 May 2009, 9645/09.
Council of the EU (2009b), Information note on the Small Business Act for Europe (SBA), Brussels, 26 May 2009, 10283/09.
Council of the EU (2009c), Preparation of the Council meeting ('Competitiveness') on 3–4 December 2009 – Proposal for a Council Regulation on a European private company (SPE)=Political agreement, Interinstitutional file 2008/0130 (CNS), Document partially accessible to the public, Brussels, 9 November 2009, 15355/09, ADD 1.
Council of the EU (2009d), Preparation of the Council meeting ('Competitiveness') on 3–4 December 2009 – Proposal for a Council Regulation on a European private company (SPE)=Political agreement, Interinstitutional File: 2008/0130 (CNS), Document partially accessible to the public, Brussels, 20 November 2009, 16155/09, ADD 1.
Council of the EU (2009e), Proposal for a Council Regulation on a European private company – Political agreement, Brussels, Interinstitutional File: 2008/0130 (CNS), 27 November 2009, 16115/09, ADD 1.
Council of the EU (2011), Council (Competitiveness), Council Conclusions on the Review of the 'Small Business Act' for Europe, Brussels, 31 May 2011, 10975/11.
Council of the EU (2013), Preparation of the Council ('Competitiveness') of 18–19 February 2013, Action Plan for Entrepreneurship – Presentation by the Commission – Exchange of views, Brussels, 1 February 2013, 5862/13.
Council of the EU (2014a), Draft Council conclusions on promoting youth entrepreneurship to foster social inclusion of young people – Adoption, Brussels, 30 April 2014, 8378/14.
Council of the EU (2014b), Press Release, 3316th Council meeting, Education, Youth, Culture and Sport, Brussels, 20 and 21 May 2014, 10023/14.

Council of the EU (2014c), Promoting a youth entrepreneurial mindset – Policy debate (Public debate pursuant to Article 8(2) CRP [proposed by the Presidency]), Brussels, 2 May 2014, 9012/14.

Djankov, S., R. La Porta, F. Lopez-de-Silanes and A. Shleifer (2002), 'The regulation of entry', *Quarterly Journal of Economics*, 117(1), 1–37.

Euractiv (2008), Ministers give green light to Small Business Act, 2 December 2008, accessed 31 March 2017 at http://www.euractiv.com/section/innovation-industry/news/ministers-give-green-light-to-small-business-act/.

EUR-Lex (2017), Procedure: COM (2008) 394: Communication from the Commission to the Council, the European Parliament, the European Economic and Social Committee and the Committee of the Regions – 'Think Small First' – A 'Small Business Act' for Europe (SEC[2008] 2101) (SEC[2008] 2102), accessed 29 March 2017 at http://eur-lex.europa.eu/legal-content/en/HIS/?uri=CELEX:52008DC0394.

European Commission (2007), Communication from the Commission to the Council, the European Parliament, the European Economic and Social Committee and the Committee of the Regions. Small and medium-sized enterprises – Key for delivering more growth and jobs. A mid-term review of Modern SME policy, Brussels, 4.10.2007, COM(2007) 592 final.

European Commission (2008a), Communication from the Commission to the Council, the European Parliament, the European Economic and Social Committee and the Committee of the Regions – 'Think Small First' – A 'Small Business Act' for Europe, Brussels 25.6.2008, COM(2008) 394 final.

European Commission (2008b), Proposal for a Council Regulation on the Statute for a European private company, Brussels, 25.6.2008, COM(2008) 396 final, 2008/0130 (CNS).

European Commission (2011), Communication from the Commission to the European Parliament, the Council, Economic and Social Committee and the Committee of the Regions, Review of the 'Small Business Act' for Europe, Brussels, 23.2.2011, COM(2011) 78 final.

European Commission (2016), Public Procurement Reform, Fact Sheet No 1: General Overview Ref. Ares(2016)782979 – 15/02/2016.

Fabbrini, S. (2013), 'Intergovernmentalism and its limits: assessing the European Union's answer to the Euro crisis', *Comparative Political Studies*, 46(9), 1003–1029.

Hardy, C. and S. Maguire (2008), 'Institutional entrepreneurship', in: R. Greenwood, C. Oliver, R. Suddaby and K. Sahlin-Andersson (eds), *The Sage Handbook of Organizational Institutionalism*. London: Sage.

Kingdon, J. W. (2011), *Agendas, Alternatives, and Public Policies*, updated 2nd edition. Longman Classics in Political Science. Boston, MA: Pearson.

Méndez-Picazo, M. T., M. A. Galindo-Martín and D. Ribeiro-Soriano (2012), 'Governance, entrepreneurship and growth', *Entrepreneurship & Regional Development*, 24(9–10), 865–877.

North, D. C. (1990), *Institutions, Institutional Change and Economic Performance*. Cambridge: Cambridge University Press.

North, D. C. (1991), 'Institutions', *Journal of Economic Perspectives*, 5(1), 97–112.

Pelkmans, J. and A. Renda (2014), 'Does EU regulation hinder or stimulate innovation?' *Centre for European Policy Studies, Special Reports*, November (No. 96).
Pollack, M. A. (1999), 'Delegation, Agency and Agenda Setting in the Treaty of Amsterdam', *European Integration Online Papers (EIoP)*, 3(6), accessed 8 March 2018 at http://eiop.or.at/eiop/pdf/1999-006.pdf.
Puetter, U. (2012), 'Europe's deliberative intergovernmentalism: the role of the Council and European Council in EU Economic Governance', *Journal of European Public Policy*, 19(2), 161–178.
Ribeiro-Soriano, D. and M. A. Galindo-Martín (2012), 'Government policies to support entrepreneurship', *Entrepreneurship & Regional Development*, 24(9–10), 861–864.
Roper, S. (2013), *Entrepreneurship. A Global Perspective*. New York: Routledge.
Sabatier, P. A. and H. C. Jenkins-Smith (1999), 'The advocacy coalition framework: an assessment', in: P. A. Sabatier (ed.) *Theories of the Policy Process*. Boulder, CO: Westview Press.
Silander, D. (2016), 'The political entrepreneur', in: C. Karlsson, D. Silander and C. Silander (eds) *Political Entrepreneurship – Regional Growth and Entrepreneurial Diversity in Sweden*. Cheltenham and Northampton: Edward Elgar.
Steyaert, C. and J. Katz (2004), 'Reclaiming the space of entrepreneurship in society: geographical, discursive and social dimensions', *Entrepreneurship & Regional Development*, 16(3), 179–196.
UEAPME – The voice of SMEs in Europe (2008), SBA: Competitiveness Council conclusions must be endorsed by Heads of State, accessed 31 March 2017 at http://www.ueapme.com/IMG/pdf/081202_pr_SBA_conclusions.pdf.
Verdun, A. (2013), 'The European currency in turbulent crisis – austerity policy made in Brussels as the only way out?', in: D. Schiek (ed.) *The EU Economic and Social Model in the Global Crisis: Interdisciplinary Perspectives*. Farnham: Ashgate.
Verdun, A. (2015), 'A historical institutionalist explanation of the EU's responses to the Euro area financial crisis', *Journal of European Public Policy*, 22(2), 219–237.
Weible, C. M., P. A. Sabatier and J. Flowers (2008), 'Advocacy coalition framework', *Encyclopedia of Public Administration and Public Policy*, 2nd edition, 1(1), 1–10.
Zahariadis, N. (2014), 'Ambiguity and multiple streams', in: P. A. Sabatier and C. M. Weible (eds) *Theories of the Policy Process*, 3rd edition. Boulder, CO: Westview Press.

6. Debating the economic crisis in the European Parliament: enriching the discourse

Brigitte Pircher

INTRODUCTION

As we have already pointed out in the previous chapters, institutions may have the potential to act as a political entrepreneur. Our definition of a political entrepreneur includes a structural perspective by focusing on institutions within the publicly funded sector that encourage entrepreneurship through innovative approaches (see Chapter 1 in this volume). Therefore, European Union (EU) institutions may serve as a political entrepreneur. Researchers have predominantly applied the concept of policy or political entrepreneur to the European Commission, whereas to date there has been no detailed examination of the European Parliament (EP) as a possible political entrepreneur. Up to now, far too little attention has been given to the EP's potential to promote entrepreneurship or to shape entrepreneurial policies. The current chapter fills this gap by focusing on the parliamentary debates on the main entrepreneurial action plans.

The EP is a place where publicly funded politicians, bureaucrats, and officials work and cooperate closely in various informal and formal ways. If we apply an actor-centric approach, political entrepreneurs are actors within an institution who challenge the existing structures and launch innovative programmes and policies favourable to entrepreneurship. However, the EP also encompasses different political groups, standing committees, political arenas, and discussion forums that may be supportive of fostering entrepreneurship. In this case, a more structural perspective enables us to examine certain overarching institutional aims that shape entrepreneurship policy.

As crises have the potential to create a window of opportunity for certain policies to be pushed through (Kingdon, 2011), this chapter deals with the question of how and to what extent the EP has had an impact on entrepreneurship policy in times of economic crisis. How has the EP contributed to policy on entrepreneurship, and has the EP behaved as a political entrepreneur? Even though the role of the EP in times of economic crisis was restricted, important policies and policy programmes were significantly affected by its policy-influencing instruments. The first part of the chapter explores the potential of the EP to act as an entrepreneur in times of economic crisis. By defining entrepreneurship at EU level in the following section, the main body of the chapter examines the parliamentary debates on the main entrepreneurial action plans, and demonstrates the extent to which the EP has contributed to an innovative entrepreneurship policy. In conclusion, the study assesses whether the EP was in fact able to act as a political entrepreneur.

EUROPEAN PARLIAMENT'S POTENTIAL TO ACT AS A POLITICAL ENTREPRENEUR

This section combines the theoretical work on policy and political entrepreneurs with the literature on agenda-setting and decision-making in the EP in times of economic crisis. A successful policy entrepreneur, according to Kingdon (2011), needs the combination of the problem, policy, and political streams. The onset of the financial crisis in 2008, as an external shock (Baumgartner and Jones, 1993; Weible et al., 2008; Zahariadis, 2014), led to a perception of the problem at EU level, and placed entrepreneurship on the political agenda. The policy stream consists of the 'solutions' developed by the EP, while the politics stream involves the decision-making stage. The research also operationalises when and under which conditions an entrepreneur is effective. Moreover, it describes the motivations that trigger policy entrepreneurs to advocate certain policies (Kingdon, 2011).

Successful political entrepreneurs use the window of opportunity and are taken seriously in advocating their interests (Kingdon, 2011: 165). They are innovative in promoting new policies, norms, and values, and in using channels and networks to improve conditions for entrepreneurs and for the common good (Silander, 2016), and they encourage entrepreneurship through innovative approaches (see Chapter 1 in this volume). Kingdon (2011: 122–124) argues that the incentives for entrepreneurs can be personal interest (to strengthen their own position), the promotion of their values, or simply enjoying the 'game' – that is, that they enjoy taking part in the policy process. Even though this concept is generally applied to individuals, we argue that it is equally applicable to institutions.

There is an extensive literature in which this concept is applied to the European Commission (Copeland and Scott, 2014; Laffan, 1997; Moravcsik, 1999; Pollack, 1997; Schön-Quinlivan and Scipioni, 2017). The president of the Commission, Jean-Claude Juncker, recently called the current situation a 'window of opportunity' that 'will not stay open forever' in his speech on the State of the Union 2017 (European Commission, 2017). Evidence indicates that the economic crisis increased the power of the European Commission and the European Council in particular, whereas the role of the EP turned out to be weak (Bauer and Becker, 2014). Even though deeper European integration has always been accompanied by the EP's extension of its role and competencies (Burns, 2016; Shackleton, 2000, 2017; Hix, 2002), its power in adopting economic measures such as the European Semester, the Euro-Plus pact, the Treaty on the European Stability Mechanism, and the Treaty on Stability, Coordination and Governance was limited (Shackleton, 2017: 150–154; Fabbrini, 2013; Hodson, 2015; Rittberger, 2014). The EP came out with strong statements relating to these measures, but the lack of decision-making competencies severely restricted their impact (Fabbrini, 2013; Fasone, 2013). The new measures were finally decided on without much involvement of the EP, and provided only a marginal role for the institution.

Therefore, is there any potential for the EP to act as a political entrepreneur? The EP, as a co-legislator, plays a central role in the formulation of policies. Draft legislation is delivered and assigned to one main responsible committee. At the committee level, one member of the EP (MEP) is appointed as rapporteur, the main person in charge of dealing with the act (Versluis et al., 2010: 35–37). The strong standing committees are regarded as the legislative backbone of the EP (Neuhold, 2001). It is assumed that MEPs in the plenary sessions support their party colleagues in the relevant committees (Ringe, 2010). In times of economic crisis, the EP exercised legislative power while adopting economic measures under the co-decision procedure. The six-pack and two-pack legislative measures, aimed at introducing greater macroeconomic surveillance, are prime examples of the EP's having shaped legislative acts by improving democratic commitments and economic surveillance (Fasone, 2013; Hodson, 2015; Manoli and Maris, 2015; Rittberger, 2014).

In addition to its legislative function, another relevant aspect is the EP's potential ability to shape policies and strengthen its influence in the decision-making process by applying institutional bargaining pressure via policy-influencing instruments. When adopting the single supervisory mechanism (SSM), for example, the EP had to deliver a non-binding opinion. Due to the fact that the SSM was linked to another legislative act decided by co-decision, the EP managed to put bargaining pressure on the Council and to introduce enhanced scrutiny (Rittberger, 2014). Moreover, the EP created fora to discuss the economic crisis and its economic and social impact on the EU member states (for example, the special Committee on the Financial, Economic and Social Crisis) and formulated policy recommendations to overcome the crisis situation (European Parliament, 2011c).

In times of economic crisis, the EP commanded flexible policy-influencing rather than policy-making instruments. These policy-influencing instruments included various initiatives such as reports, resolutions, opinions, public hearings, and open debates. These different channels of parliamentary commitment also served to guide values for civil society organisations (Manoli and Maris, 2015). When it comes to the EU policy on entrepreneurship, the EP faces a similar position. Besides legislative acts adopted by co-decision aimed at introducing favourable conditions for entrepreneurs, the role of the EP in launching specific entrepreneurial plans is limited. It is therefore important to examine how the EP shaped the discourse and influenced policy on entrepreneurship in times of crisis. Consequently, the next section focuses on the general definition of entrepreneurship at EU level, with a view to establishing whether the EP's contribution had an impact on this concept.

DEFINING ENTREPRENEURSHIP AT EU LEVEL

From the onset of the financial crisis in 2008, EU institutions were faced with the challenge of taking swift action to overcome the crisis situation. As a result, new provisions, regulations, and policies aimed at fostering economic growth and entrepreneurship were adopted and implemented.

However, does the boosting of entrepreneurship really assist member states? It could be argued that the answer to this question depends primarily on the definition of entrepreneurship. Entrepreneurship at EU level is conceptualised as an economic phenomenon and focuses on the business context. For example, the Council recommendations suggest that as many people as possible – including so-called 'specific groups' such as women, seniors, migrants, unemployed, and young people – should enter the market in order to 'realise untapped entrepreneurial potential' and intensify competition (Council of the EU, 2013: 7). First, this offers evidence that entrepreneurship is conceptualised from an economic or enterprise perspective. Second, however, by classifying so-called 'specific groups', it reflects that, at EU level, an entrepreneur is seen as an employed, middle-aged male, with no migration background. Moreover, the Commission's principal perspective on entrepreneurship is that '[e]very young person should have an entrepreneurship experience before completing their studies' (Council of the EU, 2013: 16). The following statement emphasises the EU's entrepreneurship approach:

> Androulla Vassiliou, former Commissioner for Youth, highlighted that 'entrepreneurship has to be cultivated very early at all levels of education. Young people must understand that you need more than just a job to have a nice life but also the opportunity and determination to create one's own business'. (*Agence Europe*, 2014)

In this sense, entrepreneurship is predominantly equated with self-employment.

As Berglund and Johansson (2007: 500) point out in their analysis of the Green Paper on Entrepreneurship, entrepreneurship might also occur in different contexts, but it is only of interest when connected to economic actions. They call this the dominant enterprise discourse. However, research suggests that entrepreneurship should be conceptualised in a broader sense, by including geographical, cultural, ecological, civic, and social dimensions (Steyaert and Katz, 2004). Berglund and Johansson (2007) even demonstrate that a dominant enterprise discourse suppresses entrepreneurial initiatives relevant to regional development.

In their Special Issue of Entrepreneurship and Regional Development, Steyaert and Katz (2004, p. 180) contend that entrepreneurship takes place in multiple sites and spaces. These spaces are political spaces that are 'constituted through a variety of discourses overcoming the sole economic definition'. In relation to this understanding, the EP becomes an interesting research object, as it provides a number of different discussion arenas (for example, party, committee, plenary or working group level) that have the potential to overcome a purely economic perspective on entrepreneurship. However, was the EP really able to shape the entrepreneurship debates and discourse at EU level?

ANALYSING PARLIAMENTARY DEBATES

In order to establish how and to what extent entrepreneurship was discussed in the EP during the economic crisis, how the EP shaped entrepreneurship policy, and whether it behaved as a political entrepreneur, the following section analyses the parliamentary debates – at both committee and plenary level – on the main entrepreneurial action plans, that is, the Small Business Act (SBA) for Europe and its review, and the Entrepreneurship 2020 Action Plan. This has two main advantages – first, the action plans deal exclusively with the promotion of entrepreneurship as a policy strategy, including policy measures; and second, the action plans cover a long investigation period (from the end of 2008 until 2014) during a time of economic crisis (see also Chapter 2 in this volume).

This investigation makes use of official reports, recommendations, parliamentary resolutions, protocols, committee and plenary debates, minutes, voting results, explanations of votes, and general discussions that are officially available on the EP's website. Moreover, *Agence Europe* articles were also analysed. As this kind of analysis is comprehensive, the study is limited to the main entrepreneurial action plans, but provides a qualitatively in-depth analysis of the policy debates. The various documents are assessed via content analysis. The following section deals with the parliamentary engagement and debates on the most relevant entrepreneurial action plans, and reveals how the EP has shaped entrepreneurship policy through policy-influencing instruments.

The Small Business Act (SBA) for Europe

As seven parliamentary committees dealt with the Commission's communication on the SBA, a broad policy debate on the action plan has taken place in the EP (European Parliament, 2009e). The Committee on Industry, Research and Energy (ITRE) was primarily responsible for the report drafted by Edit Herczog, a former Hungarian member of the Party of European Socialists (PES)[1] (European Parliament, 2009g). In March 2009, the plenary voted on the committee report, and adopted a resolution by 536 votes in favour, 47 votes against, and 47 abstentions (European Parliament, 2009f).

The EP supported aspects of the SBA, such as the renewal of the directive on value added tax, the new provisions on access by SMEs to state aid, the revision of the late payment directive, and the creation of a European Private Company (EPC) statute – although the latter has led to heated and controversial debate (*Agence Europe*, 2009). However, while

[1] Officially renamed the Progressive Alliance of Socialists and Democrats (S&D) in July 2009.

the Council of the EU rapidly decided upon swift policy measures with regard to the SBA, the EP, backed by the European Economic and Social Committee and the Committee of Regions, criticised core elements of the measures. A main point of criticism put forward by the three institutions was the non-legally binding character of the legislation (Official Journal of the EU, 2009a, 2009b, 2010). The EP called on the Council to establish the 'think small first' principle as a binding rule with regard to all policies. Further, appropriate SBA implementation measures at the member-state level were regarded as crucial (Official Journal of the EU, 2010).

The final adoption was preceded by controversial debates at both committee and plenary levels (for a summary of the different political views, see also Table 6.1). The two largest groups in the EP, the European People's Party (EPP) and the PES, widely supported the resolution. Nevertheless, some members of the EPP expressed their reservations, and highlighted the need for actions to be implemented at the member-state level in order for the SBA goals to be achieved (European Parliament, 2009a, 2009b). Further, members appealed for the 'think small first' principle to be made a permanent feature for future legislation (European Parliament, 2009a).

In contrast to the EPP, which focused on economic aspects and the implementation of the SBA, the PES emphasised SMEs' access to funding, entrepreneurial education, and aspects relating to labour law and social protection. One core topic was the need to strengthen SMEs' access to financing and funding, especially in times of crisis, and to encourage the lending of money to SMEs within the different EU programmes. The PES emphasised the protection of SMEs when engaging in cross-border trading, and stressed the problem faced by enterprises in the area of employment (European Parliament, 2009a, 2009b).

Entrepreneurial education appeared to be an important topic in the debates on the SBA. Members from the EPP, the Alliance of Liberals and Democrats for Europe Party (ALDE), the Union for Europe of the Nations (UEN) – a former national-conservative and Eurosceptic group, the PES, and the Greens-European Free Alliance (Greens-EFA) all stressed the need to promote entrepreneurial mindsets (European Parliament, 2009a). The Greens-EFA drafted the opinion of the Committee on Culture and Education, which emphasised the need to take the creative and cultural sector into account as well, the importance of entrepreneurial education, and the facilitation of mobility programmes for artists, the self-employed, and entrepreneurs (European Parliament, 2009g: 38–40). The access of SMEs to public procurement was another crucial topic, supported by representatives from the EPP, ALDE, PES, European United Left-Nordic Green Left (GUE/NGL), and non-attached members (European Parliament, 2009a, 2009b).

Strong statements were made by Gerard Batten, Nigel Farage, Jeffrey Titford, and Derek Roland Clark from the UK Independence Party, affiliated to the Independence/Democracy (IND/DEM) group, a former Eurosceptic political group and successor to the Europe of Democracies and Diversities (EDD) which in 2009 became the Europe of Freedom and Democracy (EFD). They officially stated that although some measures 'might' be supportive of SMEs, the overarching objectives of the SBA were to 'promote EU control, churning of the businesses, feminist agendas and infiltration of businesses by EU officials' (European Parliament, 2009b).

The deregulation of labour markets has been vigorously taken up by the GUE/NGL. In her statement, Ilda Figueiredo (GUE/NGL, Portugal) explained that the main objective of the SBA was to encourage free competition. This would lead to support for larger companies and 'insisting on the liberalisation of services' behind a 'façade of pseudo-help' for SMEs (European Parliament, 2009b). She highlighted the risk of destroying public services, deregulating the labour market, and removing social and working rights, and stated that it was on the basis of these concerns that the group was voting against the report.

Unlike the Council, the EP also discussed entrepreneurship from a social perspective and included a strong commitment to labour law, social protection, and aspects of entrepreneurial diversity. The insistence of certain members and groups in the EP that labour rights should be included was a thread that ran through the entire debate. That is why the EP contended that the SBA had failed to develop a clear strategy for the self-employed, aimed at improving their legal status and rights in view of standard tariffs and collective agreements. The EP further advocated the creation of a social security network for SMEs, which often encounter unstable working conditions (European Parliament, 2009g; Official Journal of the EU, 2010).

The European Private Company (EPC) Statute

The EPC statute, which was part of the initial SBA plan, is a further example of legislation where the EP demanded labour and social law protection (European Parliament, 2009d). The EPC statute provided a common legal form for limited liability companies. The proposal targeted the creation of jointly simplified legal principles for starting small and medium-sized businesses in the EU, with a view to reducing the existing administrative load (European Commission, 2008).

Two core aspects were the subject of heated debate: the cross-border transfers of companies' registered offices, and the participation of employees on the boards of private companies (European Parliament, 2009a). The most relevant question was whether SMEs would be allowed to register their headquarters in one country, while conducting business in another. Individual MEPs, entire political parties and, specifically, trade unions feared an attack on national labour rights (European Parliament, 2009a). Harald Ettl (PES, Austria) – drafter of the opinion of the Committee on Employment and Social Affairs – criticised the 'envisaged minimum capital of EUR 1 and, in addition, inadequate registration procedures, no requirement for cross-border activity, and the separation of the articles of association, the seat and the actual place of business'; he stated that the 'latter would have led to the circumvention of employee participation' (European Parliament, 2009a). The PES urged the Commission to simplify companies' mobility without curtailing national labour rights, and appealed for greater involvement of, and consultation with, social partners.

In the debate, rapporteur Klaus-Heiner Lehne (EPP, Germany), a former MEP and current president of the European Court of Auditors, stressed that such a statute benefiting SMEs was long overdue. The EPP regarded the final report as a solution for protecting employees' rights. Members even stated that trade unions would raise a false alarm, as labour law aspects would have been included. Some members of the EPP underlined the vital role of SMEs – enterprises that would experience serious credit problems in times of crisis – and regarded the statute as an important means of facilitating SMEs' access to funding and markets. Georgios Papastamkos (EPP, Greece) regarded the legal simplification and the starting capital of 1 Euro as the main tenets of a 'new momentum to the development of intra-Community entrepreneurship' (European Parliament, 2009a).

The GUE/NGL group held a more critical view. Members stressed that the vague definition of SMEs would result in larger companies also being supported. Like the PES and the trade unions, the GUE/NGL criticised the approach that it would be possible to create a fictitious registered office and conduct business elsewhere, where the lowest level of wage protection and social rights would be applicable. They warned that companies would use the statute to evade protective legislation for workers, and even called the statute a 'damage on [sic] workers' social and labour rights' (European Parliament, 2009a). The group therefore resolved to vote against the proposal in order to send a clear signal to the Commission and the Council.

Another topic was the participation of employees on the boards of European private companies. This employee participation takes place in accordance with national legal regulations, but it is in only a few member states (for example Sweden and Denmark) that there is employee participation in small companies (European Commission, 2008). Particular groups and members were in favour of ensuring employee participation on boards, whereas the Commission and the EPP opposed such a measure.

Despite harsh criticism, the EP adopted a resolution amending the Council proposal on the EPC statute by 578 votes to 72, with 25 abstentions. The main amendments involved new provisions on flexible cross-border elements and the need for labour law aspects, measures to combat undeclared work, and measures to increase the level of under-represented societal groups in SMEs (European Parliament, 2009c).

When debating the SBA review in 2011, the EP urged member states to adopt the statute and put pressure on the Council to find a compromise (European Parliament, 2011d). In the parliamentary discussion of March 2011, the Council – represented by a former MEP and member of the Fidesz party, Enikő Győri, as the President-in-Office – said that the Hungarian presidency would strive for a compromise on the statute and that MEPs should 'be able to exercise some sort of political pressure and motivate through their own channels in order to generate the necessary majority' (European Parliament, 2011b).

During the Council debates, some national delegations took over the concerns of individual members and groups, and blocked the statute. Ultimately, the Council, as the main legislator (the EP was only consulted), failed to reach a unanimous agreement. After several attempts to adopt the statute, Germany and Sweden opposed the measure in 2011. Germany opposed it on the very question of the separation of management offices from head offices that had been so heatedly debated in the EP (see also Chapter 4 in this volume).

ENRICHING THE ENTREPRENEURSHIP DISCOURSE

It is clear from the debates on both the SBA and the EPC statute that the EP added another dimension to the discussion on entrepreneurship by vigorously advocating labour law and social aspects. One core topic was the regulation of labour markets. The labour market strongly influences entrepreneurship policy in two ways. As was foreseen in the initial SBA plan, a low level of labour market regulation increases the flexibility of companies and is regarded as a desirable condition for people to become entrepreneurs and to hire employees. Moreover, weak employment protection reduces the advantage of being an employee, making it more favourable to become self-employed (Henrekson and Stenkula, 2010: 614). However, the deregulation of labour markets means at the same time that hard-earned national labour rights are watered down, and entrepreneurs themselves face weak employment protection, which heightens the risk of entrepreneurial precarity and lowers the incentive to become an entrepreneur.

While the Council pursued the Commission's position to deregulate labour markets with a view to boosting competition, the EP was more aware of possible negative impacts in other policy areas, such as employment. Individual groups and members opened the debate to a more social concept of entrepreneurship, overriding the dominant enterprise discourse.

This confirms that political differences between the Council and the EP are ideological and often relate to issues of regulation rather than of European integration, which is along the traditional political left–right axis (Tsebelis and Garrett, 2000). In many different policy areas '[t]he right-wing Council is against regulation, whereas the left-wing EP is in favor of it' and it is especially the left wing within the EP that pushes for common regulations (Kreppel and Tsebelis, 1999: 963). The analysis of the SBA and the EPC statute confirms this phenomenon. In presenting the various political differences and ideologies, Table 6.1 focuses on the degree of intended regulation and the various definitions of entrepreneurship of the main political groups.

The whole political spectrum is mirrored in this discussion: the conservative and liberal groups are in line with the Commission and the Council in striving primarily to boost the internal market by deregulation. In their definition, entrepreneurship is equated with self-employment. The more social democratic or socialist of groups emphasise the social dimension of entrepreneurship by focusing on labour rights, social protection, and the promotion of entrepreneurial diversity and entrepreneurial training. Entrepreneurship in this context is also seen as a concept aimed at improving working conditions and contributing to the common good. This definition broadens the discussion to include more innovative and green companies, or even new job markets or a sustainable concept of social entrepreneur. Unlike the situation in the case of the Council and the Commission, this social dimension of entrepreneurship is not limited to the enterprise context; it also includes the question of

Table 6.1 Summary of political positions on entrepreneurship of the Council, the Commission, and the main political groups in the EP

	Council/ Commission	EPP	PES/S&D	ALDE	GUE/ NGL	The Greens
Regulation level	Deregulation	Deregulation	Maintaining national labour rights	Deregulation	Regulation	Maintaining national labour rights
Defining Entre-preneurship (ES)	ES as self-employment	ES as self-employment	ES as self-employment and a concept for the promotion of improved working conditions for self-employed	ES as self-employment	ES seen as a pretext for deregulation of labour markets and public services	ES as a concept for innovative and green approaches

how entrepreneurship contributes to the common good. These considerations were taken up in the SBA review and especially in the Entrepreneurship 2020 Action Plan, which are dealt with in the next section.

STRENGTHENING THE OPEN METHOD OF COORDINATION

The SBA review and the Entrepreneurship 2020 Action Plan are both instances with regard to which the EP strengthened the open method of coordination. In certain policy areas, where the EU competencies are limited and where the main responsibilities lie at the member-state level – for example education and training, and enterprise policy – this soft legal instrument, organised as a voluntary mutual learning process, is used to launch specific guidelines and indicators for certain policies, to enhance cooperation, and to share best practice among member states (Kröger, 2009). As it is an intergovernmental mechanism, the involvement of the EP is weak and its legitimacy questionable (Büchs, 2008). However, the EP did promote this method in the field of entrepreneurship.

Small Business Act Review

As the 2010–2011 annual report on SME performance revealed that the positive impacts of the SBA measures on SMEs had come to a halt (European Commission, 2011), six political groups jointly tabled a resolution to put pressure on the Council and the Commission (European Parliament, 2011e, 2011f). The authors, on behalf of their groups, stressed the need for concrete action to ensure proper implementation (European Parliament, 2011b). Under pressure from the EP, the Commission launched plans to introduce a new governance system, to facilitate an exchange between member states, and to fully apply the 'think small first' principle at the member-state level (European Parliament, 2011b). These measures were later put into effect by the Commission, together with the EP.

During the parliamentary discussions, the members of the various parties strove for the increased promotion of entrepreneurship. At the top of the agenda were entrepreneurial education and training, and measures to boost young entrepreneurship (European Parliament, 2011b). Unlike the case of the SBA in 2009 – and despite some critical statements on social and environmental issues made by the GUE/NGL – the review enjoyed broad support in the EP (European Parliament, 2011a).

In October 2012, the EP adopted a resolution on competitiveness and business opportunities for SMEs in order to promote the SBA objectives. Again, the resolution received significant support. Only two members from the S&D and GUE/NGL expressed reservations (European Parliament, 2012a). Shortly thereafter – in February 2013 – the EP also adopted a resolution on improving SMEs' access to finance (European Parliament, 2013b). This resolution, too, resulted in a broad-based consensus (European Parliament, 2013d), and critical statements ceased.

This may be explained on the basis of three main arguments. First, as mentioned in the explanations of the votes, the enduring intense economic situation in the EU member states triggered a consent; second, the majorities in the EP had drastically changed after the EP election in June 2009: the more right-oriented parties made gains, while the more left-oriented parties – the parties that had introduced the social dimension of entrepreneurship in the SBA debates – suffered significant losses; and third, the role of the EP when launching the action plans was restricted.

Entrepreneurship 2020 Action Plan

The Entrepreneurship 2020 Action Plan is another example where the EP succeeded in enhancing the open method of coordination. The main objectives of the Commission's communication were to boost entrepreneurship in Europe by entrepreneurial education and training, and to reignite the culture of entrepreneurship (European Commission, 2013).

On behalf of the ITRE Committee, Paul Rübig (EPP, Austria) officially put five questions to the Commission relating to the objectives of the action plans and their realisation, especially with regard to the fact that member states were responsible for education and training programmes. Other questions were related to the reduction of administrative, regulatory, and taxation burden, and increased funding for SMEs within the multiannual financial framework (European Parliament, 2013c). The Commissioner in charge, Antonio Tajani, replied during the debate that the entrepreneurial objectives should be implemented via the national education and school systems. He stated that excellent programmes promoting the development of entrepreneurial skills already existed in schools and universities, and that these programmes should serve as best practice examples and be transferred to other educational systems. Member states should be encouraged to effectively implement the action plan (European Parliament, 2013a). Certain measures have therefore been developed and institutionalised by the Commission, together with the EP, which have led to a strengthening of the open method of coordination in this area.

Under pressure from the EP and the Council, the Commission also proposed new legislation in the area of taxation and SMEs' access to funding. A major landmark in this area was the Competitiveness of Enterprises and Small and Medium-sized Enterprises (COSME) programme 2014–2020, which was the first SME-specific funding programme in Europe, and finally adopted by ordinary legislative procedure in 2013 (European Parliament, 2012b; Official Journal of the EU, 2013). The EP debate on the COSME programme and the Entrepreneurship 2020 Action Plan was dominated by a common understanding of promoting SMEs and entrepreneurship in Europe, especially in view of the intense economic situation in the member states (European Parliament, 2013a). Another milestone in this context was the establishment of the Erasmus for Young Entrepreneurs programme. The EP initiated this mobility exchange programme for young entrepreneurs across the member states, by introducing a budget line for it in 2007. It was subsequently taken up by the Commission and institutionalised at EU level.

CONCLUSION

This chapter demonstrates that the EP shaped the EU policy on entrepreneurship. When we return to our definition of a successful entrepreneur, we might argue the EP used the crisis as a policy window and was innovative in promoting new policies, norms, and values and in using channels and networks to improve the conditions for the common good (Silander, 2016). The incentives for the EP were the strengthening of its own position and the promotion of its values (see also Kingdon, 2011: 122–124). The EP acted as a political entrepreneur when debating the relevant entrepreneurial action plans in three respects.

First, the EP was able to influence the decision-making process in this field and enhance the open method of coordination, despite a restricted legislative role. In the case of the EPC statute, concerns about the effects on the labour market expressed during parliamentary debates were taken into account at Council level, and finally led national delegations to block the statute and prevent its becoming law. When debating the SBA review and the Entrepreneurship 2020 Action Plan, the EP put pressure on the Council and the Commission by asking parliamentary questions, which resulted in a strengthening of the open method of coordination.

Second, the EP used policy-influencing instruments, such as resolutions, opinions, debates, and parliamentary questions, in order to advocate a certain entrepreneurship policy. Whereas the Commission and the Council were in favour of boosting competition by encouraging people to become self-employed and by deregulating labour markets, critical statements by the more left-oriented groups (PES, S&D, Greens-EFA, GUE/NGL) led to a broad discussion on labour law, social aspects, and entrepreneurial diversity. The far-reaching societal consequences of the dominant business approach of encouraging individuals and specific groups to enter markets and start their own businesses have been discussed exclusively in the EP. Therefore, the fact that the enterprise discourse has been expanded is indicative of an innovative approach, and may lead to a different understanding of entrepreneurship in the future, which will include a more social and innovative definition of the concept. In this respect, the EP acted as political entrepreneur by enriching the entrepreneurship discourse.

Third, the initiatives of certain parliamentary committees and individual members resulted in a number of landmarks being achieved for entrepreneurs. A good example is the Erasmus for Young Entrepreneurs programme. However, in defining political entrepreneurship and in examining the role of the EP in acting as a political entrepreneur as explained above, one might also argue that those incidents where the EP served as political entrepreneur constitute – at least to some extent – the daily working life of the EP. This is due to the fact that the established parliamentary policy-influencing instruments might be already regarded as 'entrepreneurial'. In lack of decision-making competences in the past, the EP continuously developed innovative instruments to create possibilities aimed at shaping certain policies. Nonetheless, when it comes to the entrepreneurship policy, the economic crisis enabled the momentum to broadly discuss the topic within the parliamentary arena and to initiate various policy-influencing instruments within a certain time period.

However, and as the debates indicate, the potential of the EP to act as a political entrepreneur has its limitations, as the EP is ultimately determined by its political majorities, which provide the basis for and direction of its entrepreneurship policy.

REFERENCES

Agence Europe (2009), EP/INTERNAL MARKET: Parliament disappointed that Small Business Act is not legally binding, Brussels, 09/03/2009, AE 9857, 10.3.2009.

Agence Europe (2014), YOUTH: Council stresses developing spirit of enterprise among youth, Brussels, 20/05/2014, AE 11083, 21.5.2014.

Bauer, M. W. and S. Becker (2014), 'The unexpected winner of the crisis: the European Commission's strengthened role in economic governance', *Journal of European Integration*, 36(3), 213–229.

Baumgartner, F. R. and B. D. Jones (1993), *Agendas and Instabilities in American Politics*. Chicago, IL: University of Chicago Press.

Berglund, K. and A. W. Johansson (2007), 'Entrepreneurship, discourses and conscientization in processes of regional development', *Entrepreneurship & Regional Development*, 19(6), 499–525.

Büchs, M. (2008), 'How legitimate is the open method of co-ordination?', *Journal of Common Market Studies*, 46(4), 765–786.

Burns, C. (2016), 'The European Parliament', in: M. Cini and N. Perez-Solorzano Borragan (eds) *European Union Politics*. Oxford: Oxford University Press, pp. 155–166.

Copeland, P. and J. Scott (2014), 'Policy windows, ambiguity and commission entrepreneurship: explaining the relaunch of the European Union's Economic Reform Agenda', *Journal of European Public Policy*, 21(1), 1–19.

Council of the EU (2013), Preparation of the Council ('Competitiveness') of 18–19 February 2013, Action Plan for Entrepreneurship – Presentation by the Commission – Exchange of Views, Brussels, 1 February 2013, 5862/13.

European Commission (2008), Proposal for a Council Regulation on the Statute for a European private company, Brussels, 25.6.2008, COM(2008) 396 final, 2008/0130 (CNS).

European Commission (2011), *Are EU SMEs recovering from the crisis? Annual Report on EU Small and Medium sized Enterprises 2010/2011, Ref. Ares(2016)1077412-02/03/2016*. Rotterdam, Cambridge, Ecorys.

European Commission (2013), Communication from the Commission to the European Parliament, the Council, the European Economic and Social Committee and the Committee of the Regions, Entrepreneurship 2020 Action Plan, Reigniting the Entrepreneurial Spirit in Europe, Brussels, 9.1.2013, COM(2012) 795 final.

European Commission (2017), President Jean-Claude Juncker's State of the Union Address 2017, Brussels 13 September 2017.

European Parliament (2009a), *Debates, Monday, 9 March 2009 – Strasbourg, 18. Statute for a European private company–Cross-borders transfers of companies' registered offices – Small Business Act – Workers' participation in companies with a European Statute (debate)*, accessed 30 October 2017 at http://www.europarl.europa.eu/sides/getDoc.do?type=CRE&reference=20090309&secondRef=ITEM-018&language=EN&ring=A6-2009-0074.

European Parliament (2009b), *Debates, Tuesday, 10 March 2009 – Strasbourg, 9. Explanations of vote, Oral explanations of vote, Report: Edit Herczog (A6-0074/2009)*, accessed 30 October 2017 at http://www.europarl.europa.eu/sides/getDoc.do?type=CRE&reference=20090310&secondRef=ITEM-009&language=EN&ring=A6-2009-0074#2-199.

European Parliament (2009c), *Legislative Observatory, 2008/0130(NLE) – 10/03/2009 Text adopted by Parliament, 1st reading/single reading*, accessed 30 October 2017 at http://www.europarl.europa.eu/oeil/popups/summary.do?id=1070520&t=d&l=en.

European Parliament (2009d), *Legislative Observatory, Procedure file, Document reference 2008/0130(NLE), Company law: statute for a European private company*, accessed 30 October 2017 at http://www.europarl.europa.eu/oeil/popups/ficheprocedure.do?lang=en&reference=2008/0130(NLE).

European Parliament (2009e), *Legislative Observatory, Procedure file, Document reference 2008/2237(INI), Small Business Act*, accessed 30 October 2017 at http://www.europarl.europa.eu/oeil/popups/ficheprocedure.do?reference=2008/2237(INI)&l=en.

European Parliament (2009f), *Legislative Observatory, Statistics-2008/2237(INI), A6-0074/2009, Results of vote in Parliament, Final vote 10/03/2009*, accessed 30 October 2017 at http://www.europarl.europa.eu/oeil/popups/sda.do?id=16781&l=en.

European Parliament (2009g), Report on Small Business Act (2008/2237(INI)), Committee on Industry, Research and Energy, Rapporteur: Edit Herczog, A6-0074/2009, 18.2.2009.

European Parliament (2011a), *Debates, Thursday, 12 May 2011 – Strasbourg, 13. Explanations of vote, Motion for a resolution B7-0286/2011, Part 2*, accessed 30 October 2017 at http://www.europarl.europa.eu/sides/getDoc.do?type=CRE&reference=20110512&secondRef=ITEM-013&language=EN&ring=B7-2011-0286#4-236-000.

European Parliament (2011b), *Debates, Wednesday, 11 May 2011 – Strasbourg, 12. Small Business Act review (debate)*, accessed 30 October 2017 at http://

www.europarl.europa.eu/sides/getDoc.do?type=CRE&reference=20110511&secondRef=ITEM-012&language=EN&ring=B7-2011-0286.

European Parliament (2011c), European Parliament Special Committee on the Financial, Economic and Social Crisis. Documentation relating to the Committee's work from October 2009 to July 2011, Chairman Wolf Klinz, Rapporteur Pervenche Berès, Brussels, July.

European Parliament (2011d), Motion for a Resolution, further to Questions for Oral Answer B7-0301/2011 and B7-0302/2011 pursuant to Rule 115(5) of the Rules of Procedure on the Small Business Act Review, B7-0286/2011, 4.5.2011.

European Parliament (2011e), *Parliamentary questions 12 April 2011, O-000089/2011, Question for oral answer to the Council, Rule 115*, accessed 30 October 2017 at http://www.europarl.europa.eu/sides/getDoc.do?pubRef=-//EP//TEXT+OQ+O-2011-000089+0+DOC+XML+V0//EN&language=EN.

European Parliament (2011f), *Parliamentary questions, 12 April 2011, O-000090/2011, Question for oral answer to the Commission, Rule 115*, accessed 30 October 2017 at http://www.europarl.europa.eu/sides/getDoc.do?pubRef=-//EP//TEXT+OQ+O-2011-000090+0+DOC+XML+V0//EN.

European Parliament (2012a), *Debates, Monday, 22 October 2012–Strasbourg, 23. SMEs: competitiveness and business opportunities (short presentation)*, accesssed 30 October 2017 at http://www.europarl.europa.eu/sides/getDoc.do?pubRef=-//EP//TEXT+CRE+20121022+ITEM-023+DOC+XML+V0//EN&language=EN.

European Parliament (2012b), Report on the proposal for a regulation of the European Parliament and of the Council establishing a Programme for the Competitiveness of Enterprises and small and medium-sized enterprises (2014–2020), (COM(2011)0834 – C7-0463/2011 – 2011/0394(COD)), Committee on Industry, Research and Energy, Rapporteur: Jürgen Creutzmann, A7-0420/2012, 13.12.2012.

European Parliament (2013a), *Debates, Wednesday, 20 November 2013–Strasbourg, 13. Competitiveness of enterprises and small and medium-sized enterprises (2014 – 2020) – Entrepreneurship 2020 action plan – Reigniting the entrepreneurial spirit in Europe (debate)*, accessed 30 October 2017 at http://www.europarl.europa.eu/sides/getDoc.do?pubRef=-//EP//TEXT+CRE+20131120+ITEM-013+DOC+XML+V0//EN&language=EN.

European Parliament (2013b), *Legislative Observatory, Procedure file 2012/2134(INI), Improving access to finance for SMEs*, accessed 30 October 2017 at http://www.europarl.europa.eu/oeil-mobile/fiche-procedure/2012/2134(INI).

European Parliament (2013c), *Parliamentary questions 10 October 2013, O-000110/2013, Question for oral answer to the Commission Rule 115, Paul Rübig, on behalf of the Committee on Industry, Research and Energy, Subject: Entrepreneurship 2020 Action Plan – Reigniting the entrepreneurial spirit in Europe*, accessed 30 October 2017 at http://www.europarl.europa.eu/sides/getDoc.do?type=OQ&reference=O-2013-000110&language=EN.

European Parliament (2013d), *Statistics 2012/2134(INI)|A7-0001/2013, Results of vote in Parliament, Final vote 05/02/2013*, accessed 30 October 2017 at http://www.europarl.europa.eu/oeil-mobile/sda/22402?l=en.

Fabbrini, S. (2013), 'Intergovernmentalism and its limits: assessing the European Union's answer to the Euro crisis', *Comparative Political Studies*, 46(9), 1003–1029.

Fasone, C. (2013), 'European economic governance and parliamentary representation. What place for the European Parliament?' *European Law Journal*, 20(2), 164–185.

Henrekson, M. and M. Stenkula (2010), 'Entrepreneurship and public policy', in: Z. J. Acs and D. B. Audretsch (eds) *Handbook of Entrepreneurship Research.* New York: Springer.

Hix, S. (2002), 'Constitutional agenda-setting through discretion in rule interpretation: why the European Parliament won at Amsterdam', *British Journal of Political Science*, 32(2), 259–280.

Hodson, D. (2015), 'Policy-making under economic and monetary union. Crisis, change, and continuity', in: H. Wallace, M. A. Pollack and A. R. Young (eds) *Policy-Making in the European Union*, 7th edition. Oxford: Oxford University Press.

Kingdon, J. W. (2011), *Agendas, Alternatives, and Public Policies*, updated 2nd edition. Longman Classics in Political Science, Boston, MA: Pearson.

Kreppel, A. and G. Tsebelis (1999), 'Coalition formation in the European Parliament', *Comparative Political Studies*, 32(8), 933–966.

Kröger, S. (2009), 'The open method of coordination: underconceptualisation, overdetermination, depoliticisation and beyond', Special Issue 1, in: S. Kröger (ed.) *What we have learnt: Advances, pitfalls and remaining questions in OMC research.* European Integration online Papers, 13(5), accessed 8 March 2018 at http://eiop.or.at/eiop/texte/2009-005a.htm.

Laffan, B. (1997), 'From policy entrepreneur to policy manager: the challenge facing the European Commission', *Journal of European Public Policy*, 4(3), 422–438.

Manoli, P. and G. Maris (2015), 'The role of the European Parliament in managing the international economic crisis', in: S. Stavridis and D. Irrera (eds) *The European Parliament and its International Relations.* Abingdon and New York: Routledge.

Moravcsik, A. (1999), 'New statecraft? Supranational entrepreneurs and international cooperation', *International Organization*, 53(3), 267–306.

Neuhold, C. (2001), 'The "Legislative Backbone" keeping the Institution upright? The Role of European Parliament Committees in the EU Policy-Making Process', *European Integration online Papers (EIoP)*, 5(10), accessed 8 March 2018 at http://eiop.or.at/eiop/pdf/2001-010.pdf.

Official Journal of the EU (2009a), Opinion of the Committee of the Regions on 'Think Small First' – A 'Small Business Act for Europe', (2009/C 120/04), 28.5.2009.

Official Journal of the EU (2009b), Opinion of the European Economic and Social Committee on the Communication from the Commission to the Council, the European Parliament, the European Economic and Social Committee and the Committee of the Regions – 'Think Small First': A 'Small Business Act for Europe', COM(2008) 394 final, (2009/C 182/06), 4.8.2009.

Official Journal of the EU (2010), Small Business Act, European Parliament resolution of 10 March 2009 on the Small Business Act (2008/2237(INI)), P6_TA(2009)0100, (2010/C 87 E/11).

Official Journal of the EU (2013), Regulation (EU) No 1287/2013 of the European Parliament and of the Council of 11 December 2013 establishing a Programme for the Competitiveness of Enterprises and small and medium-sized enterprises (COSME) (2014–2020) and repealing Decision No 1639/2006/EC, L 347/33-49, 20.12.2013.

Pollack, M. A. (1997), 'Delegation, agency and agenda-setting in the European community', *International Organization*, 51(1), 99–135.

Ringe, N. (2010), *Who Decides, and How? Preferences, Uncertainty, and Policy Choice in the European Parliament*. Oxford: Oxford University Press.

Rittberger, B. (2014), 'Integration without representation? The European Parliament and the reform of economic governance in the EU', *Journal of Common Market Studies*, 52(6), 1174–1183.

Schön-Quinlivan, E. and M. Scipioni (2017), 'The Commission as policy entrepreneur in European economic governance: a comparative multiple stream analysis of the 2005 and 2011 Reform of the Stability and Growth Pact', *Journal of European Public Policy*, 24(8).

Shackleton, M. (2000), 'The politics of codecision', *Journal of Common Market Studies*, 38(2), 325–342.

Shackleton, M. (2017), 'The European Parliament: the power of democratic ideas', in: D. Hodson and J. Peterson (eds) *The Institutions of the European Union*, 4th edition. Oxford: Oxford University Press.

Silander, D. (2016), 'The political entrepreneur', in: C. Karlsson, C. Silander and D. Silander (eds) *Political Entrepreneurship. Regional Growth and Entrepreneurial Diversity in Sweden.* Cheltenham, Northampton: Edward Elgar.

Steyaert, C. and J. Katz (2004), 'Reclaiming the space of entrepreneurship in society: geographical, discursive and social dimensions', *Entrepreneurship & Regional Development*, 16(3), 179–196.

Tsebelis, G. and G. Garrett (2000), 'Legislative politics in the European Union', *European Union Politics*, 1(1), 9–36.

Versluis, E., M. Van Keulen and P. Stephenson (2010), *Analyzing the European Union Policy Process*. Basingstoke: Palgrave Macmillan.

Weible, C. M., P. A. Sabatier and J. Flowers (2008), 'Advocacy coalition framework', *Encyclopedia of Public Administration and Public Policy*, 2nd edition, 1(1), 1–10.

Zahariadis, N. (2014), 'Ambiguity and multiple streams', in: P. A. Sabatier and C. M. Weible (eds) *Theories of the Policy Process*, 3rd edition. Boulder, CO: Westview Press, pp. 25–58.

PART III

EU embedded policies on entrepreneurship and regional growth

7. Industrial policy in the post-industrial society: is the EU on the right track?

Charlie Karlsson and Sam Tavassoli

INTRODUCTION

There are only few policy areas in recent decades that have attracted more interest among economists than industrial policy. Moreover, there is probably no other policy area where economists disagree more than the area of industrial policy. They all agree on the importance of macro-economic stability, high rates of physical, R&D and human capital investments and well-functioning institutions as critical components of success, but are unable to agree on the proper role of industrial policy in developed as well as developing economies. Today we can observe a high interest among economists in the role of industrial policy (Chimoli et al., 2009; Naudé, 2010; Lin, 2012; OECD, 2012, 2013) and according to Google Scholar the interest in industrial policy seems to have started in the early 1980s, possibly because of the discussion about deindustrialisation that has been intensified in the 1970s (Appendix 7.1). However, this great interest in industrial policy among economists does not imply that there is any agreement among economists on the role and importance of industrial policy, not even on how to define the policy area of industrial policy.

As shown in Appendix 7.1, the interest among economists started to grow rapidly in absolute terms in the early 1980s. We may now ask why the interest is even larger today? This is because of several policy challenges that governments are presently facing. First, it is due to globalisation and a new geography of growth, production and trade that has emerged, not least due to the rise of China as an industrial powerhouse and its growing integration into world trade and foreign direct investments (Karlsson et al., 2015). Second, it is due to a new geography of innovation with an increased diffusion of information technologies and a growing priority given to science and technology not least in developing countries, which is contributing to new micro-dynamics of learning and knowledge circulation, generating new hubs of innovation in the world (Karlsson et al., 2012). Third, a major challenge is climate change and the need to develop new infrastructures, goods and services that can handle negative environmental externalities and increase the production of renewable energy. Fourth, another major challenge is the financial and economic crisis that started in 2008 and, in many countries, has stimulated a related search for new growth mechanisms. This has been obvious in countries with financial problems. The crisis also led many politicians and some economists to question the capacity of free markets to secure economic growth and led to a re-opening of a debate on the role of the state in contemporary capitalist economies (Skidelsky, 2009; Griffith-Jones et al., 2010).

After the crisis, there has emerged a growing feeling that markets alone do not always perform optimally for society, which has generated a demand for new forms of economic thinking. It has also generated a demand for new policy models that consider the specificities of the new economic landscape characterised by a higher integration of global economies not least financially; an increasing importance of (local, regional and international) networks for innovation and production; a higher speed of diffusion of information, knowledge and innovations; and a higher mobility of capital and talents. Furthermore, today policymakers have access to a much richer flow of evidences on the nature and performance of past industrial policies, which might give a feeling that they can avoid some of the earlier mistakes in industrial policy.

Thus, there are strong motives for economists to study industrial policies and to evaluate their effects and costs. There is also a need for *all* governments, with regular intervals, to go through their industrial policies and evaluate and compare them with what other governments do, since industrial policies often relate to vested interests, difficult problems and substantial costs and risks including rent-seeking (Krueger, 1990; Ades and Di Tella, 1997; Pack and Saggi, 2006). The main question for governments is not whether or not they should engage in industrial policies but *how to do it in the right manner and efficiently*. Hence, the discussion tends to shift towards a more pragmatic level where economists and policymakers discuss not about the need (or not) for industrial policy, but on "what" to do and on "how" to do it (Chang, 2011).

Today, policymakers in different countries and not least in the European Union (EU) are hunting for new approaches to industrial policy to meet the challenges they are facing. The financial crisis of 2008 has stimulated an intensive debate on the role of industrial policy (Pianta,

2014). Two main questions are increasingly asked about the appropriate scale and scope of industrial policy: (i) should industrial policies be "vertical" and target sectors, industries or even firms? Or (ii) should industrial policies be "horizontal" and focus on the general economic conditions that affect all sectors, industries and firms? Interestingly, there are two questions that are asked much more seldom and they are: (i) What are the spatial implications of current "vertical" and/or "horizontal" industrial policies? And (ii) should industrial policies focus on regions, possibly targeting specific clusters of firms?

The threefold purpose of the current chapter, against the above background, is: (i) to discuss how the views on industrial policy have changed in a long-term perspective with a special focus on the post-war period up to the current post-industrial society; (ii) to present arguments and motivations for the reasons why industrial policies in the current post-industrial society should mainly be regional policies or rather industrial policies at the regional level; and (iii) to briefly evaluate the EU's current approach to industrial policy, the so-called "smart specialisation".

The chapter is organised as follows: in Section 2, we discuss what should be understood with industrial policy and in Section 3 we present the arguments for and against industrial policy. In Section 4, we highlight some of the problems related to industrial policies and in particular "vertical" industrial policies. The next section – Section 5 – is devoted to a short discussion about industrial policies in the era before the industrial society and during the industrial society. Then follows in Section 6 a presentation of industrial policies during the transition from the industrial to the post-industrial society and how the views on industrial policy changed during this period. In Section 7, we present our arguments and motivations for regional policies as the main industrial policy in the post-industrial society and discuss the conditions for industrial policy in small and medium-sized regions as well as in large urban regions. This section also contains a discussion of the EU's new approach to industrial policy – smart specialisation. Section 8 concludes.

WHAT IS INDUSTRIAL POLICY?

The Oxford Dictionary of Economics (2003) defines industrial policy as "official policies concerning the direction of economic activity to particular parts of the economy". This definition is very close to the definition of industrial policy provided by Stiglitz et al. (2013: 2), "government policies directed at affecting the structure of the economy". A similar sector/industry-oriented definition is used by the US International Trade Commission. According to them industrial policy involves "coordinated government action aimed at directing production resources to domestic producers in certain industries to help them become more competitive" (Tyson, 1992). Lakshmanan (1994: 105) uses the definition: "the state's use of its power and resources to develop and administer policies intended to meet the needs of specific sectors and industries (and in some cases those of individual firms) to promote the efficient use of resources". According to Porter (2000), industrial policy rests on a view of competition in which some industries and firms offer greater wealth-creating prospects than others and are therefore the target for support.

All the above definitions are about what is called "vertical" industrial policy, which implies that benefits are given to certain sectors, industries or firms but not to all (Beason and Weinstein, 1996). However, there also exists a "horizontal" definition of industrial policy. The EU has in its Lisbon Agenda been pursuing such an approach and according to their definition "the main role of industrial policy [...] is to proactively provide the right framework conditions for enterprise development and innovation in order to make the EU an attractive place for industrial development and job creation, taking account of the fact that most businesses are small or medium-sized enterprises (SMEs)" (European Commission, 2007). It is obvious that the existence of two main approaches to industrial policy – "vertical" and "horizontal" – is contributing to the disagreement among economists concerning industrial policy. The existence of two different main definitions of industrial policy is also making research on, as well as the political discussion of, industrial policy more complicated.

Industrial Policy: Why and Why Not?

We can observe that several scholars forcefully argue that governments can help industries and firms to grow and that rapid industrial development is often backed with government subsidies and protective tariffs that deliberately distort markets to incentivise local investment and entrepreneurship (Amsden, 1989; Rodrik, 1995, 2004). The theoretical arguments for industrial policy can be summarised as follows:

(i) the infant industry argument, which can be supported with Arrow's learning-by-doing argument;
(ii) various neoclassical theories of market failure, especially those related to knowledge-generation and the market for capital;

(iii) the interdependence arguments in terms of the need for a "big push" (Rosenstein-Rodan, 1943) and/or the role of market linkages (Hirschman, 1958);
(iv) theories of collective production and innovation in national systems of innovation and industrial districts generating positive externalities (Tavassoli and Tsagdis, 2014);
(v) Oliver Williamson's theory of asset specificity motivating a defensive industrial policy; and
(vi) the existence of tacit knowledge.

The study by Chimoli et al. (2009) argues that industrial policy plays a critical role in economic growth. They claim that no country has moved from being a backward economy to an industrial economy without extensive involvement from the state in the form of tariffs, subsidies, and targeted sector-level support. In the nineteenth and early twentieth centuries, all of today's rich countries, except the Netherlands and pre-World War I Switzerland, practised protectionism and other forms of industrial policy (subsidies, state-owned enterprises, regulation of FDIs, investments in infrastructure, etc.). Even the rapid growth of the US economy owes much to temporary protection against manufacturing products from Britain in the nineteenth century (Chang, 1994) and to government-sponsored research and targeted initiatives in sectors such as agriculture, computing, health and military equipment (Mowery, 1984; Graham, 2010; Mazzucato, 2013). It was only after World War II, when the US successfully had established its dominance behind protectionist barriers, that the US started to reduce its tariffs from averages of 20–50 per cent.[1] Also, Great Britain – the other supposed home of free trade – had the world's highest levels of tariff protection during its industrialisation period.

The fact that Japan (Johnson, 1982), South Korea (Amsden, 1989) and Taiwan (Wade, 1990) have been able to catch up with the developed economies in the West has been seen as empirical evidence for these claims. The argument is extended by claims that successful experiences of industrial policy in the post-war period are not confined to East Asia but also include: (i) national industrial policies in France, Finland, Norway and Austria; (ii) regional industrial policies in Italy and Germany; and (iii) industrial policy in the form of government R&D funding

[1] This argument is failing. Simply that the US had high tariffs while it was developing into a world power does not prove that it developed due to high tariffs. It might have grown more rapid with lower tariffs. Without a proper randomised trial, we cannot prove the effects of this industrial policy.

in the US. It is against this background that we ask whether industrial policy is always the right policy to solve growth problems. We may observe that the widespread failure of developing countries to catch up with advanced economies is at least partly due to the failure of their institutions to push productivity growth in the learning industries (Acemoglu and Robinson, 2013). The institutions for inducing learning must both provide incentives for learning and have the credibility to impose costs and sanctions on industries and firms that fail to achieve the required rate of learning. If the state doesn't have the credibility and the instruments to withdraw a subsidy when there is underperformance, there will be both a short-term and a permanent cost, because the infant industries will never mature.

In the debate, we can see that some economists accept industrial policy if it is "horizontal", that is, if it is non-targeted (Chang, 2003, 2008). They have been heavily criticised by the proponents for an "activist industrial policy", who claim that: (i) in a world with scarce resources, targeting is inevitable; (ii) in such a world, every policy choice you make, however "general" it may look, has discriminatory effects that amount to targeting; (iii) it is not necessarily true that less targeted policies are better due to leakages, monitoring costs, etc.; and (iv) the debate should not be on whether we target, but on how well we target. Against this background it is interesting to observe that many mainstream growth and trade economists are, and have been for the most part, sceptical of activist industrial policy for two main and mutually reinforcing reasons: first, while it is possible to write down fully articulated models in which industrial policies are welfare-increasing, this is only true under circumstances that are somewhat special, such as the existence of productivity externalities or rents; and second, the existence of these conditions is extremely difficult to establish empirically.

Another group of economists that have been sceptical to industrial policy are those within the Austrian school, who view competition as a type of discovery process, propelled by rivalrous entrepreneurs who generate and disseminate new knowledge about what products customers want, how much they are willing to pay and how existing products can be produced at lower costs (Hayek, 1978). Within an institutional framework of private property rights and freedom of making contracts, the establishment of a price structure provides both the incentives and the necessary information for entrepreneurs to search and exploit potential opportunities for mutually beneficial exchanges (Boettke and Prychitko, 1998). Thereby, these market processes will foster mutual learning that in general will tend to coordinate the expectations and the plans of the economic agents. According to this perspective the central function of the market is interpreted as a coordination instrument rather than an instrument for efficient resource allocation (Kirzner, 1973) and since the market takes care of the coordination problem there is no need for any industrial policy. Expressed in another way, the argument here is that there exist no theoretical justifications for industrial policy – everything is a matter of getting the prices right.

Industrial Policy – A Risky Policy Area

There are many problems related to industrial policies, which makes it a risky policy area (cf. Karlsson and Andersson, 2009). All too often policymakers don't seem to be aware of the problems and risks involved. A first hurdle is that what might be an optimal policy for one industry might not be optimal for the whole economy, if other industries function in a non-optimal way. A second hurdle is that even if economists should be able to design an optimal industrial policy, politicians may for ideological and/or other reasons, such as popularity among voters, choose another less optimal policy and keep it for a very long time. There may also be the case where politicians pursue policies just to demonstrate to voters that they are active and doing something for the voters. This may lead to all too frequent changes of laws, regulations, taxes and subsidies. What complicates the picture is that we can't assume that the main objective of politicians is to increase general welfare. Their main objective is normally to secure their re-election. The picture is further complicated by the fact that we can't assume that civil servants have as their main objective the efficient implementation of policies to increase general welfare. We can't exclude the possibility that their main objective is to maximise their own utility (Buchanan, 2003). A further problem to consider is that many vested interests in many countries are well organised and have large financial resources, which they may use in lobbying campaigns to influence politicians and civil servants to take decisions concerning industrial policy in line with the wishes of these groups.

These problems related to implementing industrial policy were taken up by Page and Campos (1993), who concluded that industrial policy is uniquely exposed to government failure, so an exceptional government capacity is necessary for it to work. The first problem related to the implementation of industrial policy is policy irrelevance. Government policies implemented in the public sector often do not fully consider that the responses of the economic agents in the private sector can lead to unintended or even perverse consequences. The responses of the targeted economic agents can be such that their actions weaken, undo or even reverse the government's intended outcomes. A second and partly related problem is the issue with perverse incentives. Industrial policies might encourage potential entrepreneurs as well as incumbents to engage in unproductive rent-seeking activities, such as subsidy maximisation, rather than in productive economic activities. This might have negative effects on productivity, innovation, competition and eventually on economic growth. The third problem in this category is the crowding-out problem. Many industrial policies are expensive to implement. Thus, governments must spend tax money to finance their industrial policies – tax money that could have been used for other types of public spending or to reduce the tax burden for households and/or firms. The crowding-out effect generates an opportunity cost, which can be larger than the value of the new industrial policy.

There are also technical problems related to industrial policymaking. One major problem is that policymaking is a slow process that is delayed due to the existence of many lags, such as an observation lag, an analysis lag, a policy-formulation lag, a policy decision-making lag, an implementation lag and finally an effect lag. Taken together these lags imply that when an industrial policy is starting to have effects the problem might be gone or other policy problems might have become more urgent. Another technical problem is the problem related to the fact that different processes in society run with different speeds. Policymakers don't have the necessary tools to influence rapid or very rapid process, such as changes in currency values or stock prices during the day or daily traffic flows. They have some tools to influence slower processes, such as migration or changes in industrial structure but their best tools concern slow processes such as changes in transport systems, investments in transport, communication and technical infrastructures, systems of higher education, and changes in formal institutions. This implies that policymakers are best equipped to deal with long-term industrial policies and must be careful the more rapid processes they try to influence.

A problem with the very rich literature on industrial policy is that it gives little practical guidelines to policymakers on how to successfully address market failures and to minimise rent-seeking from unproductive entrepreneurs. However, one advice from the literature in the field is to ensure that all industrial policies are conducted in a highly competitive environment (Aghion et al., 2012). Nevertheless, the proponents for an activist industrial policy admit that political conditions matter, but that we should not let the best be the enemy of the good. They actually maintain that in the real world, (i) successful countries are the ones that have managed to find "good enough" solutions to their political economy problems and that have implemented policies, rather than sitting around bemoaning the imperfect nature of their political system; (ii) it is not true that industrial policy is uniquely difficult; (iii) industrial policy does *not* require a sophisticated knowledge of economics, as often is believed; (iv) high-quality bureaucracies are not as difficult to build, as people think; (v) without trying out "difficult" policies, like industrial policy, capabilities cannot be improved through "learning-by-doing"; and (vi) the fact that something is difficult cannot be the reason not to recommend it (Chang, 1994, 2003).

INDUSTRIAL POLICY IN THE INDUSTRIAL SOCIETY

Industrial policy is by no means a new invention. It had already been practised during the mercantilist era by means of the regulation of imports, subsidies to exports and the granting of monopoly rights to manufacturers. Industrial policy has had many proponents over the centuries. Even Adam Smith, who strongly attacked the mercantilist philosophy, recognised a significant but selective industrial policy role for governments in providing the necessary infrastructures. Since Alexander Hamilton in 1791 wrote his "Report on the Subject of Manufactures", US governments have tried to actively stimulate one or more sectors of the economy to grow. In Germany, List (1841) argued that Germany could hope to overcome Great Britain's large lead in manufacturing but demanded policies that protected the infant industries in Germany. Most (if not all) of today's rich countries practised industrial policy in the nineteenth and early twentieth centuries as well as in the inter-war period, that is, during the early industrial society. After World War II, the use of industrial policy continued in what are now mature industrial societies. Moreover, currently the use of industrial policy also has spread to developing countries. The period from the late 1940s to the 1970s has been termed the global age of industrial policy (Primi, 2013).

In the early post-war period in Europe, industrial policies were used to stimulate the development of a large manufacturing base within industries such as steel, auto and chemicals (Pianta, 2014). In the early 1970s, industrial policy in Europe turned its focus to new industries, such as electronics and aircraft. Industrial policy in this period included, in particular, protectionism for infant industries but also agriculture with high tariff levels. It also included other forms such as industrial and R&D subsidies, public procurement of high-technology goods including weapons, state-owned enterprises in strategic industries, market protection, regulation of FDIs, specific support for the development of new firms, technologies and products, development of institutions, and development of national innovation systems. The provision of critical infrastructures, such as transport and communication networks also played an important role as well as the stable provision of energy. At the European level, we also got a coordination of industrial policies through the creation of the European Coal and Steel Community (ECSC) 1951 and the European Economic Community (EEC) 1957 with (mostly) free internal trade and a high trade protection from outside producers. Later, the European cooperation was enlarged to include common regulation and cooperation programmes in R&D and technology. The objectives of industrial policy in this period included (i) achieving static efficiency, (ii) achieving dynamic efficiency, and (iii) addressing market failures.

As the industrial society matured, industrial policy in the rich countries became more and more directed towards combatting market failures, specifically static market failures, but also to a certain extent dynamic market failures. These market failures included lack of/imperfect information, asymmetric information, dysfunctional capital markets/imperfect risk markets, public goods, semi-public goods and merit goods, positive and negative pecuniary and technological externalities, monopolies and other forms of competition limitation, such as oligopolies, economies of scale and other barriers to entry, under-investment in private R&D, market equilibria that are not efficient (Greenwald and Stiglitz, 1986), such as unemployment and unequal distribution. The industrial policies induced in rich countries by market failures during the mature industrial society were characterised by several clear limitations. The focus was often on one industry/sector at a time with no systems' perspective. Sometimes the focus was on "hitting the winners", which has turned out to be extremely difficult. The policies in this period were based upon the idea of social engineering and the belief that it was possible to "fine tune" economies. The policies that were implemented were based upon assumptions about perfect policy interventions and the possibilities of government failure were neglected as well as the risks for corruption. Moreover, the total cost of the interventions was often disregarded. The focus was very clearly on existing industries and firms, and policymakers showed very little interest in emerging industries and entrepreneurship.

We can observe that, from the late 1940s and onwards, most of the developing countries had introduced strategies to foster the creation of endogenous technological and production capabilities to shift from agricultural to industrialised societies (Amsden, 1989; Wade, 1990; Reinert, 2007). However, the industrial policies in developing countries during this period had a different focus and used means other than those used in the industrialised countries. A major one of those means was the establishment of state-owned enterprises and another was what turned out to be unsustainable import-substitution policies. The latter type of policy included market monopoly for non-viable firms in prioritised industries, suppression of interest rates, over-valuation of the domestic currency, price controls for raw materials and preferential access to credit for non-viable firms in prioritised industries.

INDUSTRIAL POLICY IN THE TRANSITION FROM THE INDUSTRIAL TO THE POST-INDUSTRIAL SOCIETY

The economic crisis in the 1970s and the associated deindustrialisation led to a change in the focus of industrial policies. This change was supported by new developments in economic theory such as the new trade theory, which provided theoretical arguments reinforcing the political arguments for industrial policy. Here, we present two different lines of theoretical arguments for industrial policy: the "National Innovation Systems" approach and the "infant industry" approach.

First, the national innovation systems approach was inspired by the industrial policies pursued by the Ministry of Industrial Trade and Industry in Japan. This approach addresses several issues: (i) infrastructural and institutional problems; (ii) technological lock-in, path dependence and transition failures; (iii) the quality of linkages and network configuration failures; and (iv) learning dynamics at the firm-, local network- and system levels (Andreoni, 2014). Many politicians, but also several economists in other rich countries, were amazed by the success of Japanese manufacturing in the decades after World War II and a search for possible reasons for this success started. One answer that emerged and that was accepted by many politicians was that the secret behind the Japanese success was the development of a national innovation system in Japan. According to this approach, industrial policy should focus on patent laws, support company R&D, increase the investments in higher education and university R&D, including the start-up of new universities and university colleges, use public procurement to support innovation and product development and generally make the government a promoter of new technologies.

Certainly, there are theoretical arguments for an industrial policy focusing on the production and diffusion of knowledge. Most increases in per capita incomes come from knowledge-based advances in technology. It is well established that markets on their own fail to maximise knowledge production and learning due to insufficient incentives for knowledge investments in a market economy. They are also incapable of handling important knowledge spillovers. At the same time, we know that knowledge spillovers are a critical source for knowledge-based entrepreneurship (Karlsson and Gråsjö, 2013). We also know that industries where knowledge is critical for competitiveness tend to be imperfectly competitive, leading to a restrained output in these industries. Furthermore, the production of knowledge is often conjoined with the production of goods and services, which implies that the production of goods and services themselves will not in general be (inter-temporally) efficient.

A second new approach to industrial policy in this transition period was based on the old infant industry argument, which had experienced a renaissance due to the development in international trade theory leading to the so-called new trade theory, which stressed that scale economies are fundamental to the competitiveness of firms in the international market. However, the infant industry argument could also be based upon Arrow's learning-by-doing argument and the existence of externalities in learning and discovery. The infant industry argument in principle says that new industries in the tradeable sector should be protected by tariffs, etc. until they are big enough to reap substantial scale economies and thus able to compete with the same industries in other countries (Feldman and Tavassoli, 2015). Such protection is feasible today even if WTO rules set some limits for the policy options. However, in the 1980s a totally different approach to industrial policy emerged, both in Europe and the US, based upon a critique of the established industrial policies as inefficient and inappropriate (Lerner, 2009). The counter movement to industrial policies that became popular in the 1980s stressed that government failures are a bigger problem than market failures. The underlying motivation was that economic agents operating in free markets behave rationally. The recipe for economic success and growth was liberalisation, privatisation and deregulation. The new approach said that markets should be left on their own to increase economic growth and welfare. This market fundamentalism approach was backed up theoretically not least by Milton Friedman and other Chicago-economists and is associated with Margaret Thatcher and Ronald Reagan. The main argument was that government failures are very serious and that markets operate efficiently (i) in allocating resources in the short run, and (ii) in developing new products, activities, resources and markets in the long run. The theoretical policy recommendations that included privatisation of firms owned by the public sector, of infrastructure and of public sector production and deregulation of trade, capital flows, domestic markets, etc. was to a large extent implemented in many countries. What remained of industrial policies were mainly some horizontal policies, which implied that few possibilities remained for the politicians to influence the direction of development in different sectors and industries.

However, in recent decades a widespread rethinking of the importance of industrial policy and of not least the manufacturing industry has emerged. Several restatements of the need for industrial policy have been presented (Chang, 1994; Hausmann and Rodrik, 2003; Rodrik, 2008; Wade, 2012; Greenwald and Stiglitz, 2013). The re-evaluation of the role of industrial policy has been stimulated by the changes in global manufacturing, including (i) a declining share of manufacturing activity in OECD countries, (ii) growing competition from emerging economies, (iii) the growing demands for resource-efficient manufacturing, (iv) the increased complexity and importance of global manufacturing chains, (v) the increased emphasis on engineering skills and vocational education, (vi) the increased importance of manufacturing R&D, and (vii) the accelerating pace of technological change (O'Sullivan et al., 2013). The effect of these changes is that the global manufacturing landscape has become both complex and increasingly fragmented in stages and tasks, which has led to a reshaping of the global industrial structures in terms of relations, location, governance, business models, and ownership of production (Pilat et al., 2008). The new industrial policy should be based on new technologies and support society's long-term targets (Aiginger, 2007). The new argument is that the question is not whether industrial policy makes sense, but the best way it can be carried out. This debate has particularly focused on newly industrialised countries, where extensive industrial policies have been used to combine public and private efforts in acquiring and developing new knowledge and technologies, invest in new activities and capacities and expanding exports and FDIs (Chimoli et al., 2009; Lee, 2013a, 2013b; Freire, 2013).

Analyses of the experiences of the US and Europe[2] have emphasised a need for 'transformative' public action in innovation and industrial and structural change (Mazzucato, 2013) and for mechanisms for controlling and targeting industrial policies (Aghion et al., 2011; Aghion et al., 2012). Several issues have also contributed to a resurgence of the interest in industrial policy in developing economies: (i) globalisation has opened up for new opportunities as well as threats for job creation and is requiring new strategic approaches to be able to benefit from the new conditions (Dahlman, 2011); (ii) growth in emerging and developing

[2] There exist a number of analyses and assessments of industrial policy in Europe (Coriat, 2004; Pianta, 2010; Lucchese and Pianta, 2012; WIIW, 2013; Reinstaller et al., 2013; Aiginger, 2014).

economies has opened up spaces for proactive policies, which were not available 20 to 30 years ago; and (iii) the costs of poor industrial and innovation capabilities have become more visible.

INDUSTRIAL POLICY IN THE POST-INDUSTRIAL SOCIETY: REGIONAL POLICY

Before presenting our argumentation that industrial policy in the post-industrial society must mainly be a policy at the regional level, we must clarify how we define a functional economic region (or functional urban region, since functional regions are normally centred in an urban area). The functional region is a geographical area for knowledge creation, appropriation, diffusion, absorption and use, as well as for the transformation of knowledge to innovations via entrepreneurial initiatives (Karlsson et al., 2009). A functional region can encompass these activities because it is an arena for exploiting communication externalities, which requires that the spatial extent of the region must be limited so that the economic agents in the region can and do exercise frequent face-to-face communication.

A functional economic region is characterised by a common labour market in which knowledge spreads as individuals change their job affiliation and place of employment, a common housing market, a common market for consumer services, a common market for business services and by being the market for most firms in the region. It is common to use commuting regions as the basis for delineating functional economic regions. Functional economic regions differ in terms of their political, economic and social history, their social capital (and its depth), and their informal institutions, such as customs, norms and traditions. Our basic argument is that industrial policies must be tailored to fit the specific circumstances in each individual functional economic region.

The economic development of functional economic regions is to a substantial extent governed by the location advantages they offer. There are two fundamental types of location advantages, namely (i) fixed and semi-fixed location factors and (ii) the regional market potential (Johansson and Karlsson, 2001). First, the fixed and semi-fixed location factors consist of geographical location, natural resources, hard and soft infrastructures, the current industry structure, the current labour force with its education, skills and experiences, the prevailing formal and informal institutions, regional industrial structure and portfolio in terms of specialisations and diversity, and the regional market potential (Tavassoli and Carbonara, 2014). Typical for these location factors is that they are either fixed or change only slowly. Second, the regional market potential measures the total purchasing power that firms in the functional economic region can access and consists of both the intra-regional and inter-regional accessibility to purchasing power.

The long-term economic development of functional economic regions is dependent upon three critical scale economies generating increasing returns (Karlsson et al., 2005). These are:

(i) the internal scale economies of firms;
(ii) location economies, that is, the co-location scale economies of individual industries in terms of a common labour market (static), a common pool of suppliers (static), and a common information and knowledge pool (dynamic); and
(iii) urbanisation economies, that is, the scale economies generated by the co-location of many clusters of different industries in larger (urban) functional economic regions (static and dynamic).

The spatial patterns that emerge over time are to a high extent the result of self-organised but interdependent location processes. Households themselves decide where to live and where to work based upon the availability of jobs and the supply of consumer services, amenities and household infrastructure. Entrepreneurs and firms on the other hand decide on locating, growing and contracting firms based upon demand conditions, the availability of labour, and the supply of business services and business infrastructures. The key role of policymakers within this context is to supply framework conditions important for the location decisions of households, entrepreneurs and firms. The existence of location and/or urbanisation economies in a functional region implies that there exist externalities within and between industries (Marshall, 1920; Krugman, 1993; Harrison and Rodríguez-Clare, 2010; Tavassoli and Carbonara, 2014), which are not considered in the decisions by firms and households. This implies that we here have a theoretical motivation for industrial policy initiatives in many functional regions, and hence it is natural in the post-industrial society that industrial policy has a strong local and/or regional component (Primi, 2013).

"SMART" REGIONAL SPECIALISATION AS INDUSTRIAL POLICY WITHIN THE EU

In this section, we briefly present and comment upon the idea of "smart" regional specialisation that has been developed as a combined horizontal and vertical industrial policy within the EU. This is the latest of a series of EU initiatives with the goal to encourage innovation and economic growth at the regional level (Mastroeni et al., 2013) and to reduce the centre-periphery polarisation and national fragmentation of the EU's innovation efforts. The purpose of smart specialisation policies is to increase the innovation capability of the EU's regions and to enhance local expertise in knowledge production and use, acting on local specificities and on the characteristics, strengths and weaknesses of already established innovation patterns in each region (Camagni and Capello, 2013). Its overall purpose is to meet some of the major challenges in terms of rapid technological change, globalised markets, migration, poverty, unemployment, an ageing society and climate change that the EU is facing. The policy efforts are targeting technological innovation and new governance processes with the purpose of delivering economic growth that is smart (i.e. knowledge- and innovation-based), sustainable and inclusive so that the EU can become the knowledge-based and competitive economy envisaged in the Lisbon Strategy. The expectations are that the innovations that address these challenges will likely emerge in areas of converging technologies, where technologies are combined to generate new applications. The focus is on general purpose technologies (Bresnahan and Trajtenberg, 1995; Feldman and Tavassoli, 2015) – platform technologies according to the EU – which are transformative and enabling, since they open opportunities for innovation complementarities and facilitate further innovation (Tavassoli and Karlsson, 2016; Karlsson and Tavassoli, 2016). The overall ambition of the smart specialisation strategy is (i) to coordinate the research, development and innovation efforts in the EU's regions, (ii) to reduce waste and unnecessary duplication, and (iii) to enable the development of thriving regional innovation systems. Its theoretical foundations are (i) general purpose technologies as engines for growth, (ii) the economic and social value in discovering product specialisation and having this geared towards economic development (Hausmann and Rodrik, 2003), and (iii) entrepreneurship as the mechanism that transfers knowledge from economic agents generating it to economic agents that can commercialise it successfully (Audretsch and Keilbach, 2008).

There are nine underlying ideas behind this industrial policy (Karlsson, 2016):

(i) a more productive use of the potentials of each region;
(ii) a simultaneous "polarisation" and "distribution" of R&D activities across space;

(iii) the development of a cumulative learning in advanced R&D activities and the consequent exploitation of increases in R&D productivity;
(iv) that a region can discover new specialisation fields inside its "knowledge domain" with local entrepreneurs as leading actors;
(v) a consistent matching between investments in knowledge and human capital and the present industrial and technological "vocations" and competencies of regions;
(vi) the conviction that context and inherited structures matter for the potential evolution of regional innovation systems;
(vii) that policies must be embedded in the local reality, in local assets and strategic design capabilities, and must guarantee the access of external knowledge through strong and virtuous linkages with other regions (McCann and Ortega-Argilés, 2013);
(viii) that policies must consider the heterogeneity of regional research and specialisation patterns; and
(ix) that it is possible to set up criteria to judge which specialisations, and consequently, which policy targets are "smart" for each region.

The method to pursue this policy builds upon the identification of existing specialised sectors and technological domains in different regions and the design of policies tailored to promote local innovation processes in these specialisation fields. A basic thought is that these should be different policies for core and peripheral regions with a concentration of efforts and resources in core regions to develop general purpose technologies, and investments in peripheral regions to develop applications of general purpose technologies for sectors that have a historical specialisation in these regions (Foray et al., 2009). The areas of specialisation shall be determined by local entrepreneurs who can recognise how general purpose technologies may be developed to benefit locally based industries.

However, this policy approach relates to five risks:

(i) it is questionable whether the smart specialisation approach really can provide generalisable principles that can be adapted to fit the variety of regional contexts and development paths, and provide stakeholders and policymakers with the means on how to manipulate different variables so that their target sectors make a transition to a higher level of productivity and competitiveness;
(ii) there is much more focus on enhancing the efficiency and innovativeness of existing industries than on nurturing new ones;

(iii) the focus on smart specialisation may reduce the variety that is a source of scientific novelty and innovation and may lead to a lock-in that could affect the resilience of different regions to economic change (Cooke, 2009);
(iv) there is little empirical research regarding the relationship between the policy objectives and the policy instruments; and
(v) the focus is not on functional economic regions but overwhelmingly on much larger administrative regions.

We may conclude that if smart specialisation is to be an efficient industrial policy, it will need to encourage and harness the relevant differences of each region's economy as well as secure access to useful knowledge in other regions. This might lead to the discovery of new market niches and avoid limiting the variety of each region's economy through counter-productive specialisation. Regional governments will need to supply proper incentives to entrepreneurs to find new niche areas and to identify complementary and supporting investments in, for example, training and education for these niches. Entrepreneurship tends to flourish in economic milieus that offer complementary resources and organisations, such as education and training, financing, skilled labour supplies and support for new firm formation and firm growth on the supply side; and on the demand side, a sufficient market potential and efficient channels for innovation adoption and distribution. This implies that governments at least partially can shape the pre-conditions required for innovation and entrepreneurship. However, it is important to observe that the knowledge and complementary technologies necessary to launch innovations will not be present in all (any?) of the regions. This implies that regions must have networks, inter-regional labour mobility and access to communication networks to facilitate inter-regional and international knowledge exchange and the import of other innovative inputs necessary for the recognition and exploitation of opportunities (Hausmann and Rodrik, 2003). However, the absorption of knowledge generated in other regions is a function of not only the geographical proximity but also of the institutional, technological, cognitive, social and organisational proximity (Marrocu et al., 2013). These different proximities are a crucial condition for firms' interaction and cooperation with firms in the location region as well as in other regions aimed at innovation. The problem here is that governments have limited instruments to influence several of these proximities.

In the post-industrial society, there are two major arenas for developing such framework conditions, namely on the one hand, small and medium-sized functional economic regions and on the other hand, large urban functional economic regions.

"INDUSTRIAL POLICY" IN SMALL AND MEDIUM-SIZED FUNCTIONAL ECONOMIC REGIONS

Industrial policy in small and medium-sized functional economic regions faces a fundamental problem in the sense that the intra-regional market potential is too small to allow firms in many different industries with distance-sensitive products, that is, products that require frequent face-to-face interaction between seller and buyer, to exploit their internal scale economies to such a degree that they become profitable. For such regions, there are two major options for industrial policy: (i) the development of large-scale plants producing products with a low distance-sensitivity; or (ii) the nurturing of a cluster in one industry or of clusters in a small number of industries producing products with low distance-sensitivity. Here we limit the discussion to industrial policies suitable for nurturing clusters (cf. Cornett, 2014).

We can distinguish three major types of cluster policies. First, there are industrial policies to initiate new clusters. However, the potential of policymakers to initiate new clusters is seriously questioned in the literature. Second, there are industrial policies to support clusters in normal operation to (i) take full advantage of existing potential positive external economies, and (ii) avoid the development of structural rigidities. Third, there are industrial policies for clusters in crises.

There are many problems associated with developing and implementing industrial cluster policies. There is a lack of generally accepted good criteria for identifying the existence of clusters not to mention the identification of new potentially emerging clusters. There usually exists too little information and knowledge about the clusters that are identified, since statistical bureaus normally don't collect data specifically for clusters. Furthermore, it is difficult to generalise industrial cluster policies, since different clusters have different histories and different specialisations and are in different life-cycle stages (Tavassoli and Tsagdis, 2014). Since the processes that policymakers can influence are slow, industrial cluster policies must be proactive. The existence of asymmetric information – the firms in a cluster are better informed about their current situation than the policymakers – puts the policymakers in a disadvantageous situation. They don't have access to all the information they need to design and implement industrial cluster policies and they risk being captured by the vested interests of the cluster firms. A general problem with industrial cluster policies is the risk of lock-in effects and obsolescence in terms of products, technologies, skills and infrastructures.

Before any industrial cluster policy is designed there is a need to answer many questions: What factors gave rise to the emergence of the cluster? What factors are keeping it together? Which are the key actors? What are the long-term prospects of the cluster? How strong is its competitiveness? Are there any fundamental arguments for or against policy interventions, such as unexploited location economies, actual or potential cost externalities, and actual or potential coordination failures? What are the proper policy interventions? What problems and costs are associated with these interventions? Are the benefits of intervention larger than the costs?

To design and implement industrial cluster policies, the policymakers must first understand the cluster production system. This implies that they must clarify what the actual cluster networks look like, which firm and non-firm actors within and outside the cluster are involved and which type of networking is taking place and to what extent. They must also examine what the cluster innovation system, that is, the learning and R&D system, look like and which actors inside and outside the region are involved. How do the coordination and governance mechanisms within the cluster function? The functioning of the cluster labour market must also be analysed. The integration of the cluster in the interregional and international export and import networks must be specified. Furthermore, the role of existing institutions and public policies for the structure and functioning of the cluster must be explicated.

Given that there are underlying motivations for implementing a cluster policy and that the cluster production system is relatively well understood, a cluster policy may consist of the following six elements (Karlsson, 2008; Tavassoli and Tsagdis, 2014):

(i) the creation of optimal conditions for entrepreneurship, that is, for start-ups, spin-offs, spin-outs and firm growth through measures that lower the fixed start-up costs for new firms, through the provision of early stage and venture financing, primarily through former successful entrepreneurs, and through the provision of incubators and co-working spaces for new firms;
(ii) measures that reduce the geographical transaction costs, for example, investments in and improvements of transportation and communication infrastructures and transport systems;

(iii) stimulation of the formation of networks and trust of linked firms and associated services;
(iv) support of cluster-relevant education, skills and R&D;
(v) the promotion of university–industry links; and
(vi) help for firms to forge international import and export links.

"INDUSTRIAL POLICY" IN LARGE URBAN FUNCTIONAL ECONOMIC REGIONS

Turning now to industrial policies for large (and dense) urban functional economic regions, we formulate the underlying principle that the fundamental industrial policy here is horizontal policies that make these regions function better in encouraging entrepreneurship and firm growth and productivity, and in attracting highly educated and skilled labour. Large regions offer special advantages in terms of knowledge flows and spillovers, since they combine the localisation of clusters in specific industries with industrial diversity, that is, a range of different industrial clusters (Karlsson and Johansson, 2006). A fundamental factor here is density, since density improves productivity. Thus, it is important to pursue a planning and construction policy that increases the density of households and firms. Furthermore, it is important to improve the speed and capacity of inter-regional transport infrastructures to enlarge the geographical surface of large urban regions, since this increases the intra-regional market potential and makes it possible for more firms – new firms as well as incumbents – to exploit their internal economies of scale. A geographical enlargement also increases the urban labour market and makes it easier for firms to find exactly the kind of workforce they are looking for, at the same time making it easier for the workforce to find the "right" job and to forge a career, without having to move to another region.

Another critical factor for large urban regions is to increase the attractiveness of the region to keep the existing knowledge-intensive and skilled workforce and firms, and to attract such labourers and firms from other regions (Karlsson et al., 2014). Critical factors here are attractive housing areas with a suitable housing infrastructure and accessibility to consumer services and jobs, a rich supply of household amenities, attractive business locations with good opportunities for networking and a rich supply of meeting places and arenas for business interaction, such as conference centres and trade fairs. Large urban regions must also develop and strengthen their function as international gateways by offering good international air connections, high-capacity and high-speed intra-regional and international broadband connections, and excellent facilities, such as congress hotels and centres and trade fairs for international meetings. They also need to facilitate and stimulate the imports of knowledge-intensive and high-tech products to get access to the latest ideas and technologies to promote intra-regional product development.

The last point above relates to the fact that a major function of large urban regions is to function as incubator cities or nursery cities, that is, as birth places for new technologies, innovations and new knowledge-intensive and high-tech firms (Duranton and Puga, 2001). To perform that function well, they must be attractive to highly educated and highly skilled people, offer good opportunities for intensive and frequent face-to-face interaction, offer good opportunities for new firms to enter the market, offer a rich and varied supply of knowledge-intensive business services, and offer a rich and varied supply of higher education and R&D.

BACK TO NATIONAL INDUSTRIAL POLICIES: SOME BASIC GUIDELINES

There seems to exist a consensus concerning the need for broad neutral, "horizontal" industrial policy, that is, one that does not target specific industries or firms. However, even if there exists no consensus concerning vertical industrial policy, we must accept that both types of industrial policy exist and then it becomes important to find ways to make it work better from a pragmatic point of view. To achieve this, it is very important to learn lessons from real-life examples. To secure long-term learning-by-doing it is essential that policies go through *ex ante* and *ex post* evaluations by independent evaluators. In connection with this, it is important to have a vision, to choose the right targets, which are neither too far nor too close in the future, and to *ex ante* design clear performance targets, not least regarding exports. Macroeconomic stability is of course a critical prerequisite. Furthermore, industry wants stable long-term rules of the game and proper formal institutions with well-defined property rights and low transaction costs. It is also important to have low barriers for firm entry, growth and exit as well as entrepreneur-friendly bankruptcy laws and procedures; and more classical factors such as scale economies, export marketing and extension services. It is also possible to reduce the political economy problems by building consensus, and design and implementation capabilities inside and outside government.[3]

In other words, we could say that the objective of industrial policies is to stimulate a dynamic, self-renewing market economy with a sound mix of small and medium-sized firms as well as large multinational firms in which entrepreneurship plays a key role. This implies the development of formal institutions that, for example, reduce the barriers and the costs of entry and growth of firms, facilitate the sectoral and spatial mobility of resources, labour and capital, stimulate investments in R&D, innovation and education, and increase the openness of the national economy to international competition.

CONCLUSIONS

The threefold purpose of this chapter was to (i) briefly discuss how the views on industrial policy have changed from a long-term perspective with a special focus on the post-war period up to the current post-industrial society; (ii) to present arguments and motivations for industrial policies in the current post-industrial society, in that they should mainly be regional policies or rather industrial policies at the regional level; and (iii) to briefly evaluate the EU's current approach to industrial policy, the so-called smart specialisation. In the chapter, we started with clarifying what should be understood with industrial policy and discussing the arguments for and against industrial policy as well as the problems involved in implementing regional policy. Then we gave an overview of the use of industrial policy during the time of the industrial society. The overview was followed by a discussion of how the use of industrial policy and the views on industrial policy changed during the transition period between the industrial society and the post-industrial society. We characterised the post-industrial society and made an argument for

---

[3] We may in this connection observe that it is often claimed that industrial policy has become impossible due to changes in the global WTO-rules. However, WTO-rules are not as restrictive as believed (Chang, 2003, 2008): (i) tariffs are allowed including emergency tariffs, (ii) subsidies for the environment, agriculture, R&D, regional policies, etc., (iii) TRIPS (Trade-Related Aspects of Intellectual Property Rights) are constraining but not for older technologies, and (iv) TRIMS (Trade-Related Investment Measures) are constraining but performance requirements for local labour, technology transfer, R&D, etc. are allowed. Bigger restraints are aid/loan conditionalities and bilateral/regional trade/investment agreements. However, all these rules are man-made and can be changed if it is deemed necessary.

industrial policies during the post-industrial society, that they should, to a large extent, be implemented in the form of regional policies, since the conditions for industrial development exhibit such strong spatial variations. Furthermore, it was argued that small and medium-sized regions need quite different policies to large urban regions. We followed up this discussion with a short presentation about the new industrial/regional policy initiative within the EU, known as smart specialisation. In the presentation, we noted that there are some distinct problems related to this policy initiative, such as (i) the idea that one policy model fits all regions, (ii) a strong focus on existing industries and too little focus on the need for a structural transformation to new industries in many regions, and (iii) the focus on large administrative regions instead of on functional economic regions.

The overall discussion of industrial policy prompts the need to make several observations. First, it seems as if the discussion is often held at some meta-level without sufficient consideration of the decision makers that the industrial policy should influence. Decisions on organisational factors within companies, such as vertical integration or disintegration and choices on R&D, innovation and location are strategic decisions, which evolve as markets, technologies and politics in different countries change. Second, the focus is, to a great extent, on existing industries and incumbent firms. Thus, there seems to be too little interest in how industrial policy can stimulate structural change as well as innovation, entrepreneurship and firm growth. It might be that the discussion suffers from a basic static bias and tends to neglect the life-cycle stage within which different industries are operating (Tavassoli, 2015). Furthermore, the discussion is, to a high degree, centred at the national level and on policies without a geographical dimension. It neglects to mention where innovative and entrepreneurial activities take place. This is striking, given the observation made by Krugman (1991: 55): "What is the most striking feature of the geography of economic activity? The short answer is certainly concentration … production is remarkably concentrated in space". If we look back on the period after 1991, we can observe that the concentration of production has continued. If industrial policy shall be relevant in the future it needs, to a much higher extent, to have a strong spatial component. In this respect the EU is on the right track, even if several reservations can be raised against the approach chosen with the smart specialisation strategy.

REFERENCES

Acemoglu, D. and Robinson, J.A. (2013). *Why Nations Fail: The Origins of Power, Prosperity, and Poverty*. New York: Crown Business.

Ades, A. and Di Tella, R. (1997). "National champions and corruption: some unpleasant interventionist arithmetic". *Economic Journal* 107, 1023–1042.

Aghion, P., Boulanger, J. and Cohen, E. (2011). "Rethinking industrial policy". *Bruegel Policy Brief*, Issue 2011/04.

Aghion, P., Dewatripont, M., Du, L., Harrison, A. and Legros, P. (2012). "Industrial policy and competition". *NBER Working Paper No. 18048.*

Aiginger, A. (2007). "Industrial policy: a dying breed or a re-emerging phoenix". *Journal of Industry, Competition and Trade* 7, 297–323.

Aiginger, A. (2014). "Industrial policy for a sustainable growth path". *WIFO Working Papers No. 469.*

Amsden, A.H. (1989). *Asia's Next Giant: South Korea and Late Industrialization*. New York: Oxford University Press.

Andreoni, A. (2014). "Structural learning: embedding discoveries and the dynamics of production". *Structural Change and Economic Dynamics* 29, 58–74.

Audretsch, D. and Keilbach, M. (2008). "Resolving the knowledge paradox: knowledge-spillover entrepreneurship and economic growth". *Research Policy* 37, 1697–1705.

Beason, R. and Weinstein, D.E. (1996). "Growth, economies of scale, and targeting in Japan (1955–1990)". *Review of Economics and Statistics* 78, 286–295.

Boettke, P.J. and Prychitko, D.L. (1998). "Introduction: varieties of market process theories". In Boettke, P.J. and Prychitko, D.L. (eds). *Market Process Theories, Classical and Neoclassical*, Vol. 1. Cheltenham: Edward Elgar.

Bresnahan, T. and Trajtenberg, M. (1995). "General purpose technologies 'engines of growth'". *Journal of Econometrics* 65, 83–108.

Buchanan, J. (2003). "Public choice – politics without romance". *Policy* 19, 13–18.

Camagni, R. and Capello, R. (2013). "Regional innovation patterns and the EU regional policy reform: towards smart innovation policies". *Growth and Change* 44, 355–389.

Chang, H.-J. (1994). *The Political Economy of Industrial Policy*. Basingstoke: Macmillan.

Chang, H.-J. (2003). *Kicking Away the Ladder. Development Strategy in Historical Perspective*. New York: Anthem Press.

Chang, H.-J. (2008). *Bad Samaritans. The Guilty Secrets of Rich Nations & The Threat to Global Prosperity*. London: Random House Business Books.

Chang, H.-J. (2011). *Industrial Policy. Can We Go Beyond an Unproductive Confrontation?* Annual World Bank Conference on Development Economics 2010. Washington, DC: World Bank.

Chimoli, M., Dosi, G. and Stiglitz, J.E. (2009). *Industrial Policy and Development*. Oxford: Oxford University Press.

Cooke, P. (2009). "The economic geography of knowledge flow hierarchies among internationally networked medical bioclusters: a scientometric analysis". *Tijdschrift voor Economische en Sociale Geographie* 100, 332–347.

Coriat, B. (2004). *Politique de la concurrence et politique industrielle dans l'Union européenne. Un rééquilibrage est-il possible? Cahiers français*, La Documentation français, Paris.

Cornett, A.P. (2014). "Cluster development policy as a tool in regional development and ccmpetitiveness policy: theoretical aspects and empirical evidence". In Karlsson, C., Johansson, B., Kobayashi, K. and Stough, R.R. (eds). *Knowledge, Innovation and Space*. Cheltenham: Edward Elgar.

Dahlman, C. (2011). *The World under Pressure: How China and India are Influencing the Global Economy and the Environment*. Stanford, CA: Stanford University Press.

Duranton, G. and Puga, D. (2001). "Nursery cities: urban diversity, process innovation, and the life cycle of products". *American Economic Review*, 1454–1477.

European Commission (2007). *Report – State Aid Scoreboard*, COM (2007), 347, Final.

Feldman, M.P. and Tavassoli, S. (2015). *Something New: Where do New Industries Come from? Oxford Handbook of Local Competitiveness*. Oxford: Oxford University Press.

Foray, D., David, P. and Hall, B. (2009). "Smart specialization – the concept". *Knowledge Economists Policy Brief No. 9*, June.

Freire, C. (2013). "Strategies for structural transformation in South Asian countries". *Seoul Journal of Economics* 26, 311–336.

Graham, M.B.W. (2010). "Entrepreneurship in the United States, 1920–2000". In Landes, D.S., Mokyr, J. and Baumol, W.J. (eds). *The Invention of the Enterprise: Entrepreneurship from Ancient Mesopotamia to Modern Times*. Princeton, NJ: Princeton University Press.

Greenwald, B.C. and Stiglitz, J.E. (1986). "Externalities in economies with imperfect information and incomplete markets". *Quarterly Journal of Economics* 101, 229–264.

Greenwald, B.C. and Stiglitz, J.E. (2013). "Industrial policies, the creation of a learning society, and economic development". In Stiglitz, J.E. and Yifu, L. (eds). *The Industrial Policy Revolution I: The Role of Government Beyond Ideology*. Basingstoke: Macmillan.

Griffith-Jones, S., Ocampo, J.A. and Stiglitz, J.E. (2010). *Time for a Visible Hand: Lessons from the 2008 World Financial Crisis*. Oxford: Oxford University Press.

Harrison, A. and Rodríguez-Clare, A. (2010). "Trade, foreign investment and industrial policy for developing countries". In Hall, P.A. and Rosenzweig, M. (eds). *Handbook of Development Economics*. Amsterdam: Elsevier.

Hausmann, R. and Rodrik, D. (2003). "Economic development as self-discovery". *Journal of Development Economics* 72, 603–633.

Hayek, F.A. (1978). *New Studies in Philosophy, Politics, Economics, and the History of Ideas*. London: Routledge and Kegan Paul.

Hirschman, A.O. (1958). *The Strategy of Economic Development*, New Haven, CT: Economics, Yale University Press.

Johansson, B. and Karlsson, C. (2001). "Geographical transaction costs and specialization opportunities of small and medium-sized regions: scale economies and market extension". In Johansson, B., Karlsson, C. and Stough, R.R. (eds). *Theories of Endogenous Regional Growth. Lessons for Regional Policies*. Berlin: Springer-Verlag.

Johnson, C. (1982). *MITI and the Japanese Miracle: The Growth of Industrial Policy, 1925–1975*. Stanford, CA: Stanford University Press.

Karlsson, C. (ed.) (2008). *Handbook of Research on Innovation and Clusters: Cases and Policies*. Cheltenham: Edward Elgar.

Karlsson, C. (2016). "Political entrepreneurship, industrial policy and regional growth". In Karlsson, C., Silander, C. and Silander, D. (eds). *Political Entrepreneurship: Regional Growth and Entrepreneurial Diversity in Sweden*. Cheltenham: Edward Elgar.

Karlsson, C. and Andersson, M. (2009). "Entrepreneurship policies: principles, problems, and opportunities". In Leitão, J. and Baptista, R. (eds). *Public Policies for Fostering Entrepreneurship. A European Perspective*. Dordrecht: Springer.

Karlsson, C. and Gråsjö, U. (2013). "Entrepreneurial knowledge, technology and the transformation of regions. An introduction". In Karlsson, C., Johansson, B. and Stough, R.R. (eds). *Entrepreneurial Knowledge, Technology and the Transformation of Regions*. Abingdon: Routledge.

Karlsson, C. and Johansson, B. (2006). "Dynamics and entrepreneurship in a knowledge-based economy". In Karlsson, C., Johansson, B. and Stough, R.R. (eds). *Entrepreneurship and Dynamics in the Knowledge Economy*. New York: Routledge.

Karlsson, C. and Tavassoli, S. (2016). "Innovation strategies of firms: what strategies and why?". *The Journal of Technology Transfer* 41(6), 1483–1506.

Karlsson, C., Gråsjö, U. and Wixe, S. (2015). (eds). *Innovation and Entrepreneurship in the Global Economy. Knowledge, Technology and Internationalization*. Cheltenham: Edward Elgar.

Karlsson, C., Johansson, B. and Stough, R.R. (2005). "Industrial clusters and inter-firm networks". In Karlsson, C., Johansson, B. and Stough, R.R. (eds). *Industrial Clusters and Inter-Firm Networks*. Cheltenham: Edward Elgar.

Karlsson, C., Johansson, B. and Stough, R.R. (2009). "Introduction: innovation and entrepreneurship in functional regions". In Karlsson, C., Johansson, B. and Stough, R.R. (eds). *Entrepreneurship and Innovations in Functional Regions*. Cheltenham: Edward Elgar.

Karlsson, C., Johansson, B. and Stough, R.R. (eds) (2012). *The Regional Economics of Knowledge and Talent. Local Advantage in a Global Context*. Cheltenham: Edward Elgar.

Karlsson, C., Johansson, B. and Stough, R.R. (eds) (2014). *Agglomeration, Clusters and Entrepreneurship. Studies in Regional Economic Development*. Cheltenham: Edward Elgar.

Kirzner, I.M. (1973). *Competition and Entrepreneurship*. Chicago, IL: University of Chicago Press.

Krueger, A.O. (1990). "Government failures in development". *Journal of Economic Perspectives* 4, 9–23.

Krugman, P. (1991). *Geography and Trade*. Cambridge, MA: MIT Press.

Krugman, P. (1993). "The current case for industrial policy". In Salvatores, D. (ed.). *Protectionism and World Welfare*, Cambridge: Cambridge University Press.

Lakshmanan, T.R. (1994). "State market networks in Japan: the case of industrial policy". In Johansson, B., Karlsson, C. and Westin, L. (eds). *Patterns of a Network Economy*. Berlin: Springer-Verlag.

Lee, K. (2013a). "Capability future and industrial policy to move beyond the middle-income trap: from trade-based to technology-based specialization". In Stiglitz, J.E. and Yifu, L. (eds). *The Industrial Policy Revolution I: The Role of Government Beyond Ideology*. Basingstoke: Macmillan.

Lee, K. (2013b). *Schumpeterian Analysis of Economic Catch-Up. Knowledge, Path-Creation, and the Middle-Income Trap*. Cambridge: Cambridge University Press.

Lerner, J. (2009). *Boulevard of Broken Dreams. Why Public Efforts to Boost Entrepreneurship and Venture Capital Have Failed and What to Do About It*. Princeton, NJ: Princeton University Press.

Lin, J. (2012). *New Structural Economics: A Framework for Rethinking Development and Policy*. Washington, DC: World Bank.

List, F. (1841). *The National System of Political Economy*. London and New York: Longmans Green and Co.

Lucchese, M. and Pianta, M. (2012). "Industrial and innovation policies in the European Union". In Garibaldo, F., Baglioni, M., Casey, C. and Telljohann, V. (eds). *Workers, Citizens, Governance: Socio-Cultural Innovation at Work*. Berlin: Peter Lang.

Marrocu, E., Paci, R. and Usai, S. (2013). "Proximity, networking and knowledge production in Europe: what lessons from innovation policy?". *Technological Forecasting and Social Change* 80, 1484–1498.

Marshall, A. (1920). *Principles of Economics*. London: Macmillan.

Mastroeni, M., Tait, J. and Rosiello, A. (2013). "Regional innovation policies in a globally connected environment". *Science and Public Policy* 40, 8–16.

Mazzucato, M. (2013). *The Entrepreneurial State. Debunking the Public vs. Private Myth in Risk and Innovation*. London: Anthem Press.

McCann, P. and Ortega-Argilés, R. (2013). "Transforming European regional policy: a results-driven agenda and smart specialization". *Oxford Review of Economic Policy* 29, 405–431.

Mowery, D.C. (1984). "Firm structure, government policy, and the organization of industrial research: Great Britain and the United States, 1900–1950". *Business History Review* 58, 504–531.

Naudé, W.A. (2010). "Industrial policy: old and new". *UNU-WIDER Working Paper 106*, Helsinki.

OECD (2012). Beyond Industrial Policy – Emerging Issues and Trends, *Draft STI Working Paper on Industrial Policy DSTI/IND(2012)19*. Paris: OECD.

OECD (2013). *Perspectives on Global Development 2013 – Shifting Up the Gear: Industrial Policies in a Changing Economic Landscape*. Paris: OECD.

O'Sullivan, E., Andreoni, A., López-Gómez, C. and Gregory, M. (2013). "What is new in the new industrial policy? A manufacturing systems perspective". *Oxford Review of Economic Policy* 29, 432–462.

Oxford Dictionary of Economics (2003). Oxford: Oxford University Press.

Pack, H. and Saggi, K. (2006). "Is there a case for industrial policy? A critical survey". *World Bank Research Observer* 21, 267–297.

Page, J. and Campos, E. (1993). *The East Asia Miracle: Economic Growth and Public Policy*. Washington, DC: World Bank.

Pianta, M. (2010). "Industrial and innovation policies in Europe". In Watt, A. and Botsch, A. (eds). *After the Crisis; Towards a Sustainable Growth Model*. Brussels: ETUI.

Pianta, M. (2014). "An industrial policy for Europe". *Seoul Journal of Economics* 27, 277–305.

Pilat, D., Cimper, A., Olsen, K. and Webb, C. (2008). "The changing nature of manufacturing in OECD economies". In *Staying Competitive in the Global Economy. Compendium of Studies on Global Value Chains*. Paris: OECD.

Porter, M. (2000). "Location, competition, and economic development: local clusters in a global economy". *Development Quarterly* 14, 15–34.

Primi, A. (2013). "The return of industrial policy: (what) can Africa learn from Latin America?". *Working Paper Prepared for JICA/IPD Africa Task Force Meeting, Yokohama, Japan, June 2–3, 2013.*

Reinert, E. (2007). *How Rich Countries Got Rich and Why Poor Countries Stay Poor.* London: Constable & Robinson.

Reinstaller, A., Hölzl, W., Kutsam, J. and Schmid, C. (2013). The Development of Productive Structures of EU Member States and their International Competitiveness, *WIFO Research Study.*

Rodrik, D. (1995). "Getting interventions right: how South Korea and Taiwan grew rich". *Economic Policy* 20, 55–107.

Rodrik, D. (2004). "Industrial policy for the twenty-first century". *CEPR Discussion Paper No. 4767*, London: Centre for Economic Policy Research.

Rodrik, D. (2008). "Normalizing industrial policy". *Working Paper No. 3*, Commission on Growth and Development, The International Bank for Reconstruction and Development/The World Bank.

Rosenstein-Rodan, P.N. (1943). "Problems of industrialization of Eastern and South-Eastern Europe". *Economic Journal* 53, 202–211.

Skidelsky, R. (2009). *Keynes: The Return of the Master: Why, Sixty Years after his Death, John Maynard Keynes Is the Most Important Economic Thinker for America*. New York: Public Affairs Press.

Stiglitz, J.E., Lin, J.Y. and Monga, C. (2013). "The rejuvenation of industrial policy". *Policy Research Working Paper 6628*. Washington, DC: The World Bank.

Tavassoli, S. (2015). "Innovation determinants over industry life cycle". *Technological Forecasting and Social Change* 91, 18–32.

Tavassoli, S. and Carbonara, N. (2014). "The role of knowledge variety and intensity for regional innovation". *Small Business Economics* 43(2), 493–509.

Tavassoli, S. and Karlsson, C. (2016). "Innovation strategies and firm performance: simple or complex strategies?". *Economics of Innovation and New Technology* 25(7), 631–650.

Tavassoli, S. and Tsagdis, D. (2014). "Critical success factors and cluster evolution: a case study of the Linköping ICT cluster lifecycle". *Environment and Planning A* 46(6), 1425–1444.

Tyson, L.D. (1992). *Who Is Bashing Whom? Trade Conflicts in High-Technology Industries*. Washington, DC: Institute for International Economics.

Wade, R.H. (1990). *Governing the Market: Economic Theory and the Role of Government in East Asia Capitalism*. Princeton, NJ: Princeton University Press.

Wade, R.H. (2012). "Return to industrial policy?". *International Review of Applied Economics* 26, 223–239.

WIIW (2013). *European Competitiveness Report. A "Manufacturing Imperative" in the EU – Europe's Position in Global Manufacturing and the Role of Industrial Policy*. Vienna: WIIW.

Appendix 7.1 Number of hits for the term "industrial policy" using Google Scholar (14 March 2017)

Period	*No. of hits*	*Δ No. of hits*	*Δ No. of hits (%)*
2012–2016	21,100	+900	+4.5
2007–2011	20,200	+1,900	+10.4
2002–2006	18,300	+1,800	+10.9
1997–2001	16,500	+1,100	+7.1
1992–1996	15,400	+5,000	+48.1
1987–1991	10,400	+3,680	+54.8
1982–1986	6,720	+4,290	+176.5
1977–1981	1,350	+1,080	+80.0
1972–1976	1,350	+636	+89.1
1967–1971	714	+376	+113.1
1962–1966	335	+117	+53.7
1957–1961	218	+37	+20.4
1952–1956	181	–	–

8. The social efficiency of entrepreneurship education

Charlotte Silander and Caroline Berggren

INTRODUCTION

Entrepreneurship education is on the educational and political agenda in most European countries. This chapter deals with European Union (EU) policy towards entrepreneurship with a focus on ideological perspectives. Entrepreneurship is increasingly put forward in policy as a way to ensure future prosperity and growth for Europe. One important solution to the European economic crisis is to increase the number of small businesses and to encourage more people to become self-employed. At the same time, recurrent investigations report a lower rate of self-employment in the EU compared to the US and (European Commission, 2004a; Braunerhjelm et al., 2016) on a perceived lack of entrepreneurial spirit among Europeans. One proposed way to change this is to educate people to become entrepreneurs (see also Chapter 4 in this volume). Entrepreneurship education aims to stimulate economic development (O'Connor, 2013), and policies related to entrepreneurship education and training are viewed as efficient mechanisms to increase entrepreneurial activity. Although the impact of entrepreneurship education is unclear (Pittaway and Cope, 2007; Oosterbeek et al., 2010), it is widely perceived as a central policy for many governments (Hannon, 2006; Minniti and Lévesque, 2008).

Since the start of the Lisbon process in 2000, entrepreneurship has increasingly been put forward as a "key competence" that needs to be taught (European Commission, 2004b). Entrepreneurship has taken a central position in EU ambitions for schools and has indeed been introduced into the school curricula in many European countries (Olofsson, 2012; Nordin, 2012). Policies to promote entrepreneurship have also come to be more directed towards higher education (Nyström and Karlsson, 2008; European Commission, 2010). This is partly because investments in entrepreneurship in higher education are expected to create long-term results in terms of self-employment (Galloway and Brown, 2002; Hegarty and Jones, 2008) and partly because higher education is considered to be close to the labour market in terms of pay-off. University graduates are expected to start a business, and by doing so, employ others. This approach has resulted in an increase in the number of entrepreneurship education programmes at universities and university colleges (Olofsson, 2012).

Here it is proposed that entrepreneurship education is one way to understand the educational policy of the EU as it combines two central solutions to the European crises: *entrepreneurship* and *education*. Entrepreneurial competence is seen as a main policy issue for governments striving for economic growth (Acs, 2008). Among policymakers there is a common belief that entrepreneurship education will help to influence culture and build enterprising economies (McKeown et al., 2006; Martinez, et al., 2010). In a similar way, there is a growing interest in education as a tool to guarantee economic growth. The EU has called for educational reforms to help Europe maintain its position in the world, highlighting globalisation and the knowledge-driven economy as the main reasons for the need for radical reforms (Robertson, 2008; Alexiadou, 2014; Nordin, 2012). Entrepreneurship thus becomes a key ingredient in the educational policy of the EU, and education is an important part of the policy of promoting entrepreneurship.

Traditionally, educational policy has been seen in a national context and has only been influenced to a limited extent by transnational policy flows, which are often discussed in terms of "policy borrowing" and "policy learning" (Dale, 1999). International influences have primarily affected limited aspects of education such as individual programmes or the kinds of instruments used, and they have had less of an impact on the overall goals of policy (Dale, 1999). Globalisation has challenged the idea of education as a national phenomenon (Dale, 1999). Deepening processes in the EU have included the transfer of sovereignty from member states to the EU level in an expanding number of areas (Grek and Lawn, 2009). The role of the EU as an important actor has increased as education has become more related, step by step, to employment and social policy, areas in which the EU has strengthened its role as an agenda-setter and policymaker (Rhodes, 2010), thereby emphasising the role of entrepreneurship in strategies for European growth (European Commission, 2010). European higher education is currently undergoing profound changes, in which policy produces processes and modifies aspects of educational practices involving teachers and students. This tendency has been further emphasised by policy programmes in which EU member states have agreed on certain common educational policy objectives which have an influence at both the national and supranational level (European Commission, 2004a, European Commission, 2010).

Dale (1999) argues that globalisation causes transnational policy to also influence the way we think about education. If we make a distinction between policy ideas, programmatic ideas and philosophical ideas (Schmidt, 2008, 2011), policy ideas are more limited and may change rapidly; meanwhile, programmatic ideas can be described as the general ideas underlying policy. Philosophical ideas, on the other hand, are thought of as broad concepts tied to values and moral principles, which underlie a policy or a programme and guide and define the problem (Schmidt, 2008). In line with this, we need to understand the deeper underlying philosophical ideas of the EU concerning the purpose of higher education. In this chapter, policy on entrepreneurship education will be reviewed from a critical perspective using ideologies of education as a lens through which policy towards entrepreneurship education is viewed.

The aim of the chapter is to contribute to the understanding of the EU's role in higher education by reviewing EU policy from a critical perspective using ideologies of education as an analytical framework. There is a great variation in the kinds of entrepreneurship education, from smaller business courses that cover a shorter period of time to longer programmes at the postgraduate level. In the first part, the EU policy of entrepreneurship will be described by referring to previous research, and a thematic analysis will be applied to the existing policy in order to point out aspects of the focus of EU policy towards entrepreneurship. Based on the assumption that philosophical ideas matter for understanding policy and, according to Blyth (2010), even more so in periods of crises, the second part seeks to understand the underlying assumption of policy formulation in the area of higher education and entrepreneurship by exploring the ideological bases of EU educational policy. Policy is here generally understood as public policy, referring to guidelines, programmes, or courses of action decided and adopted by the government. In this way policy is more comprehensive than a single statement, because it refers to a chain of decisions and various measures taken to implement public policies or programmes. Policy can be understood as loaded with value in contrast to representing a neutral solution to existing problems or as something that is being constructed and which shapes the policy process (Bacchi, 2009; Ball, 1994). In this way, policy expresses an existing discourse, but it is also involved in the shaping of this discourse. The "taken for granted truth" presented in policy documents needs to be deconstructed to explain the discourses manifested in the formulations of the documents and to analyse the underlying logic of the problem. The review is based on an analysis of documents originating from the European Commission and its DGs, and documents from the Council of Ministers or related working groups.[1]

RESEARCH ON ENTREPRENEURSHIP AND EDUCATION

Entrepreneurship education is a broad term referring to many different forms of programmes with various objectives. Distinguished from general education, entrepreneurship education focuses on the "promotion of entrepreneurship and stimulating entrepreneurial skills and knowledge" (Verheul et al., 2001: 34). According to Pittaway and Cope (2007: 500), there is no consensus on what entrepreneurship education actually "is", and "policy is generally unclear about what outputs are to be created when such education is promoted". Bennett (2006) argues that this confusion is due to the lack of a common definition of entrepreneurship and the absence of a cohesive theoretical framework in entrepreneurship education. One reason for this is the persisting disagreement about the concept of entrepreneurship itself and who is an entrepreneur (Cunningham and Lischeron, 1991; Gartner, 1990).

Although there is no consensus in the basic definitional issues, some features seem to be possible to identify. There is a common understanding that the major rationale of entrepreneurship education is more economical than social, in that entrepreneurship is seen as a solution to economic problems, especially employment. This means that the driving force behind other objectives for entrepreneurship education (such as start-ups, self-employment, job creation, knowledge advancement and skill development) is to achieve economic growth (Mwasalwiba, 2010). Recognising the overall objective of economic growth, two major educational objectives can be identified. The first is a broader conception of education that *encourages entrepreneurial attitudes and skills* in general

[1] A strategic selection is used, and central EU documents frequently referred to within the policy area are analysed. The identification and choice of EU policy documents was carried out by identification of the most central documents and texts in reference threads, favouring those that frequently reoccurred and those that were given special attention. This snowball method allows for mapping out documents central to both the area of education (documents describing the Lisbon process and *Europe 2020*) and documents in the area of entrepreneurship. In total, 16 EU documents were analysed, covering the period 2000 to 2017.

and involves developing certain personal qualities by creating an orientation to and awareness of entrepreneurship (Mwasalwiba, 2010; Kirby, 2004; Stevenson and Lundström, 2002). This version is not directly focused on the creation of new businesses but relates to a broader context. The second is the more specific concept of *training people how to start new businesses* through programmes that seek to develop competences for enterprise formation, self-employment or economic self-sufficiency (Mwasalwiba, 2010).

Another distinction that needs to be made is between *education in general* as a way to increase entrepreneurship and specific *entrepreneurship education*. The connection between entrepreneurship and education in general is not straightforward. Important findings in research have shown that entrepreneurs seem to be more successful when they have higher levels of education (Foley and Griffith, 1998; Lee, 1997; Leffler and Svedberg, 2005) and that this group is also more frequently found in start-ups (Minniti et al., 2006). This result indicates that the level of general education is central. On the other hand, a literature review conducted by Dickson et al. (2008) concluded that there was no clear link at all between general education and choosing to become an entrepreneur.

The impact of focused entrepreneurship education is limited to having an effect on attitudes and intentions, but less evidence exists with regard to actual self-employment (Fayolle et al., 2006; Souitaris et al., 2007; Pittaway and Cope, 2007). Bae et al. (2014) conducted a meta-analysis of 73 studies and found a small but positive correlation between entrepreneurship education and entrepreneurial intentions. However, when controlling for the intention to become self-employed before the entrepreneurship education, the education as such was found not to have any influence. Moreover, this positive attitude is not always put into practice. Dickson therefore refers to it as an assumed link between entrepreneurship education and self-employment, a link that "must exist" but about which evidence is inconclusive (Dickson et al., 2008: 252).

The link between education and entrepreneurship also differs depending on the national setting. In some countries, such as the US, the prevalence of entrepreneurship was highest among professionals and those with a doctorate (Hipple, 2010), while in Sweden (Hammarstedt, 2009), self-employment was more common among people with only compulsory or a short education. In a comparison of European countries, Sweden has the lowest rate of graduates who are self-employed, while Italy is among those with the highest rate (Zamfir et al., 2013). Despite this finding, among Italian graduates, it was those with the highest degrees who chose employment before self-employment (Castagnetti and Rosti, 2011).

Studies have also pointed out that it is not only the level of education that may influence the likelihood of self-employment, but also the sector in which people are active. Commonly, students educated in the STEM fields (science, technology, engineering and mathematics) are often perceived as being most likely to start businesses (European Commission, 2004a, 2012b). However, studies from Sweden (Hammarstedt, 2009) show that it is instead the agriculture and trade sectors that have a comparatively large proportion of self-employed workers. In an Austrian study (Falk and Leoni, 2009) (in which the agriculture sector was excluded), graduates in medicine, law and arts subjects were most likely to become self-employed. Bridgstock (2013: 128) writes that "... artists are often 'pushed' to entrepreneurship through necessity ...". They have to be self-employed to make a living. It is also important to keep in mind that the financial rewards are generally poorer for most entrepreneurs compared to those who seek employment (Shane, 2008).

If higher levels of education are more important than specific entrepreneurship education for business start-up and performance (O'Connor, 2013), the line between the need for education in general and focused entrepreneurship education remains unclear. Some authors argue that if policy is about enhancing entrepreneurship through education, it should first of all aim to raise the educational level in general (Kolstad and Wiig, 2014; Wennekers and Thurik, 1999) and should secondly support educational contexts in which entrepreneurship appears naturally (Falck et al., 2012; Falck and Woessmann, 2013).

Entrepreneurship education is often divided into three elements: to teach *about*, *for* or *through* entrepreneurship (Scott et al., 1998; Jamieson, 1984; Kirby, 2004; Hytti and O'Gorman, 2004). To teach *about* entrepreneurship is to obtain a general understanding of entrepreneurship as a phenomenon (Hytti and O'Gorman, 2004). This means mediating theoretical perspectives to create awareness and to teach students different aspects of setting up and running a business. This can take place in higher education in the form of special university entrepreneurship courses and programmes. Teaching *for* entrepreneurship seeks to prepare potential students for a career as a self-employed worker by teaching practical skills about how to set up a business, how to abide by regulations and how to write a business plan. This can take the form of shorter, more practical and business-oriented education. To educate for entrepreneurship means to create an entrepreneur; that is, an individual who is destined to start a new venture. Co and Mitchell (2006) view education for entrepreneurship as addressing both present and potential entrepreneurs with the aim of stimulating the entrepreneurial process, providing them with the tools to start a business. Teaching *through* entrepreneurship involves promoting students' entrepreneurial abilities through internships or within an existing company; this can either consist of students participating in entrepreneurship programmes or educating already established entrepreneurs, focusing on development and growth.

Another categorisation, based on the view of what an entrepreneur is, relates to "different worlds of entrepreneurship education" (Neck and Greene, 2011). In the *entrepreneur's world*, the focus is on the individual entrepreneur as a hero figure. However, research has failed to establish the traits necessary to become an entrepreneur, as many characteristics described as important for entrepreneurship (risk-taking, self-confidence, etc.) are traits of successful people in many lines of work. This world represents a fixed view of the entrepreneur: a person either does or does not fit into the description of an entrepreneur. Here, entrepreneurship education serves to present role models to students and to teach them about the proper behaviour to follow to become successful. However, this approach risks reducing the role of the teacher and the role of provisional knowledge and instead favours "real entrepreneurs" before academic teachers (Farny et al., 2016). Instead, case studies often draw upon entrepreneur biographies, characteristics and behaviours and invite entrepreneurs into the classroom, while encouraging students to learn from and imitate their example (Farny et al., 2016: 525). This approach privileges practical knowledge over academic knowledge, suggesting that entrepreneurship cannot be learned but is an innate behaviour (Farny et al., 2016: 245).

In comparison to the former approach, the *process world* approach focuses more on the process of entrepreneurship and on the firm. Here, education seeks to teach opportunity evaluation, feasibility analysis, business planning and financial forecasting. The focus is on prediction and entrepreneurship viewed as a linear process that, if followed correctly, will increase the likelihood of a venture's success. The problem with this perspective, according to Neck and Greene, is that it fails to address the fact that entrepreneurship is neither linear nor predictable (Neck and Greene, 2011: 60). In the *cognitive world* of entrepreneurship, the focus is on both the person and the team but in a more dynamic way. This perspective recognises the potential for learning how to think entrepreneurially in order to be successful. Finally, Neck and Greene (2011) propose *entrepreneurship as a method*, consisting of a set of ideas about how entrepreneurship can be taught, which moves beyond the process world. In this approach, the learning method is argued to be more important than the content. By referring to Van de Ven and Johnson

(2006), they argue that: "In an ever-changing world, we need to teach methods that stand the test of dramatic changes in content and context. Rather than viewing practical or pedagogical knowledge as derivative of scientific knowledge, it is more appropriate to view practice and teaching as distinct modes of knowing in their own respects" (Neck and Greene, 2011: 62). This method is applicable to all students and all levels of organisations; the focus is on doing and then learning.

ENTREPRENEURSHIP EDUCATION PROMOTED BY THE EU

EU policy promotes a variety of educational initiatives. Examples of policy include the promotion of shorter business-oriented courses and start-up training (teaching *for* entrepreneurship). At the level of tertiary education, entrepreneurship education is supposed to provide specific training on how to start and run a business, including the capacity to draft a real business plan and the skills associated with identifying and assessing business opportunities (ENQHEEI, 2006). The EU also provides a number of possibilities for internship to teach entrepreneurship (teaching *through* entrepreneurship) – for example, the Commission's launching of the "Erasmus for Young Entrepreneurs" programme, which aims to promote exchanges of experience and training by giving young entrepreneurs the possibility to learn from experienced host entrepreneurs (European Commission, 2008: 6). The Commission criticises the existing systems of higher education, as they

> continue to fall short in providing the right skills for employability, and are not working adequately with business or employers to bring the learning experience closer to the reality of the working environment. These skills mismatches are a growing concern for European industry's competitiveness. (European Commission 2012b: 2)

Four aspects stand out as the focus of EU policy on entrepreneurship education: (i) the universities as educators of entrepreneurship; (ii) the integration of entrepreneurship into the whole educational system; (iii) entrepreneurship as a priority; and (iv) a special focus on STEM disciplines, and these will be discussed below:

(i) *The universities as educators of entrepreneurship*: Higher education is perceived as an important tool in the support for entrepreneurship and self-employment. As entrepreneurship programmes in higher education are considered to have an immediate effect (European Commission,

2015: 34), universities are perceived as playing an important role in stimulating entrepreneurship and growth. Hence, universities should be given the role of educating young people in entrepreneurship (European Commission, 2006; European Commission, 2012a), and all students should be exposed to entrepreneurship in their courses (European Commission, 2012a). The European Commission defines 'entrepreneurship' as: "The mindset and process [needed] to create and develop economic activity by blending risk-taking, creativity and/or innovation with sound management, within a new or an existing organisation" (European Commission, 2003: 6). This means that entrepreneurship refers to an individual's ability to turn ideas into action and includes creativity, innovation and risk-taking. It is also related to the creation of economic activity.

(ii) *The integration of entrepreneurship into the whole educational system*: The main EU strategy to promote entrepreneurship is to reform the educational system and embed entrepreneurship in all types of education at all levels. Since the introduction of the Lisbon process, EU policy for entrepreneurship education has increasingly worked to embed entrepreneurship deeply into the whole educational system and into higher education curricula, thereby making it a natural part of all educational activities.

> The important point here is one of progression, not only through university, but also through the whole education system at all levels. Integration of entrepreneurship into the curriculum needs to be the vision for a higher education institution as part of its wider mission. (European Commission, 2012a: 23)

This means that the policy of entrepreneurship education is not about promoting smaller business-oriented courses or temporary initiatives, but instead the Commission intends to integrate entrepreneurship into education and "support Member States in developing a more systematic strategy for entrepreneurship education" (European Council, 2000: 4). The strategy is about offering special courses on entrepreneurship and business-related issues to students at all levels to ensure that all pupils leaving the education system have had access to entrepreneurship courses (European Commission, 2012a). The primary aim of the strategy is to integrate entrepreneurship and the teaching of entrepreneurial skills into regular programmes and the overall curriculum:

> Currently the teaching of entrepreneurship is not yet sufficiently integrated in higher education institutions' curricula. Available data show that the majority of entrepreneurship courses are offered in business and economic studies.

> However, it is questionable whether Business Schools are the most appropriate place to teach entrepreneurship: innovative and viable business ideas are more likely to arise from technical, scientific and creative studies. So the real challenge is to build inter-disciplinary approaches, making entrepreneurship education accessible to all students. (European Commission, 2012a: 10)

The aim of the strategy is as comprehensive as follows:

> the concrete objective is to bring entrepreneurship into the mainstream of national educational policy and practice in every country in the EU, to enhance the understanding of education as growth-friendly investment and inspire long-term policy reform at the Member State level. (Thematic Working Group on Entrepreneurship Education 2013: 4)

Universities and technical institutes are therefore expected to "integrate entrepreneurship as an important part of the curriculum, spread across different subjects, and require or encourage students to take entrepreneurship courses" (European Commission, 2006: 9).

(iii) *Entrepreneurship as a priority*: Entrepreneurship stands out as an overall objective that is given priority over other educational aims. "Entrepreneurship education is not just a module or a teaching method. The entrepreneurial approach needs to be core to the way education operates. It is a stance; a culture of leadership, learning and teaching" (Thematic Working Group on Entrepreneurship Education, 2013: 15).

(iv) *A special focus on STEM disciplines*: EU policy is directing a special focus towards the academic disciplines of science, technology, engineering and mathematics (STEM) (European Commission, 2006), as "special attention should be paid to systematically integrating entrepreneurship training into scientific and technical studies and within technical institutions" (European Commission, 2012a: 11). Resting on the idea that entrepreneurship education will produce extra added value in the area of technology and science:

> Entrepreneurship education in universities should be available for students and researchers from all fields, notably in technical universities. Matching scientific potential with entrepreneurial skills will contribute to better commercialisation of research results through spin-offs and more start-ups in knowledge-based sectors. (European Commission, 2004a: 7)

It seems as if education is foremost about nature and technology-oriented knowledge and is for people who can use it for the demands of the labour market, "to ensure a sufficient supply of science, maths and engineering graduates and to focus school curricula on creativity, innovation, and entrepreneurship" (European Commission, 2010: 11). These thoughts rest on the traditional idea that the main role of universities in relation to entrepreneurship is that their research and innovation should result in self-employment through spin-offs. A second explanation for the focus on STEM can be traced to an assumption that it is disciplines such as maths and science that will contribute to European growth.

IDEOLOGIES OF EDUCATION

The idea of higher education in relation to society will have consequences for educational initiatives and is likely to influence the higher education sector (Schmidt, 2008). This final part will discuss educational ideologies as expressed in EU policy documents. How does EU policy present the role of education in society? Educational ideologies relate education to society, to work and to human and social development (Fanghanel, 2012). Does education fulfil a higher purpose of liberating the human mind and making the world a better place to live in, or is education primarily about producing skilled people for the labour market to bring about economic growth and welfare? Acknowledging that the economic, social and individual motives for education are related and that economic needs and social justice and personal development concerns are complex and interconnected, as employment often contributes to personal fulfilment (Jary and Thomas, 1999), it is still possible to detect distinct ideas about education's main purpose. The literature provides several different presentations of educational ideologies (for example, see Fanghanel, 2012; Schiro, 2008; Young, 2007; Trowler, 1998; Burgess, 1977). The following categorisation of four educational ideologies is inspired by Trowler (1998) and Schiro (2008), who made distinctions between the *Traditional ideology*, the *Social efficiency ideology*, the *Learner-centred ideology* and the *Social reconstruction ideology*. These categories are ideal types that represent basic beliefs that will shape attitudes, actions and practices within higher education and can help researchers to understand educational philosophies. An important distinction for typology is the one between *content* (i.e., if education has a value of its own) or if it serves a *function* (Schiro, 2008). The perspective that education has personal, social and cultural benefits that add to or supersede economic benefits comes in different forms. The Humboldt tradition gives education a value of its own; education becomes important "for its own sake" (Hirst, 1974). Education can also be seen as a basis for liberation and empowerment and therefore of benefit for the individual (Freire, 1972). Another distinction can be made between focus on the discipline and propositional knowledge on one hand and on general transferable skills on the other. Both content and function are related to how knowledge is viewed and from where it derives its authority. According to the traditional ideology of education, the virtue of education exists for its own sake; cultural and disciplinary heritage is valued and advancement in the field is emphasised in order to find new knowledge and produce new experts (Schiro, 2008; Trowler, 1998). In line with the Humbolt ideal of *Bildung*, education should not provide professional skills but should rather allow students to build individual characters by choosing their own ways (Michelsen, 2010). This is the ideology underlying the liberal art idea of education (Burman and Mehrens, 2011), where students learn out of curiosity and interest in the subject as such, and the primary role of the university is to find and transmit knowledge (Fanghanel, 2012; Troiano and Elias, 2014). Knowledge gives the student the ability to understand, and authority is derived from the discipline where the truth has been verified through scientific methods. In this way, knowledge is viewed as something objective (Schiro, 2008: 176), and the focus is on content (Trowler, 1998). Learning means transmitting knowledge to the student who lacks it, and teachers are authorities who are to pass the knowledge of a discipline to the student. The traditionalists view learning as a function of teaching (Schiro, 2008: 42); the teaching is in focus more than is the learning. Students are shaped by the intellectual structures of the discipline. The source of knowledge is outside the student and is actively transmitted from the teacher to the student. Learning is something that is unique for the discipline; therefore, the discipline carries within itself a methodology for teaching and learning (Schiro, 2008: 43). The traditionalists worry about epistemic drift and are afraid that the discipline will vanish because of increased focus on transferable skills (Trowler, 1998). A traditionalist version of entrepreneurship education teaches *about* entrepreneurship as a phenomenon.

The social efficiency ideology (production perspective or enterprise perspective) instead places education in relation to its functions and views knowledge as a way to build capability for action. The authority is derived from the impact it can have on society by providing individuals with the skills they need in order to function (Burgess, 1977; Trowler, 1998; Schiro, 2008: 177). According to Schiro, the main purpose of education is to be useful in general for a client and often for society as a whole (Schiro, 2008: 176); meanwhile, Fanghanel (2012) focused on efficiency in economic terms, referring to a human capital theory in which higher education can translate into economic capital and serve as an entry into the labour market (Becker, 1993). According to a neoliberal ideology, higher education supplies the knowledge economy with employable people by providing them with marketable skills (Jankowski and Provezis, 2014). Education is viewed as something instrumental, "context-dependent" and is treated as an economic investment, which in return gives employability and higher income (Troiano and Elias, 2014). This perspective is also in line with a functional perspective on education, in which the student is viewed as a "consumer" (Jungblut et al., 2015). Student needs are understood to be facilitating knowledge useful for employment, and the curriculum becomes a package that is predictable (Fanghanel, 2012: 56). The Social Efficiency ideology views learning as a process in which behaviour is to be changed (Schiro, 2008: 180), and the emphasis is on the stimuli that make the learner change, the responses that show change and the relation between the two (Schiro, 2008: 61). Learning is only successful if it is an active process, and skills are to be developed by "learning by doing". The role of the teacher is to deliver, to act in strict accordance with directions from the curriculum and to fulfil the need of the client. The objective is to prepare the student to perform skills, and effectiveness is measured as student learning. The concept of "scientific instrumentalism" is central (Schiro, 2008: 61); this concept asserts that a curriculum can be developed in a "scientific" manner similar to the way the industry produces products. The view on propositional knowledge is that it should be useful. New technology and new approaches to teaching and learning are valued as more efficient tools for learning than traditional lectures. Entrepreneurship education in line with a social efficiency perspective would be education that changes the behaviour of students and gives them skills that will make them become entrepreneurs.

The learner-centred (or progressivist) ideology is less related to society and is more occupied with how learning should take place. Academic standards are viewed as being of less importance, and the focus is more on students' benefits. The perspective is still within the Humboldt tradition of higher education (Trowler, 1998) and differs from the social efficiency perspective in that the main objective is not vocational and instead wants to produce independent critical thinkers. This approach claims to be "student-centred", as in valuing student participation in planning and assessing courses, disciplinary knowledge and traditions are considered to be of less importance (Trowler, 1998). Students' freedom of choice and personal development is more important than is propositional knowledge. Schiro (2008) saw the approach as having focused on content and as viewing knowledge as personal meanings, which gave learners the possibility for self-development and which derived its authority from the meaning it had for its possessor. Teaching is considered successful if it makes individuals grow intellectually and emotionally (Schiro, 2008: 103). The learning-centred approach rejects elitism and favours mass access to higher education. The approach is concerned with social inequality and believes in education as a way to help disadvantaged groups as much as possible but does not wish to reconstruct society. A learning-centred perspective clashes with entrepreneurship education, as it focuses on the individual and is not concerned with output.

Finally, the social reconstruction (or transformation) ideology on education also has a functional perspective on education, but instead of economic growth, the focus is on social, personal, human transformation of individuals or society (Freire, 1972; Schiro, 2008; Fanghanel, 2012). The goal is not growth but freedom, democracy or equality. Instead of serving the society according to the social efficiency perspective, education should criticise it and reconstruct it. Education should serve as a basis for personal growth and empowerment, for development of personal capabilities that can serve to promote equality (Sen, 2002; Nussbaum, 2000). The authority of knowledge derives from its potential to shape future good society (function). Learning should change the behaviour of the student to reshape society into a better place (Schiro, 2008: 148), and it is therefore a social act rather than an individual act. The intent of teaching is to reconstruct students so they can reconstruct society, hence the focus is on skills and on active problem-solving pedagogy (Trowler, 1998). Teaching is therefore to make students know and act in line with the vision of a good society. The social reconstructionist perspective claims that education can be a force for social change and for creating improved individuals who are able to critically address prevailing norms and help change them for the better (Trowler, 1998). The social reconstruction perspective aims for change in common with the social efficiency perspective, but the nature of the desired change differs and is more radical. According to Freire (1972), education is for liberation and empowerment, which can encourage action against political oppression and cause people to question the existing society; this stands in sharp contradiction to the social efficiency perspective, which seeks to contribute to and reproduce society. In this way, education is to benefit the individual, but for purposes of empowerment, not for economic gains. Entrepreneurship education with a social reconstruction perspective would, for example, seek to educate groups in order to empower them to make change, such as encouraging entrepreneurship in order to reach equality (see Table 8.1).

Table 8.1 Framework for analysis

Perspectives	Traditional	Social efficiency	Learner-centred	Social reconstruction
Motives	Individual development related to the discipline	Institutional – to make teachers efficient in making students learn	Individual development for critical thinking and growth	Individual or institutional for liberation and empowerment
Main objective of higher education	To value cultural and disciplinary heritage and extend the existence of the discipline	To efficiently and scientifically carry out a task for a client. To equip students with skills	To stimulate the growth of people and fulfil personal needs	To reshape society and be a force for social change
Knowledge – function or content	Discipline-based propositional knowledge (content)	Knowledge as capabilities for action (function) and to keep up society through skills	Focus on personal meanings of knowledge (content)	Capabilities for liberation and empowerment (function)
Teaching and learning – (discipline-based propositional or transferable skills)	Teaching as transmission in order to advance the student	Transferable skills to prepare the student to perform	Student participation, student freedom of choice to stimulate personal growth	Skills more important than disciplinary content to acculturate the student into the vision of the educator

IDEOLOGY OF EDUCATION IN EU POLICY TOWARDS ENTREPRENEURSHIP

A review of central documents on entrepreneurship education reveals a functional approach in which the role of education is to be useful for society, as the value of knowledge derives from its functions (Schiro,

2008: 179). In line with a social efficiency perspective, the role of education is to efficiently and scientifically carry out a task for a client (Schiro, 2008):

> Investment in education and training for skills development is essential to boost growth and competitiveness: skills determine Europe's capacity to increase productivity. In the long-term, skills can trigger innovation and growth, move production up the value chain, stimulate the concentration of higher level skills in the EU and shape the future labour market. (European Commission, 2012b: 2)

The "client" in this case was European society as a whole, but in the text, the focus was mainly placed on economic growth, and education is viewed as an important way to take Europe out of the perceived economic crisis. "Smart growth means strengthening knowledge and innovation as drivers of our future growth. This requires improving the quality of our education, strengthening our research performance, promoting innovation and knowledge transfer throughout the Union" (European Commission, 2010: 9). The task that should be carried out is to teach entrepreneurial skills to Europeans. Efficiency will be guaranteed by identifying the "knowledge gaps" in the European labour market, in line with an instrumentalist view on higher education. One initiative to address this gap is the "EU skills Panorama", which will provide a single overview of "European, national and sectoral findings on the short-term to medium-term prospects for jobs and skills needs as they evolve up to 2020. The Panorama will help identify emerging skills shortages in specific occupations across or within sectors" (European Commission, 2012d: 14). Another initiative underway is the work on key competences (European Council, 2006), with the aim to point out which competences Europeans need to learn, with one of eight competences being the "Sense of initiative and entrepreneurship: ability to turn ideas into action through creativity, innovation and risk-taking as well as ability to plan and manage projects" (European Council, 2006: 1). These initiatives emphasise an instrumentalist view on education and reflect the idea of a neutral, objective and scientific way to establish the relevant knowledge and skills needed. If education systems need to be able to accommodate an increasingly flexible labour market, more adaptable education systems are needed:

> Europe's education and training systems need to adapt both to the demands of the knowledge society and to the need for an improved level and quality of employment. They will have to offer learning and training opportunities tailored to target groups at different stages of their lives: young people,

> unemployed adults and those in employment who are at risk of seeing their skills overtaken by rapid change. (European Council, 2000)

In this way, the Lisbon Strategy brought about a view on education and knowledge as both limited in time and context-dependent.

Both the social efficiency perspective and the social reconstruction perspective focus on the functions of education. In EU policy, the overall objective is economic growth, and education is perceived as a way to create growth, which also will reduce poverty and social inequalities. "Better educational levels help employability, and progress in increasing the employment rate helps to reduce poverty" (European Commission, 2010: 9). The overall objective of economic growth is legitimised, as it is also a way to reduce inequalities, "as a bonus" which stands in sharp contrast to the ideas of Freire (1972) about education for personal empowerment and liberation in order to fight oppression. This view on knowledge also reflects the social efficiency perspective on education. Knowledge is primarily a way to build a capability for action, and its authority comes from the impact it can have on society by providing individuals with the skills they need (Schiro, 2008: 177). Education should provide skills in order for people to become productive: At higher education level, the primary purpose of entrepreneurship education should be to develop entrepreneurial capacities and mindsets. The way to success is to teach students about new sources of self-employment and convince them that being a businessman or woman is one way of entering the labour market (European Commission, 2012b: 12).

It is important to point out that entrepreneurship is viewed as a way for individuals to develop and satisfy other personal needs. "Entrepreneurship education prepares people to be responsible and enterprising individuals. It helps people develop the skills, knowledge, and attitudes necessary to achieve the goals they set out for themselves" (European Commission, 2015). Entrepreneurship education can add "bonus values" in the form of self-development, (which resembles the learning-centred approach) and social cohesion (in line with the social reconstruction approach). In this way, entrepreneurship education resembles a "kinder egg" for Europe, fulfilling three wishes in one being "a major driver of innovation, competitiveness and growth, […] a vehicle for personal development … that can harness social cohesion when the opportunity of creating one's own business is offered to everybody, regardless of background or location" (European Commission, 2012c: 3). Also, the Thematic Working Group on Entrepreneurship Education (2013: 9) expresses this multi-purpose view on entrepreneurship when they state that entrepreneurship education is about "learners developing the skills and mindset to be able to turn creative ideas into entrepreneurial action. This is a key competence for all learners, supporting personal development, active citizenship, social inclusion and employability" (European Commission, 2010: 16).

According to the social efficiency perspective, the desired result of learning is to change people's behaviour rather than changing their minds. The output is in focus. Individual development is less interesting, unless it is put into entrepreneurial action (Thematic Working Group on Entrepreneurship Education, 2013: 9). Through education, the Commission can influence programmes and courses and cause them to be geared towards the acquisition of the following generic and horizontal skills, aiming to make students: more creative/innovative; highly motivated; proactive; self-aware; self-confident; willing to challenge; better communicators; decision makers; leaders; negotiators; networkers; problem solvers; team players; systematic thinkers; less dependent; less risk-averse; able to live with uncertainty and capable of recognising opportunities (European Commission, 2012a: 26). If education can serve to change these behaviours, it is expected to create a more favourable societal climate for entrepreneurship, "based on an integrated policy with a view to not only changing the mindset but also improving the skills of Europeans and removing obstacles to the start-up, transfer and growth of businesses" (European Commission, 2006: 3).

The focus on entrepreneurship in education will have implications for the forms of teaching, as the main focus in the process and intent of teaching is on preparing the students to perform transversal skills, which are seen as different to what is normally taught at universities: "... focus in training programmes targeting youth should be on the practice of non-cognitive skills such as teamwork, self-regulation, and setting increasingly ambitious goals" (OECD/European Union, 2015: 98). In order to do this, the Commission stresses the necessity for new ways of teaching in order for entrepreneurship education to be successful:

> Key actions are to ensure that measures are taken to introduce transversal skills across all curricula from early stages of education up to higher education, using innovative and student-centred pedagogical approaches, and to design assessment tools through which levels of competence can be effectively assessed and evaluated. (European Commission, 2012b: 15)

The focus is on assessment and on transversal skills, which is a clear step away from the Academic scholar approach. New forms of teaching are needed, and education should be based on entrepreneurial curricula that

> should allow flexibility and encourage educational institutions to interact and engage with the wider social and economic environment, developing an outward-facing approach in collaboration with stakeholders. Sticking to traditional classroom teaching/lecturing leaves out significant elements of entrepreneurship, such as creativity, understanding risk, collaboration and problem-solving. Emphasis should be on pedagogies and teaching methods that allow learners to develop a range of entrepreneurial learning outcomes within one activity to maximise impact on their entrepreneurial confidence. (Thematic Working Group on Entrepreneurship Education, 2013: 13)

There is a tendency to view entrepreneurs and other external experts as more important than educators, with educators rarely appearing as highly visible subjects. Where educators are specifically mentioned, they are viewed as deficient and as if they "lack motivation and specific training" (European Commission, 2006: 8). The system of higher education therefore needs to be reconstructed in order to:

> promote creativity, innovation and self-employment, which include: developing personal attributes and skills that form the basis of an entrepreneurial mindset and behaviour (creativity, sense of initiative, risk-taking, autonomy, self-confidence, leadership, team spirit, etc.); raising the awareness of students about self-employment and entrepreneurship as possible career options; and providing specific business skills and knowledge of how to start a company and run it successfully. (European Commission, 2012a: 10)

CONCLUSIONS

The EU seeks to implement policies to introduce entrepreneurship education into the education system in order to improve the entrepreneurial performance vertically (all levels of education) and horizontally (all fields and types of education) but with special attention given to the academic disciplines of science, technology, engineering and mathematics. The policies of entrepreneurship education are not about promoting smaller business-oriented courses or temporary initiatives; instead, entrepreneurship should be incorporated into all education, and the member states should be supported in developing a more systematic strategy for entrepreneurship education. Entrepreneurship education is associated with the behaviours of individuals at the micro level and reflecting the "world of the entrepreneur" but also the "cognitive world of the entrepreneur" (Neck and Greene, 2011) where the creating of an "entrepreneurial mindset" is in focus.

Schmidt (2008) argues that there seldom is only one overall paradigm, or "frame of reference", dominating, but a review of policies on entrepreneurship education shows that the social efficiency perspective, in which the overall purpose of higher education is to efficiently and scientifically contribute to economic growth and fight unemployment, dominates. Scientific instrumentalism is seen in the ambitions to find the "right skills" needed and to introduce them into the curriculum of higher education. The view on propositional knowledge is utilitarian, meaning that knowledge should be useful. Education is perceived as a tool to change people's behaviour and it should prepare students to perform skills. Knowledge must serve a function, and education should focus on transversal skills. Entrepreneurship is only, to a limited extent, discussed in terms of empowerment and as a way to reduce inequalities representing the social reconstruction perspective or with reference to the importance of discipline and provisional knowledge, reflecting a traditional approach. The learning-centred ideology approach, which is not concerned with output but individually oriented, is absent. Instead, entrepreneurship is for the collective good of saving Europe from crises; individual benefit might come as a bonus.

With the ambition to explore the underlying assumptions of a policy (Bacchi, 2009), there are primarily five points that can be highlighted. First, EU policies towards entrepreneurship education rest heavily on an objective view of knowledge. The European initiatives (the European skills panorama and the key competence project) were set out to determine the relevant skills needed by society. The assumption is that there are knowledge and skills that are "right" for economic growth and the development of society and that these can be "found" and used. The question of what is relevant knowledge for a society and who decides what is relevant is put in the background. Second, the policy reflects a "scientific instrumentalism" (Schiro, 2008), the belief that if we only incorporate these right skills into the curriculum and make sure that they are used by the teachers by setting learning objectives and by aligning teaching to the learning objectives, students will learn the right things and become entrepreneurial. The risk with this approach is that it disconnects teachers from the learning process, undermining professional roles by implying that there is a neutral "scientific" way of teaching. Third, policies supporting entrepreneurship education in several ways rest on assumptions with weak empirical bases, that is, EU policies on entrepreneurship education heavily rest on the assumption of the existence of a large group of people wishing to become entrepreneurs but who are held back by risk averseness (implicitly caused by the tradition of a strong European welfare system) and the lack of an entrepreneurial mindset. The link between entrepreneurial intentions and entrepreneurial action has, however, been heavily criticised as weak and not empirically proven. As the Eurobarometer polls only measure entrepreneurial intentions, our knowledge about real entrepreneurial potential is unknown. A similar weak empirical-based fact can be found in the focus in policy on STEM disciplines. The assumption that graduates in STEM disciplines are more inclined to choose self-employment lacks empirical evidence (Silander and Berggren, 2016). Fourth, EU policies on entrepreneurship education show scepticism towards the traditional university virtues and mark a move away from provisional knowledge, favouring role models and best practice and "real entrepreneurs" over traditional education and academic teachers. Fifth, modern research on entrepreneurship has ceased to view entrepreneurs as people who possess certain traits (self-confident, dominant, autonomous risk-takers etc.) and instead put entrepreneurship in something constructed in a social context. EU policies on entrepreneurship clearly show a belief in entrepreneurship as something that can be taught and that should not be treated as an innate behaviour. On the other hand, they seem to have moved back to the traditional focus on the individual entrepreneur as an individual who is characterised by certain traits. EU policies are situated in the "world of the entrepreneur" (Neck and Greene, 2011) where the focus is on the individual entrepreneur as a hero figure and where entrepreneurship education often is expected to present role models to students and teach them what is proper behaviour in order to become successful.

REFERENCES

Acs, Z. J. (2008). "What is the value of entrepreneurial start-ups to an economy?" In Acs, Z. J. (ed.), *Entrepreneurship, Growth and Public Policy*. Cheltenham: Edward Elgar.

Alexiadou, N. (2014). "Policy learning and Europeanisation in education: the governance of a field and the transfer of knowledge". In Nordin, A. and Sundberg, D. (eds), *Transnational Policy Flows in European Education: The Making and Governing of Knowledge in the Education Policy Field*. Oxford: Symposium Books.

Bacchi, C. (2009). *Analysing Policy: What's the Problem Represented to be?* Australia: Pearson Education.

Bae, T. J., Qian, S., Miao, C. and Fiet, J. O. (2014). "The relationship between entrepreneurship education and entrepreneurial intentions: a meta-analytic review". *Entrepreneurship Theory and Practice*, 12(2–3), 217–254, doi: 10.1111/etap.12095.

Ball, S. (1994). *Education Reform: A Critical and Post-structural Approach*. Maidenhead: McGraw-Hill Education.

Becker, G. S. (1993). *Human Capital: A Theoretical and Empirical Analysis, with Special Reference to Education.* 3rd ed. Chicago, IL: The University of Chicago Press.

Bennett, M. (2006). "Business lecturers' perception of the nature of entrepreneurship". *International Journal of Entrepreneurial Behaviour & Research*, 12(3), 165–188.

Blyth, M. (2010). "On setting and upsetting agendas: Blyth on Gofas and Hay, Tonder and Seabrooke". In Gofas, A. and Hay, C. (eds), *The Role of Ideas in Political Analysis: A Portrait of Contemporary Debates*. London: Routledge.

Braunerhjelm, P., Larsson, J., Thulin, P. et al. (2016). "The entrepreneurial challenge – a comparative study of entrepreneurial dynamics in China, Europe and the US". Stockholm: Entreprenörskapsforum.

Bridgstock, R. (2013). "Not a dirty word: arts entrepreneurship and higher education". *Arts and Humanities in Higher Education*, 12(2–3), 122–137.

Burgess, T. (1977). *Education After School.* London: V. Gollancz.

Burman, A. and Mehrens, P. (2011). *Det goda lärandet: en antologi om liberal arts education.* Lund: Studentlitteratur.

Castagnetti, C. and Rosti, L. (2011). "Who skims the cream of the Italian graduate crop? Wage employment versus self-employment". *Small Business Economics*, 36(2), 223–234.

Cunningham, B. and Lischeron, J. (1991). "Defining entrepreneurship", *Journal of Small Business Management*, 29(1), 45–61.

Co, M. and Mitchell, B. (2006). "Entrepreneurship education in South Africa: a nationwide survey", *Education & Training*, 48(5), 348–359.

Dale, R. (1999). "Specifying globalisation effects on national policy: a focus on the mechanism". *Journal of Education Policy*, 14(1), 1–17.

Dickson, P. H., Solomon, G. T. and Weaver, K. M. (2008). "Entrepreneurial selection and success: does education matter"? *Journal of Small Business and Enterprise Development*, 15(2), 239–258.

ENQHEEI – The Quality of Entrepreneurship Programmes in Europe Project (2006). Best Practices and Pedagogical Methods in Entrepreneurship Education in Europe.

European Commission (2003). "Entrepreneurship in Europe", Green Paper, Brussels, 21 January.

European Commission (2004a). "Action plan: The European agenda for entrepreneurship", COM (2004) 70 final. Brussels: European Commission.

European Commission (2004b). "Implementation of the 'Education and Training 2010' work programme. Key competences for lifelong learning – a European reference framework". Brussels: European Commission.

European Commission (2006). "Entrepreneurship education in Europe: Fostering entrepreneurial mindsets through education and learning". Brussels: European Commission.

European Commission (2008). "Think Small First – A Small Business Act for Europe". COM (2008)394. Brussels: European Commission.

European Commission (2010). "Europe 2020 – A strategy for smart, sustainable and inclusive growth". Brussels: European Commission.

European Commission (2012a). "Effects and impact of entrepreneurship programmes in higher education". Brussels: European Commission.

European Commission (2012b). "Rethinking education: Investing in skills for better socio-economic outcomes". Brussels: European Commission.
European Commission (2012c). "The Entrepreneurship 2020 Action plan – Reigniting the entrepreneurial spirit in Europe". (COM/2012/0795 final).
European Commission (2012d). "Towards a job-rich recovery". Brussels: European Commission.
European Commission (2015). "Entrepreneurship education: A road to success, a compilation of evidence on the impact of Entrepreneurship education strategies and measures". Luxembourg: Publications Office of the European Union.
European Council (2000). "Lisbon European Council 23 and 24 March 2000 Presidency Conclusions".
European Council (2006). Recommendation 2006/962/EC of the European Parliament and of the Council of 18 December 2006 on key competences for lifelong learning (OJ L 394, 30 December, pp. 10–18).
Falck, O., Heblich, S. and Luedemann, E. (2012). "Identity and entrepreneurship: do school peers shape entrepreneurial intentions?". *Small Business Economics*, 9, 39–59.
Falck, O. and Woessmann, L. (2013). "School competition and students' entrepreneurial intentions: international evidence using historical Catholic roots of private schooling". *Small Business Economics*, 40, 459–478.
Falk, M. and Leoni, T. (2009). "Characteristics of self-employment among university graduates". *Applied Economics Letters*, 16(10), 1065–1071.
Fanghanel, J. (2012). *Being an Academic*. London: Routledge.
Farny, S., Hedeboe Frederiksen, S., Hannibal, M. and Jones, S. (2016). "A CULTure of entrepreneurship education". *Entrepreneurship & Regional Development*, 28(7–8), 514–535.
Fayolle, A., Gailly, B. and Lassas-Clerc, N. (2006). "Assessing the impact of entrepreneurship education programmes: a new methodology", *Journal of European Industrial Training*, 30(9), 701–720.
Foley, A. and Griffith, B. (1998). "Education, training and the promotion of high quality entrepreneurs in the Republic of Ireland". In Scott, M.G., Rosa, P., Klandt, H. (eds), *Educating Entrepreneurs for Wealth Creation*. Aldershot: Ashgate.
Freire, P. (1972). *Pedagogy of the Oppressed*. Harmondsworth: Penguin.
Galloway, L. and Brown, W. (2002). "Entrepreneurship education at university: a driver in the creation of high growth firms"? *Education and Training*, 44(8/9), 398–405.
Gartner, W. (1990). "What are we talking about when we talk about entrepreneurship?". *Journal of Business Venturing*, 5, 15–28.
Grek, S. and Lawn, M. (2009). "A short history of Europeanizing education". *European Education*, 41(1), 32–54.
Hammarstedt, M. (2009). "Predicted earnings and the propensity for self-employment: evidence from Sweden". *International Journal of Manpower*, 30(4), 349–359.
Hannon, P. D. (2006). "Teaching pigeons to dance: sense and meaning in entrepreneurship education". *Education and Training*, 48(5), 296–308.
Hegarty, C. and Jones, C. (2008). "Graduate entrepreneurship: more than child's play". *Education and Training*, 7, 626–637.

Hipple, S. F. (2010). "Self-employment in the United States". *Monthly Labor Review*, 133(9), 17–32.

Hirst, P. (1974). *Knowledge and the Curriculum*. London: Routledge and Kegan Paul.

Hytti, U. and O'Gorman, C. (2004). "What is 'enterprise education'? An analysis of the objectives and methods of enterprise education programmes in four countries". *Education and Training*, 46(1), 11–23.

Jamieson, I. (1984). Education for Enterprise. In Watts, A. G. and Moran, P. (eds), Cambridge: CRAC Ballinger.

Jankowski, N. and Provezis, S. (2014). "Neoliberal ideologies, governmentality and the Academy: an examination of accountability through assessment and transparency". *Educational Philosophy and Theory*, 46(5), 475–487.

Jary, D. and Thomas, L. (1999). "Widening participation and lifelong learning: rhetoric or reality? The role of research and the reflexive practitioner". *Widening Participation and Lifelong Learning*, 1(1), 1–10.

Jungblut, J., Vukasovic, M. and Stensaker, B. (2015). "Student perspectives on quality in higher education". *European Journal of Higher Education*, 5(2), 157–180.

Kirby, D. (2004). "Entrepreneurship education: can business schools meet the challenge?". *Education & Training*, 46(8/9), 510–519.

Kolstad, I. and Wiig, A. (2014). "Education and entrepreneurial success". *Small Business Economics*. Online 6 December.

Lee, J. (1997). "The motivation of women entrepreneurs in Singapore". *International Journal of Entrepreneurial Behaviour and Research*, 3(2), 93–110.

Leffler, E. and Svedberg, G. (2005). "Enterprise learning: a challenge to education?". *European Educational Research Journal*, 4(3), 219–227.

Martinez, A. C., Levie, J., Kelley, D. J., Saemundsson, R. J. and Schøtt, T. (2010). *Global entrepreneurship monitor special report: A global perspective on entrepreneurship education and training*. Strathclyde: Hunter Centre For Entrepreneurship.

McKeown, J., Millman, C., Sursani, S., Smith, K. and Martin, L. (2006). "Graduate entrepreneurship education in the United Kingdom". *Education & Training*, 48(8/9), 597–613.

Michelsen, S. (2010). "Humboldt meets Bologna". *Higher Education Policy*, 23(2), 151–172.

Minniti, M. and Lévesque, M. (2008). "Recent developments in the economics of entrepreneurship". *Journal of Business Venturing*, 23, 603–612.

Minniti, M., Bygrave, W. and Autio, E. (2006). Global Entrepreneurship Monitor 2005 Executive Report, accessed 28 October 2017 at http://www.gemconsortium.org/report/47104.

Mwasalwiba, E. S. (2010). "Entrepreneurship education: a review of its objectives, teaching methods, and impact indicators". *Education & Training*, 52(1), 20–47.

Neck, H. M. and P. G. Greene (2011). "Entrepreneurship education: known worlds and new frontiers". *Journal of Small Business Management*, 49(1), 55–70.

Nordin, A. (2012). *Kunskapens politik: en studie av kunskapsdiskurser i svensk och europeisk utbildningspolicy*. Växjö: Linnaeus University Press.

Nussbaum, M. C. (2000). *Women and Human Development: The Capabilities Approach*. Cambridge: Cambridge University Press.
Nyström, K. and Karlsson, C. (2008). *Nyföretagande, näringslivsdynamik och tillväxt i den nya världsekonomin*. Underlagsrapport till Globaliseringsrådet, Stockholm: Utbildningsdepartementet, Globaliseringrådet/The Swedish Ministry of Education, The Globalisation Council.
O'Connor, A. (2013). "A conceptual framework for entrepreneurship education policy: meeting government and economic purposes". *Journal of Business Venturing*, 28(4), 546–563.
OECD/European Union (2015). *The Missing Entrepreneurs 2015: Policies for Self-employment and Entrepreneurship*. Paris: OECD Publishing.
Olofsson, A. (2012). "Konflikten mellan kontroll och förändring – exemplet entreprenörskap(sutbildning) i det svenska utbildningssystemet". In Stigmar, M. and Sandstedt, T. (eds), *Kvalitet och kollegialitet – vänbok till Leif Lindberg*. Växjö: Linnaeus University Press.
Oosterbeek, H., van Praag, M. and Ijsselstein, A. (2010). "The impact of entrepreneurship education on entrepreneurship skills and motivation". *European Economic Review*, 54(3), 442–454.
Pittaway, L. and Cope, J. (2007). "Entrepreneurship education: a systematic review of the evidence". *International Small Business Journal*, 35(5), 479–510.
Robertson, S. L. (2008). "Embracing the global: crisis and the creation of a new semiotic order to secure Europe's knowledge-based economy". *Education and the Knowledge-based Economy in Europe*. Bristol: Centre for Globalisation, Education and Societies, University of Bristol.
Rhodes, M. (2010). *Employment Policy. Policy-making in the European Union*. Oxford: Oxford University Press.
Schiro, M. (2008). *Curriculum Theory – Conflicting Visions and Enduring Concerns*. Thousand Oaks, CA: Sage.
Schmidt, V. (2008). "Discursive institutionalism: the explanatory power of ideas and discourse". *Annual Review of Political Science*, 11, 303–326.
Schmidt, V. A. (2011). "Speaking of change: why discourse is key to the dynamics of policy transformation". *Critical Policy Studies*, 5(2), 106–126.
Scott, M. G., Rosa, P. and Klandt, H. (1998). *Educating Entrepreneurs for Wealth Creation*. Brookfield: Ashgate.
Sen, A. (2002). *Rationality and Freedom*. Cambridge, MA: Belknap Press.
Shane, S. A. (2008). *The Illusion of Entrepreneurship*. New Haven, CT: Yale University Press.
Silander, C. and Berggren, C. (2016). "Political entrepreneurs and women's entrepreneurship". In Karlsson, C., Silander, D. and Silander, C. (eds), *Political entrepreneurship: Regional growth and entrepreneurial diversity in Sweden*. Cheltenham: Edward Elgar.
Souitaris, V., Zerbinati, S. and Al-Laham, A. (2007). "Do entrepreneurship programmes raise entrepreneurial intention of science and engineering students? The effect of learning, inspiration and resources". *Journal of Business Venturing*, 22(4), 566–591.

Stevenson, L. and Lundström, A. (2002). *Entrepreneurship Policy for the Future Series. Beyond the rhetoric: Defining entrepreneurship policy and its best practice*. Örebro: Swedish Foundation for Small Business Research.

Thematic Working Group on Entrepreneurship Education (2013). *Entrepreneurship education and the future of learning*. Thematic Report, Vienna: 17–19 April 2013.

Troiano, H. and Elias, M. (2014). "University access and after: explaining the social composition of degree programmes and the contrasting expectations of students". *Higher Education*, 67(5), 637–654.

Trowler, P. (1998). *Academics Responding to Change*. Ballmore: Open University Press.

Van de Ven, A. H. and Johnson, P. E. (2006). "Knowledge for theory and practice". *Academy of Management Review*, 31(4), 802–821.

Verheul, I., Wennekers, S., Audretsch, D. and Thurik, R. (2001). *An eclectic theory of entrepreneurship: policies, institutions and culture*. Tinbergen Institute Discussion Paper.

Wennekers, S. and Thurik, R. (1999). "Linking entrepreneurship and economic growth". *Small Business Economics*, 13(1), 27–56.

Young, M. (2007). *Bringing Knowledge Back In: From Social Constructivism to Social Realism in the Sociology of Education*. London: Routledge.

Zamfir, A. M., Lungu, E. O. and Mocanu, C. (2013). "Entrepreneurship among higher education graduates in 13 European countries". *Theoretical and Applied Economics*, 18(11), 588.

9. Exploring preconditions for political entrepreneurship and integration in European societies

Anna Parkhouse and Per Strömblad

INTRODUCTION

For the EU and its member states, the issue of immigration has been in political focus for quite some time. Rather to be expected, the challenges facing Europe in this respect were addressed as a top priority by Jean-Claude Juncker, in the run-up to his election campaign for Commission President in 2014. Nevertheless, eager to point out potential benefits as well, he thus identified the necessity to promote a "new European policy on legal migration to address skills shortages and attract talent to better cope with the demographic challenges facing the EU" (EC, 2016e). Reflecting Europe's reputation for prosperity and safety, a substantial part of the influx of migrants is generated by efforts to escape war, hostility and poverty. However, the extraordinarily large refugee influx in 2015 created political havoc within the EU. Although the EU asylum policy area had been one of the most rapidly developed policy areas since 1999, it became blatantly clear that the Common European Asylum System (CEAS) was not resilient enough to handle the unprecedented large refugee influx on EU territory (Constant and Zimmermann, 2016). The breakdown of the CEAS in the autumn of 2015 subsequently led some EU member states to reintroduce territorial border controls, as well as to introduce more restrictive migration policies. Arguably, such a development is not only contrary to the fundamentals of the European Union, that is, the free circulation of people, but it is also detrimental to a European labour market increasingly in need of expanding its labour force, according to the Commission (EC, 2016a, 2016c).

Apparently, a considerable part of the political dynamic of the discussion centres precisely on whether the refugee influx should be seen as a threat to the survival of the European welfare state or, rather, as a prerequisite for its survival. The latter perspective is grounded in the looming demographic crisis of Europe where the influx of migrants is seen as a vital labour force, to address the situation of an alarmingly ageing population in Europe.[1] According to the 2015 Ageing Report of the European Commission, although there will be an increase in the population of the EU member states from 507 million to 523 million between 2013 and 2060, in parallel and in the same period there will be a decrease in the working population from 211 million to 202 million (EC, 2015b: 1–2). The possible supplement of migrants, including refugees, onto the labour market would ameliorate the ratio of active workers versus inactive workers thus contributing to a stronger European economy and also to the survival of the welfare state (cf. Strömblad and Malmberg, 2016: 541–542). Reasonably, however, this would require that both the EU and its member states develop effective systems of integration, through which migrants' competencies and skills are efficiently validated and where policy initiatives would shorten their entry onto the labour market as well as into European education systems. In fact, some analysts claim that the core of the migration challenge in fact is more due to a lack of labour migration than anything else, and thus what has been called the refugee crisis is rather a migration governance crisis, or "a crisis of Europe and its institutions rather than one of European migration" (Zimmermann, 2017: 88).

Against this backdrop, we investigate institutional preconditions of political entrepreneurship within the field of EU migration and integration policies. This chapter thus entails an analysis of the potential roles that political entrepreneurs, among supranational as well as intergovernmental and non-governmental actors, may fulfil. By adhering to the definition used in the book, political entrepreneurship is viewed both from "an actor and a structure perspective by focusing on politicians/public servants/bureaucrats/institutions within the publicly funded sector that, with innovative approaches encourages entrepreneurship/business and where the goal is growth and employment" (see Chapter 1 in this volume). In addition, utilising data from the most recent round of the European Social Survey, we analyse European citizens' attitudes towards different categories of migrants, also focusing on cross-national institutional differences in this respect. Hence, disclosing potentially important disparities in the sections of this chapter, we conclude by discussing

---

[1] The demographic challenge is explicated in terms of an ageing population, longer life expectancies and a declining working-age population (EC, 2011: 2).

preconditions for efficient political entrepreneurship activities and successful integration in the European future.

THE EU MIGRATION POLICY CONTEXT

Within the framework of justice and home affairs, asylum and migration policy became a new policy area in the Maastricht Treaty in 1993 (Ucarer, 2013). The establishment of the policy area should be seen as a spillover from the completion of the single market and therefore as a logical consequence of the passport-free union (Nugent, 2010). The policy area is therefore based on a paradox: in order to guarantee the free movement of people, intra-EU, a more rigorous control of those who are outside is required; that is, of the (in EU terminology) third-country nationals (Carmel and Paul, 2013). Notably, however, in the context of the EU migration policy area, third-country nationals, or migrants, are defined as "persons born in a country outside the EU and persons born in the EU but not holding the citizenship of a Member State" (EC, 2011: 3).[2] Thus, being a "migrant" within the EU does not technically require an individual migration history. Moreover, whereas migrants may refer to people leaving a country for another (excluding intra-country relocation) for a vast number of reasons, refugees and asylum seekers are forced to emigrate in order to seek protection from another "sovereign country abroad" (Constant and Zimmermann, 2016: 3). However, with increasing and more complex migratory movements, these distinctions have arguably become less meaningful, paving the way for the term "mixed migration", referring to the fact that both the motivations and the nature of the migratory movements are becoming interconnected (Lulle and King, 2016: 23).

From having been established strictly as intergovernmental cooperation in the Maastricht Treaty, the policy area initially developed very quickly. Already in the Amsterdam Treaty in 1999—largely due to the impending Eastern enlargement and the perceived necessity to strengthen the control of borders and to counter illegal immigration—asylum, border controls, visa and migration issues were transferred to the first supranational pillar (Nugent, 2010). Subsequently, a strengthened Schengen cooperation was also integrated into the EU institutional framework. However, the effectiveness of border protection was hampered by the fact that membership

---

[2] In EU parlance, the definition of a migrant also sometimes includes second and third generation migrants, legally residing on EU territory (EC, 2016d: 9).

in Schengen is neither complete nor restricted to EU member states.[3] These shortcomings were legally reinforced by the Treaty of Nice (2003), which extended the principle of flexible integration to apply also to the area of asylum and migration policy. This meant that Ireland and the United Kingdom were given the right to stand outside the cooperation, in so-called "opt-out clauses" (Nugent, 2010).

The five-year Tampere Programme, 2000–2005, was to be the first of a number of strategic action programmes, followed by the action programmes of The Hague and Stockholm. In parallel with strengthening the rights and the free movement of those legally staying in the EU, the fight against illegal immigration would be strengthened. The Tampere Programme was also the starting point for the CEAS, designed to harmonise national asylum systems. Minimum levels of legislation, combined with poor compliance with the regulations, resulted in the Tampere Programme's goals also becoming priority objectives in the subsequent policy programmes in The Hague, 2005–2010, and Stockholm, 2010–2014 (Collett, 2014). In 2009, the CEAS was institutionalised in the Lisbon Treaty (Article 78 [1] TEU Lisbon). The right to asylum, based on the Geneva Convention,[4] is also governed by the EU Charter of Human Rights (Article 18 of the EU Charter). The Lisbon Treaty also establishes the principle of solidarity and fair division of responsibility between member states and Council conclusions on a concrete framework for solidarity with member states, particularly vulnerable to migratory strains, adopted on 8 March 2012 (Council of the European Union, 2012). Since the legislation initially had provided only minimum levels, they were to be revised with a view to strengthening the CEAS. The *qualification directive*, which was first adopted in 2004 and revised in 2011 (2011/95/EU), sets out rules for what is considered to be the basis for international protection but also expects rights to housing, access to employment and education as well as to healthcare and welfare to be

[3] The Schengen cooperation is composed of 22 EU member states and four countries not having EU membership. Apart from Ireland and the United Kingdom, having opt-out clauses, Bulgaria, Croatia, Cyprus and Romania are not part of the cooperation. When in compliance with the membership criteria, they are obliged to become members. Non-EU member states, such as Iceland, Lichtenstein, Norway and Switzerland are associate members of the Schengen cooperation. Although not *de jure* members of Schengen, Monaco, San Marino and the Holy Sea are *de facto* members, keeping their borders to neighbouring states open (Ucarer, 2013).

[4] The Geneva Convention of 1951 and its 1967 protocol are the international legal documents regulating to the rights of displaced people and the obligations of the sovereign states having signed and ratified the documents.

observed. In 2005, the EU adopted the *asylum procedures directive*, which sets out rules for a fair and efficient asylum process. The *reception conditions directive*, adopted in 2003, sets out minimum criteria for living conditions, ensuring rights to food, housing, employment and to healthcare upon arrival in the host country. Both directives were revised in 2013 (2013/32/EU; 2013/33/EU). The *Dublin convention* of 1997 and its subsequent *Dublin II regulation* of 2003 and the *Dublin III regulation*, adopted in 2013, are the basis for the CEAS and are about establishing a responsible Dublin State when it comes to the examination of the asylum application. The *Eurodac regulation* was adopted in 2000 as a fingerprint database for a more efficient implementation of the Dublin Convention (Constant and Zimmermann, 2016: 4–5). Despite the setting up of the European Asylum Support Office (EASO) in 2011, whose mandate is to enhance the cooperation between member states, the lack of cooperation and solidarity became blatant in 2015 at the height of the refugee crisis. Initiatives on how to strengthen the CEAS has been on the Commission agenda ever since (EC, 2015a).

Up until the ratification of the Lisbon Treaty, the division of competences in the policy area had been made according to the pillar structure introduced by the Maastricht Treaty. With the communitarisation of the whole policy area in the Treaty of Amsterdam, the decision-making powers of the European Parliament were equated with the Council of Ministers from 2004. The European Court of Justice was also given a mandate to interpret and judge in litigation. The Lisbon Treaty (2009) involved significant reforms also in decision-making. With the disappearance of the pillar structure, shared authority was introduced as a legislative principle. Thus, the division of competence in this policy area is shared between the EU and its 28 member states (Article 4 TFEU Lisbon) (see Chapter 1 in this volume). This means that the EU can legislate and adopt binding acts in significant parts of the policy area, such as the conditions and terms on lawful entry and residence of third-country nationals of EU member states. However, decisions regulating how many third-country nationals should be granted the right of entry to seek employment defer to member state competence.

When it comes to developing common policies for labour market immigration, in terms of making the EU more globally competitive, the process has been slow. *The blue card directive*[5] (2009/50/EC), adopted in

[5] Apart from the higher education requirement (tertiary education), three years of working experience is required to qualify for the directive (Council

May 2009, was introduced in order to facilitate for highly skilled third-country nationals to compete for qualified positions in the EU job market. In order to facilitate entry and residence of labour migrants in more low-skilled professions, especially in the sectors of services, care, industry and agriculture, the EU adopted the *seasonal workers directive*,[6] (2014/36/EU) in 2014. Other directives aimed at strengthening incentives for legal migration are about facilitating both multinational companies to temporarily relocate their staff and simplify for third-country nationals to study, research, train or volunteer in the EU. The *intra-corporate transfer directive* (2014/66/EU) was adopted in 2014 and the *recast students and researchers EU directive* (2016/801/EU) was adopted in 2016.[7] Other directives, aiming at enhancing governance of legal migration, are the *family reunification directive* (2003/86/EC), *the long-term residents directive* (2003/109/EC) as amended by directive 2011/51/EU and also the *single permit directive* (2011/98/EU).

With increasing mixed migratory movements into the EU, the Commission is emphasising that more effective integration is vital to ensure both economic growth and social cohesion. In the following, we investigate institutional preconditions for political entrepreneurship in integration policies in the EU.

POLITICAL ENTREPRENEURSHIP AND INTEGRATION IN THE EU

With the refugee crisis of 2015, in parallel with the increasing demographic crisis, calls for the strengthening of the relationship between migration and integration have been emphasised more consistently. Indeed, if effective "integration" is interpreted as the full participation of migrants, *including* refugees, in the economic and social life of host countries, promoting this is considered vital to ensuring both economic growth and social cohesion (EC, 2016c; cf. Beckman, 2011). Whereas

directive, 2009/50/EC). All member states are bound by the directive, except for Denmark, Ireland and the UK, which have opted out.

[6] The *seasonal workers directive*, which governs both housing and working conditions, is temporarily limited to the fact that the seasonal worker may legally stay in a member state between five and nine months. The time limit is, however, member state competence (Council directive, 2014/36/EU).

[7] The *intra-corporate transfer directive* (Council directive, 2014/66/EU). The *recast researcher and students directive* provides for common admission rules as well as residency rules (Council directive, 2016/81).

refugees and labour migrants historically have been categorised separately, both the nature of their migrating, as well as the measures implemented by the host societies to integrate them, tend to become intertwined.

Integration is a contested concept and in the EU member states, due to very different experiences in the level of immigration, a variety of models of integration exist, from the pure assimilationist to the pure multiculturalist.[8] Whatever the model, integration can be defined as the "process of becoming an accepted part of society" (Penninx and Garcés-Mascarenas, 2015). However, and as already emphasised by the Commission in 2005, integration should be a dynamic two-way process between immigrants and the EU citizens (EC, 2005). To facilitate the integration process, certain areas such as employment, education and skills, social inclusion, civic engagement and social cohesion, are considered to be particularly important. In order to address the accentuation of labour market shortages in the EU, in parallel to the high unemployment rate as well as the over-qualification rate of migrants, the focus on the question of how to use migrants' skills in a more efficient and sustainable manner has become prioritised (EC, 2016a). Importantly in this regard, skills in EU parlance is defined broadly as referring to "what a person knows, understands and can do" (EC, 2016a).

In the literature on political entrepreneurship, crises can create windows of opportunities where policy entrepreneurs, by innovative measures, promote formal and informal institutions in order to create favourable conditions for economic growth. However, since the decision-making power, as set out in the Lisbon Treaty (Article 79 [4] TFEU) and within the realm of integration, lies primarily at a member state level, how likely is it that innovative measures are promoted and implemented effectively?

The importance of a more efficient integration of migrants, with the view to meeting EU labour market needs, has long been at the forefront of the Commission's agendas (EC, 2005, 2011, 2014). Already in 2011, the Commission highlighted what was considered to be the five most

---

[8] Whereas France, the Netherlands and the UK are countries of extensive immigration, most countries of Eastern Europe have very little experience of immigration (Lulle and King, 2016: 52). The traditionally assimilationist policy of integrating non-French citizens was questioned after the Paris riots of 2005. The multiculturalist policy is habitually assumed to prevail in Sweden; although it has been put under pressure, its basic premises, as formulated in the early 1970s, seem to have made it considerably resistant in this country (Bengtsson and Borevi, 2015; see also Borevi, 2010).

pressing areas that needed to be addressed in view of strengthening the integration of migrants: first, the low employment rate of migrants, and especially migrant women; second, the rising unemployment rate and the problem of overqualified[9] migrants doing low-skilled work; third, the higher risks of social exclusion among migrants; fourth, the gaps in educational achievement, and finally, yet not the least important, the public attitudes on the lack of integration of migrants (EC, 2011: 3). Thus, the focus on skills as well as on measures to avoid a mismatch of competencies, in order to strengthen the competitiveness and economic growth in the EU member states, has increasingly been accentuated by the Commission. Even though the reference to a more effective integration per se was brief in the European Agenda on Migration,[10] the Commission, however, took note of the importance in strengthening the policies on legal migration and the necessity to attract both students and "other talented and highly-skilled persons" (Lulle and King, 2016: 22; EC, 2015a).

Due to the fact that much of the decision-making is member state competence, as set out in Article 79 (4), TFEU, the leeway of the Commission is undercut and limited to promoting measures and supporting member states in the area of integration (EC, 2016c). The ineffectiveness of the EU legal framework, along with the increased migratory movements, has led the Commission to promote reforms in the area of legal migration. The inefficiency of the *blue card directive* has been particularly problematic, since it has been estimated that, by 2025, nearly half of all vacant jobs will require highly skilled competencies (EC, 2016a). Particularly, there is an increasing labour shortage in professional areas, such as engineering, healthcare and ICT (EC, 2016e). In view of this, and in order to increase competitiveness and facilitate the possibilities of legal migration, in June 2016, the Commission proposed the revision of the *blue card directive* (COM [2016] 378). In addition, and with the aim of strengthening the coherence of the EU legal framework at the same time as supporting member states in improving a more comparable and consistent system for the recognition of qualifications, a

[9] In 2009, the over-qualification rate of third-country nationals was 45 per cent compared to 29 per cent for EU citizens (EC, 2011: 3).

[10] In this agenda, the Commission proposes four pillars to more effectively manage migration: i) to reduce the incentives for illegal migration; ii) to strengthen border management by creating smart borders and the better use of IT-systems, such as the Schengen Information Systems (SIS); iii) to create a more robust Common European Asylum System (CEAS); and finally, iv) to create a more effective policy for legal migration (EC, 2015a).

revision of the European Qualifications Framework has been proposed (COM [2016] 383) (EC, 2016a: 9). Also, and in view of strengthening the coherence of EU internal policies by "simplifying and streamlining the current EU framework" (EC, 2016b: 5), the Commission has launched the *Legal Migration Fitness Check (REFIT)*.[11]

It is clear that the innovative measures of the reformed *blue card* system attempt to respond to the expected demographic crisis of the EU as well as more effectively manage the refugee crisis. Hence, the proposed scope of future *blue card* holders has been extended to include highly skilled refugees as well, on condition that they are already residents in the EU as beneficiaries of international protection and therefore allowed to work according to EU asylum rules and the *qualification directive* (2011/95/EU). Another category that has been introduced in the new revised *blue card* system, in view of facilitating highly skilled mobility intra-EU, is EU citizens. Also, and in order to encourage innovation and entrepreneurship, the revised policy would allow for future *blue card* holders to be self-employed at the same time as they would hold a highly skilled employment position. Additionally, there has been a focus on strengthening the legal rights of both labour migrants and refugees, allowing for both easier access to long-term residence permits and a more flexible system where *blue card* holders would be allowed to reside in several member states (COM (2016) 378).

Another ambitious measure, which also points to the strengthening of the traditionally entrepreneurial role of the Commission, has been to make further investments in entrepreneurship. Zooming in on the importance of creating innovative measures in employment, the Commission has put to the fore the necessity to support entrepreneurship "as a vital channel to foster third country nationals' contribution to economy and society as a whole" (EC, 2016c: 9). In view of addressing the problem of the high rate of migrants being stuck as entrepreneurs in low-skilled and low-income traps, the Commission launched an *EU Guidebook to Promote and Support Migrant Entrepreneurship* (EC, 2016d). As another initiative made in this area, the Directorate General (DG) on Growth launched a call for proposals on "Entrepreneurial capacity-building for

[11] The REFIT is based on five indicators of comparison (relevance, coherence, effectiveness, efficiency and added value) and the REFIT covers the following directives: *family reunifications directive* (2003/86/EC); *long-term residents directive* (2003/109/EC) as amended by directive (2011/51/EU); *EU blue card directive* (2009/50/EC); *single permit directive* (2011/98/EU); *seasonal workers directive* (2014/36/EU); *intra-corporate transfer directive* (2014/66/EU); and the *students and researchers EU directive* (2016/801) (EC, 2016b).

young migrants". The call was explicitly focused on identifying ways to raise awareness of entrepreneurship within migrant communities; for instance, by developing training courses on entrepreneurship and setting up schemes of mentorships. The last focus was on setting up systems of best-practice exchange between actors and organisations in order to more effectively support migrant entrepreneurs (EC, 2016d). Importantly, such measures are considered relevant even though migrants account for a high proportion of entrepreneurs, compared to EU citizens. This is because migrants are expected to encounter difficulties and "fail more due to a lack of information, knowledge and language skills" (EC, 2013: 25).

It is obvious that the revised scheme and the innovative measures introduced by the Commission aim to strengthen the EU legal framework for more effective integration, in parallel to making the EU labour market more attractive and thus more competitive. It is less certain, however, that the reformed system will actually provide better possibilities of integration of highly skilled migrants and refugees on the EU labour market, while also strengthening the intra-EU labour mobility within the area of highly skilled employment. The uncertainty in this regard is hardly surprising, since decisions regulating the implementation of labour market integration programmes are member state competence. Moreover, the uncertainty is also due to the fact that more effective labour market integration, be it in self-employment or in employment, is closely interconnected with skills and competencies. According to the Commission, skills are "a pull factor for investment and a catalyst in the virtuous cycle of job creation and growth" (EC, 2016a: 2). In line with this, the proposal for a reformed European Qualifications Framework with an improved system for the recognition of qualifications is logical and necessary. However, even though many "Member States are facing similar challenges" (EC, 2016c: 3), the national contexts within the EU 28 differ in terms of national interests as well as in economic, judicial and political preconditions. Ultimately, this hampers both more effective coordination and coherence.

Specifically related to the Commission proposal for a revised and more efficient *blue card* in terms of creating a more attractive single EU-wide scheme, it certainly also opens up for more flexibility and adjustment to member states' national variations, such as flexibility in salary thresholds. The flexibility also pertains to membership as such, since the UK, Ireland and Denmark still have "opt-outs" and stand outside of the cooperation (COM [2016] 378). In addition, in terms of attracting highly skilled third-country citizens, many member state governments have introduced national schemes in parallel to the EU *blue card* and these national schemes have, in many cases, proven to be more effective (EC, 2016b). For instance, and in order to facilitate admission and labour market integration, Austria passed legislation for the mentioned group under the "Red-White-Red Card". Another separate initiative is illustrated by the Dutch example, which in 2016 had created a "hybrid entrepreneurship" scheme to facilitate highly skilled migrants and researchers to start their own business in parallel with being employed (EC, 2016b: 5). The launching of entrepreneurial activities for migrants is not exclusive to the Netherlands, however, since a significant number of member states were launching activities to facilitate for migrant entrepreneurs (EC 2016b: 5). Overall, however, regardless of EU-wide or national systems it is concluded that "only 31% of highly-educated migrants to the OECD countries, chose the EU as a destination" (EC 2016e), when compared to other seemingly more attractive destinations, such as the Asian markets. This gloomy reality points to the importance of strengthening EU competitiveness as a way of attracting highly skilled competence, but it may also be a wake-up call for member states to more effectively integrate both labour migrants and refugees who are already residing in the EU.

Particularly in the aftermath of the 2015 refugee crisis, the majority of EU member states introduced labour market integration programmes, aimed at shortening access to employment and education for both labour migrants and refugees. Even though the refugee policy historically has been based on the protection pillar, with increasing mixed migratory movements it becomes increasingly intertwined with labour market integration policies and programmes. This focus was outlined in the Commission Action Plan, which stresses the "full participation and early integration of all third-country nationals, including refugees"[12] (EC, 2016c: 3). The inefficiency of the implementation of integration programmes is, however, blatant since statistics show that even though some 25 per cent of third-country nationals are highly skilled, approximately 75 per cent of the people in this category are "inactive, unemployed or overqualified for their jobs" (EC, 2016a: 10).

The misuse, or the mismatch, of competencies is without doubt a challenge for the majority of EU member states. In terms of skills needed, it is the level of education, the level of command of the host country language and the level of work experience in the host country

---

[12] See European Parliament resolution of 12 April 2016 in connection with the situation in the Mediterranean and the necessity to take a holistic perspective on migration (2015/2095 (INI)).

that are essential in the matching of competencies (Lulle and King, 2016). The matching of competencies puts pressure on the national institutions, responsible for the recognition of foreign qualifications and the validation of skills. It is even more challenging for national authorities, however, to validate skills acquired outside "formal learning institutions" (EC, 2016a: 8). This has increasingly become a problem, especially in the case of refugees who have had to flee their homes without their belongings and so are unable to provide identification, let alone any documentation of qualifications.

To more effectively integrate both labour migrants and refugees also puts pressure on the national educational institutions, particularly in the area of more effective language learning, since command of the host language is reasonably an important key to labour market integration as well as to social cohesion. Furthermore, more effective integration of refugees requires that refugees actually have access to employment. However, as with the differences in overall migration policies, there are also national variations in the refugee policies. For instance, whereas asylum seekers have the right to start working from day one in Latvia and in Sweden, other EU member states, for instance Lithuania and Ireland, do not provide such opportunities for refugees during the asylum application period (Constant and Zimmermann, 2016: 6).

The lack of coordination and lack of coherence between EU member states can also be explained from huge discrepancies in intra-EU mobility. This has been a reality ever since the big-bang enlargement in 2004 with the EU15 having attracted a labour force from the new member states. This has created a situation of intra-EU competition between national labour markets, which in turn has created a brain-drain *problematique*, addressed recently by the Commission as something that needs to be met (EC, 2016a). Clearly, the Commission is keen to promote innovative measures and reformed policies for attracting highly skilled third-country nationals, while attempting to create a more sustainable system of the distribution of intra-EU competence. At the same time, however, implementation of integrative measures is EU Member State competence and thus carried out on the national, regional and local levels within the 28 different national contexts, wherein policymakers and bureaucrats are facing different challenges. For instance, in 2016, a few member states[13] had actively implemented measures in order to mitigate

[13] Belgium, Germany, France, Hungary, Italy and Luxembourg had implemented different measures in order to actively work to reduce brain-drain within the EU (EC, 2016b).

brain-drain. For instance, Hungary had introduced a programme to support the return of foreign students back to their home country after their study visit abroad (EC, 2016b).

It is not very far-fetched to assume that the question of success or failure in integrating third-country nationals in the EU member states is related to their different preconditions in terms of labour shortages, but also to the resilience of national welfare institutions in their support of both labour migrants and refugees. This also means that the maker or breaker of the integrative measures is closely linked to the time factor, namely the more rapidly third-country nationals can become net contributors to the host society, the better. It is also a question of strengthening the coordination between different levels of authority. Already in 2011, this was put to the fore when the Commission emphasised that "effective integration can only be realised in partnership between the whole range of stakeholders such as the European institutions, Member States and national, regional and local actors" (EC, 2011: 8). In the Skills Agenda of 2016, the Commission had pointed out that in their efforts to assist member states in reforming the national institutions, it would also become necessary to "trigger a change of mindsets in both individuals and organisations" (EC, 2016a: 3). As far as the change of individuals' mindsets, this was already raised in 2011 when the Commission identified the importance of public attitudes as one of the most pressing areas (EC, 2011: 3). In the next section, we make of use of survey data in an attempt to investigate attitudes that may affect the prospects of integration in European countries.

PROSPECTS OF INTEGRATION – VIEWPOINTS OF EUROPEAN RESIDENTS

In the light of officially stated ambitions at the EU level concerning migrant integration, we argue that there are good reasons to also pay attention to European citizens' viewpoints in this respect. For one thing, integration is hardly accomplished purely from above. Although we, in this chapter (along with the other contributions to this volume), highlight favourable conditions, potentially initiated through political entrepreneurship, the actual level of integration in a given society is arguably a net result of myriad grass-roots level social interactions (cf. Beckman, 2011).

Utilising comprehensive data from the European Social Survey (ESS),[14] we study integration-related public attitudes, in the light of which political entrepreneurship initiatives may be discussed. More precisely, this source of information allowed us to use data from 20 countries (including the European yet non-EU countries of Norway and Switzerland, but excluding Israel).

We begin by studying cross-country differences in what we may call welcoming attitudes towards migrants. Specifically, to explore the willingness to accept immigration even if, at least in the short term, it may be associated with an economic burden for the host country, we use a survey question on acceptance of migrants from "poorer countries outside Europe". Although such a category may indeed be heterogeneous, it is reasonable to assume that the question directs respondents to visualise refugees from war and persecution as well as migrants that, primarily for reasons of poverty, are seeking a better life in Europe.

Figure 9.1 shows the share of respondents, in each country, that may be regarded as positive rather than negative, when it comes to the willingness to welcome migrants from less economically prosperous parts of the world. The bars in the chart correspond to the share declaring that one's country should "allow many to come and live here" or, at least, "allow some" (rather, that is, than allowing just "a few" or "none"). Although the citizens' opinions in this respect seem to be rather similar in a number of central and western European countries, a spatial variation is clearly also discernible. In Sweden, which in this comparison stands out as a country with strikingly positive attitudes towards migrants from poor countries, nearly nine out of ten respondents (or 87 per cent) report that the country to some extent should allow such immigration.

At the other end of the bar chart, however, we may note that the shares between more and less welcoming attitudes are almost reversed in Hungary, where only a little more than one in ten respondents (or 12.7 per cent, more precisely) declare that at least some non-European

---

[14] The ESS is a biennial cross-national survey of attitudes, beliefs and patterns of behaviour, based on representative samples of the adult populations in European (along with a few other) countries, and conducted by means of face-to-face interviews. Specifically, the analyses in this section are based on ESS Round 7, conducted primarily in 2014 and provide the most recently available data. This version of the survey proved to be very well suited for our purposes, since it included a so-called rotating module, through which respondents were asked an additional set of questions on issues of migration and integration. A detailed documentation of sampling procedures and response rates is available online at the ESS website: www.europeansocialsurvey.org.

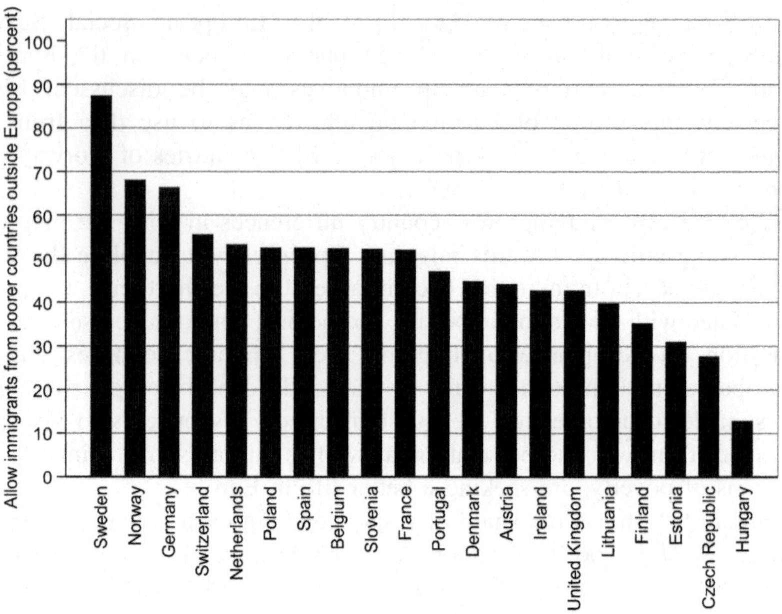

Figure 9.1 Cross-national variations in welcoming attitudes

migrants from poor countries should be allowed. Comparatively less welcoming attitudes also seem to be found in some other eastern European countries and in Finland. At the same time, however, no clear geographic pattern emerges in the graph. For instance, the residents of an eastern European country such as Poland seem to be prepared to welcome refugees at least to the same degree as the residents in Spain (and to a notably higher extent compared to the population in, for example, Austria).

Why, then, do respondents in some countries declare a significantly more generous standpoint on the reception of immigrants than the respondents in other countries? Intuitively, and indeed in harmony with the argument of many scholarly studies (cf. Hainmueller and Hiscox, 2010), one would suspect economic concerns to be an important part of the explanation. In countries facing economic recession and troublingly high levels of unemployment, native citizens may fear that immigration—particularly from far less prosperous parts of the world—will result in increased pressures on the welfare state and harmful labour market competition. Hence, anti-immigrant sentiments may develop as a result of quite rational (although, perhaps not explicitly performed) cost–benefit calculations among citizens being worried about their own economic prospects and future standard of living.[15]

Considering the overall picture, however, it is safe to say that no obvious relationship seems to exist between macroeconomic instability and the propensity to report welcoming attitudes. Relating the differences in Figure 9.1 to official economic statistics, it turns out that unemployment rates poorly predict the stated degree of hospitality towards migrants from poorer countries. According to OECD (2014) compilations, focusing on data from approximately a year before the ESS fieldwork, the rate of unemployment was, for example, significantly higher in Sweden than in Norway (8 per cent vs. 3.5 per cent, respectively), whereas the graph in Figure 9.1 suggests that the Norwegians, compared to the Swedes, clearly report less welcoming attitudes. As discussed elsewhere in this volume (see Chapter 1), the global financial crisis had a particularly severe impact on several southern European countries, including Spain and Portugal, suffering, then, from a prolonged period of very high unemployment rates. Still, as the graph makes clear, the countries representing southern Europe in this comparative analysis are rather found in the middle of the range, in terms of welcoming attitudes.[16]

Objective macroeconomic performance notwithstanding, it may of course be that inhabitants of some countries tend to make more pessimistic assessments when it comes to potential consequences of immigration. Exploring subjective forecasts of this kind, still focusing on economic conditions, we based an additive index on three survey questions aimed to tap respondents' evaluations of immigration-related economic influences in the respective countries (see note to Figure 9.2).

Once again, Figure 9.2 sorts the countries according to descending scores, this time in terms of average evaluations of how immigration influences the economic state of affairs. Yet, although the relative placement of countries is by no means identical to the one in Figure 9.1,

---

[15] Certainly, there are good reasons to assume significant differences in the degree of economic anxiety within a population, depending on the sense (whether justified or not) of socioeconomic vulnerability in various groups in society. We will return to this issue below, as we in the following analysis try to simultaneously study cross-national differences and the influence of individual-level variables on migration-related attitudes.

[16] In comparison with the seemingly most immigrant-sceptical population of Hungary, it may be noted that the unemployment rate in Spain was far more than twice as high: 26.1 per cent in the former case vs. 10.2 per cent in the latter (OECD, 2014).

some similarities are clearly observable. It is perhaps not too surprising that more welcoming attitudes towards immigrants seem to be associated with more positive economic evaluations of immigration, which—echoing the rank order of Figure 9.1—appear to be made considerably more often in Sweden, Norway and Germany than in the Czech Republic and Hungary. Still, it should be emphasised that survey questions on which the evaluation index is based do not restrict respondents to regard only migration from poor countries (assumingly often interpreted as the influx of asylum seekers). Hence, the judgement should, in this case, rather be based on how one interprets the net economic costs and benefits from all kinds of immigration in the home country.

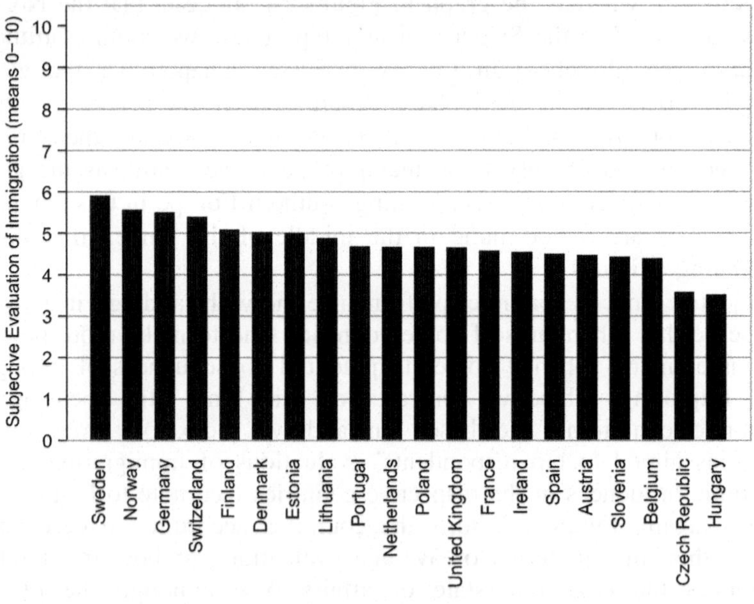

Note: The SEI index is based on the three ESS questions: (1) "Would you say it is generally bad or good for [country]'s economy that people come to live here from other countries?"; (2) "Would you say that people who come to live here generally take jobs away from workers in [country], or generally help to create new jobs?"; and (3) "Most people who come to live here work and pay taxes. They also use health and welfare services. On balance, do you think people who come here take out more than they put in or put in more than they take out?" Responses were given on 0–10 scales, anchored in: 0 = "bad for the economy" vs. 10 = "good for the economy"; 0 = "take jobs away" vs. 10 = "create new jobs"; and 0 = "Generally take out more" vs. "Generally put in more", respectively. The additive index is finally rescaled to, again, range from 0 to 10.

Figure 9.2 Cross-national variations in subjective evaluation of immigration (SEI)

It would hardly be surprising to find a correlation between, on the one hand, opinions concerning the appropriate level of immigration in a given society and, on the other, beliefs regarding how immigration influences preconditions for economic growth and welfare state redistribution. People being convinced that immigration will result in a net cost, perhaps ultimately leading to macroeconomic difficulties, are probably more likely to be reluctant to accept immigration-friendly public policies, in particular when it comes to the reception of refugees.

However, we will continue to investigate differences in subjective evaluation of immigration, along with the possibility that pessimism in this respect may be nurtured not only by economically based, but also culturally based anxiety (cf. Sides and Citrin, 2007; Weldon 2006). Moreover, we will explore to what extent the pattern of differences in public opinion, suggested in the graphs reported above, may be related to cross-country institutional differences. In the light of aforementioned reasoning, there exists at least no straightforward relationship between the current economic state of affairs and opinions on immigration.[17] At the same time, though, we know that in spite of supranational agreements on the importance of robust and efficient immigration and integration policies, considerable institutional variations in regulations prevail within the EU, as well as among European non-EU member states.

The latter mentioned differences are systematically revealed in the highly ambitious compilation of policy information known as the Migrant Integration Policy Index (MIPEX), the latest edition of which (2015) fits quite nicely with the ESS data (Huddleston et al., 2015). Based on expert consultations, the MIPEX assigns an overall score for each of the countries included in the data set (all EU member states along with several other European and OECD states, in total 38 countries) indicating to what extent present-day laws and policies meet the "highest standards" in terms of equal rights, responsibilities and opportunities for residents regardless of origin. The overall score, on a scale 0–100, is determined from grades given in the analysis of eight policy areas of integration: labour market mobility, education of children, political participation, family reunion, access to nationality, health, permanent residence and anti-discrimination (each of these areas being evaluated through an

[17] It is worth mentioning that an analogous conclusion has been put forward in research concerning electoral support for xenophobic political parties, which by definition take a highly critical stance on immigration-related issues and thus may channel popular discontent in this respect (cf. Strömblad and Malmberg, 2016; Arzheimer, 2009).

extensive set of separate indicators). Hence, a country in which immigrants, by means of regulation, for instance, enjoy better possibilities to enter the labour market and a more comprehensive judicial protection from discrimination, would score higher than a country in which the reverse is true.[18] Similarly, liberal rules for family reunification and inclusive laws concerning naturalisation of non-citizens would also render a higher MIPEX score. Following Weldon (2006), it seems reasonable that cross-national institutional differences of this kind may be reflected, also more subtly, in discourse climate and attitude formation within the general public.

In an attempt to dig further into the public opinion differences, and simultaneously assess the possible influences of nationally governed integration policies, we utilised MIPEX scores as a contextual-level variable in the ESS data set. Specifying, moreover, a set of reasonable individual-level variables in a series of multiple regression analyses, we end up with the result summarised in Table 9.1.

This table displays the estimated relationships between each of the specified independent variables and the SEI index, introduced in Figure 9.2.[19] More precisely, three models are specified, thus providing some empirical underpinnings to discuss possible internal relationships as well. Studying the estimated coefficient for the MIPEX score variable in Model 1, we note that the result suggests a positive relationship. Taking into account variation in the set of specified individual-level variables, the countries with more "generous" integration policies tend to have a citizenry that is more optimistic concerning the economic impact of immigration. Indeed, the old rule that correlation does not imply causation is important to keep in mind here. Given the cross-section feature of the data, we may not conclude that institutional design in fact influences public opinion. It might also be the other way around in the developed democracies in this study—in countries where people tend to predict that immigration will have a positive impact on the economy, they may choose to elect policymakers who declare willingness to introduce more affirmative regulations for newcomers in the country.

---

[18] It is beyond our scope in this chapter, to also include an analysis on the actual efficiency of various sets of integration policies. For a critical appraisal, however, see Koopmans, 2010.

[19] The standard errors of the reported regression coefficients are adjusted for (country-level) cluster correlation. As a robustness test, we also replicated the analyses by estimating corresponding multi-level random intercept models, the results from which proved to be virtually identical to those reported in Table 9.1.

Table 9.1 Predicting subjective evaluation of immigration, contextual and individual-level variables

	Model 1	Model 2	Model 3
MIPEX (0–100)	.025*	.017	.022*
Migrant (yes = 1; O otherwise)	.872***	.901***	.867***
Labour market position (Employed = ref.)	.00	.00	.00
Unemployed/Early retirement	–.510***	–.511***	–.540***
Pensioner	.017	.0.51	.007
Housework/Other	–.162**	–.132**	–.161**
Education (years full time)	.099***	.090***	.092***
Female (yes = 1; 0 otherwise)	–.151**	–.182***	–.159**
Age (years)	–.002	.000	.001
Skills qualification (0–10)		–.155***	
Cultural qualification (0–10)			–.161***
Constant	2.22	3.68	3.50
N	33 359	33 359	33 359
R^2	.09	.13	.14

Statistical significance: *** $p < .001$ ** $p < .01$ * $p < .05$

Note: Entries are ordinary least-squares (OLS) estimates. The dependent variable runs from 0 (maximum negative evaluation of economic consequences of immigration) to 10 (maximum positive evaluation of economic consequences of immigration). See Appendix for further information regarding coding and index construction.

Bearing this reservation in mind, the estimated MIPEX effect does appear to be substantial, in view of the quite extensive control for demographic and socioeconomic variations captured by the individual-level variables. Given the 0–100 MIPEX scale, a maximum improvement in this regard would imply an extra 2.5 points in the SEI index, all else being equal (cf. note to Figure 9.2). Yet such a massive dissimilarity is not observable among the countries reviewed for the MIPEX scoring; the variation is still considerable, with values ranging from 37 (Lithuania) to 78 (Sweden).

As for the demographic and socioeconomic control variables (see Appendix for further details and coding), we note that while age does not seem to affect the subjective evaluation of immigration, men and people of higher education tend be more optimistic. Furthermore, substantial differences in this respect seem to be related to labour market position. Unemployed respondents, or those on early retirement due to illness or disability, tend to make significantly more pessimistic scenarios when it comes to macroeconomic consequences of immigration.

As indicated in the results reported in the table, we also try to control for the uneven distribution of people who already have migrated to the countries of inquiry. Hence, a positive MIPEX effect should not be a spurious by-product of population composition (as far as this is captured by an admittedly crude dichotomous division of native-born and foreign-born). Unsurprisingly, though indicating that the control is worthwhile, we note that people who at some point have migrated to one of the European countries, tend to place themselves almost one unit higher (or 10 per cent higher) on the SEI index in comparison with native respondents, irrespective of other demographic and socioeconomic characteristics.

In the remaining Models 2 and 3 of Table 9.1, we introduce two more attitudinal variables, aiming to capture differences in views concerning reasonable demands on immigrants. Specifically, "skills qualification" is based on three survey questions regarding the importance of potential immigrants' level of education, ability to speak the official host country language, and whether she or he has the work skills needed in the host country. In harmony with the response scales of the original items, the index variable ranges from 0 to 10. A high value on this scale suggests that the respondent finds that such skills should be deemed as important when authorities regulate immigration.

The parallel "cultural qualification" variable (which is entered in Model 3) aims to capture also more subtle demands, aside from instrumental abilities in terms of the skills mentioned above. This measure is based on a question of how important it should be regarded that a potential immigrant is "committed to the way of life" in the host country. The corresponding 0–10 scale was employed in this case as well.

At first, the results from the analyses based on Models 2 and 3 appear very similar. As for the relationships between the new qualification variables and the SEI index, we note that requests for higher qualifications of would-be immigrants tend to be associated with a more pessimistic economic evaluation of immigration at large. Hence, all else being equal (and irrespective of current integration policies as reflected in a given MIPEX score), people who consider it to be important that future immigrants are prepared to adjust culturally to the new country, also tend to paint a dark picture of the economic impact of immigration.

Interestingly, however, there is also a substantial difference between the Models 2 and 3 results. Focusing on the MIPEX effect once more, we note that it is considerably reduced (by approximately one-third) and no longer statistically significant in Model 2, when accounting for different viewpoints on the importance of immigrants' skills. A possible, and arguably reasonable, causal inference may in this case be that residents of countries with generous integration policies tend to develop less restrictive instrumental demands on immigrants; that is, the right of legal entry into the country should not depend on the likely economic productivity of the migrant.

In contrast, as suggested by the Model 3 estimation results, a similar story does not hold for opinion differences in demands concerning cultural qualification. In this case, the MIPEX effect is largely unaffected, in comparison with Model 1. Hence, cross-national differences in integration policies do not seem to be associated with views on the importance of the cultural adaption of future immigrants. A reasonable conclusion is, then, that quite polarised opinions on this matter exist in the European countries—regardless of any officially declared integration policies.

CONCLUSION

In the policy domains of migration and integration, it is clear that the 2015 refugee crisis has been a catalyst for innovative measures where the Commission has taken its traditionally entrepreneurial role further, promoting measures to assist member states in their efforts to improve and speed up the integration of labour migrants and refugees in Europe. The very essence of the Commission as an institution is entrepreneurial, one may argue, since it has policy initiating power, and as such the Commission "performs an important agenda-setting role" (Egeberg, 2013: 130). The measures taken by the Commission are regarded as necessary from the perspective of labour market considerations, which in turn are believed to be dependent on social cohesion considerations. Not least important, the measures are also viewed as significant for the sake of countering the nationalistic upheavals, arguably being a threat not only to social peace in the EU member states but ultimately to the very survival of the EU.

However, as the division of competencies still means that decisions on the implementation of integration measures primarily lie on the member state level, the leeway of the Commission remains limited. Furthermore, since the 2015 refugee crisis, the political role of member state governments also seems to have been accentuated precisely when it comes to issues concerning migration and integration. A collective experience of increased pressure seems to be able to trigger retraction rather than coordination. This is reasonably hampering for innovative measures aimed at strengthening both integration and growth. True, a majority of member states has introduced integration programmes with the aim of shortening the access to employment and education for labour migrants and refugees. At the same time, though, such labour market integration programmes tend to have shortcomings that need to be addressed. For one thing, national and EU institutions need to become better equipped, in order to accomplish an effective recognition of qualifications and validation of skills. Moreover, there is clearly a need to invest further in language courses, to prevent the misuse of competencies. Moving from the institutional to the citizen level, the need for a change in mindsets has been pointed out as well. Considering the substantial attitudinal differences, suggested by our results from the survey data analyses in this chapter, however, integration from bottom-up might be at least as tricky to encourage as integration from top-down. It may be that the average level of welcoming attitudes—and perhaps also the average level of positive evaluations of immigration—has decreased in the aftermath of the 2015 refugee crisis in previously more optimistic countries, given that our analyses were based on pre-crisis survey data. In this case, it may also be true that European citizens, although they tend to be more in agreement when it comes to preconditions for integration, become more detached from institutionally driven promotion of integration.

REFERENCES

Arzheimer, K. (2009). "Contextual factors and the extreme right vote in Western Europe, 1980–2002", *American Journal of Political Science* 53: 259–275.

Beckman, L. (2011). *Den rimliga integrationen*. Stockholm: Dialogos.

Bengtsson, B. and K. Borevi (2015). "Mångfaldens vägskäl—om integrationspolitikens stigberoende", in B. Bengtsson, G. Myrberg and R. Andersson (eds) *Mångfaldens dilemman*. Medborgarskap och integrationspolitik. Malmö: Gleerups.

Borevi, K. (2010). "Dimensions of citizenship: European integration policies from a Scandinavian perspective", in B. Bengtsson, P. Strömblad and A.-H.

Bay (eds) *Diversity, Inclusion and Citizenship in Scandinavia.* Newcastle upon Tyne: Cambridge Scholars Publishing.
Carmel, E. and R. Paul (2013). "Complex stratification: understanding European Union governance of migrant rights", *Regions and Cohesion* 3(3): 56–85.
Collett, E. (2014). "Future policy development on immigration and asylum: understanding the challenge", *Migration Policy Institute Europe*, Policy Brief Series, No. 4.
Constant, A. F. and K. F. Zimmermann (2016). *Towards a New European Refugee Policy that Works, CESifo DICE Report, 4/2016.*
Council of the European Union (2012). *Council conclusions on a common framework for genuine and practical solidarity towards Member States facing particular pressures on their asylum systems, including through mixed migration flows.* Brussels, 8 March.
Council directive 2003/86/EC, Family reunification directive, 22 September 2003.
Council directive 2009/50/EC, Blue card directive, 25 May 2009.
Council directive 2011/51/EU, Amended long-term residents directive, 11 May 2011.
Council directive 2011/98/EU, Single permit directive, 13 December 2011.
Council directive 2013/32/EU, Asylum procedures directive, 26 June 2013.
Council directive 2013/33/EU, Reception conditions directive, 26 June 2013.
Council directive 2014/36/EU, Seasonal workers directive, 26 February 2014.
Council directive 2014/66/EU, Intra-corporate transferees directive, 15 May 2014.
Council directive 2016/801/EU, Recast students and researchers directive, 11 May 2016.
Egeberg, M. (2013). "The European Commission", in M. Cini and N. Pérez-Solórzano Borragán (eds) *European Union Politics*. Oxford: Oxford University Press.
European Commission (2005). *A Common Agenda for Integration Framework for the Integration of Third-Country Nationals in the European Union.* Brussels: COM(2005) 389 final. NY.
European Commission (2011). *European Agenda for the Integration of Third-Country Nationals.* Brussels: COM(2011) 455 final.
European Commission (2013). *Entrepreneurship 2020 Action Plan. Reigniting the Entrepreneurial Spirit in Europe.* Brussels: COM(2012) 795 final.
European Commission (2014). *An Open and Secure Europe: Making it Happen.* Brussels: COM(2014) 154 final. NY.
European Commission (2015a). *A European Agenda on Migration.* Brussels: COM(2015) 240 final.
European Commission (2015b). "The 2015 Ageing Report. Economic and budgetary projections for the 28 EU Member States (2013–2060)", in *European Economy* 3/2015. Luxembourg: Publications Office of the European Union.
European Commission (2016a). *A New Skills Agenda for Europe. Working Together to Strengthen Human Capital, Employability and Competitiveness.* Brussels: COM(2016) 381 final.

European Commission (2016b). *2016 Annual Report on Migration and Asylum*, European Migration Network. Brussels, 25 April 2017.
European Commission (2016c). *Action Plan on the Integration of Third Country Nationals. Brussels*: COM(2016) 377 final.
European Commission (2016d). *Evaluation and Analysis of Good Practices in Promoting and Supporting Migrant Entrepreneurship*. Guide book. Brussels, 15 September 2016.
European Commission (2016e). *Press Release on Reforming the Blue Card Directive*.
European Parliament resolution 2015/2095 (INI), 12 April 2016.
Hainmueller, J. and M. J. Hiscox (2010). "Attitudes toward highly skilled and low-skilled immigration: evidence from a survey experiment", *American Political Science Review* 104: 61–84.
Huddleston, T., Ö. Bilgili, A.-L. Joki and Z. Vankova (2015). *Migrant Integration Policy Index 2015*. Barcelona/Brussels: Barcelona Center for International Affairs and Migration Policy Group.
Koopmans, R. (2010). "Trade-offs between equality and difference: immigrant integration, multiculturalism and the welfare state in cross-national perspective", *Journal of Ethnic and Migration Studies* 36: 1–26.
Lulle, A. and R. King (2016). *Research on Migration: Facing Realities and Maximising Opportunities: A Policy Review*. Publications Office of the European Union: Luxembourg.
Nugent, N. (2010). *The Government and Politics of the European Union*. Basingstoke: Palgrave Macmillan.
OECD (2014). *OECD Employment Outlook 2014*. OECD publishing, accessed 9 March 2018 at http://dx.doi.org/10.1787/empl_outlook-2014-en.
Penninx, R. and B. Garcés-Mascarenas (eds) (2015). "The concept of integration: towards an analytical and policy framework", in R. Penninx and B. Garcés-Mascarenas (eds) *Integration of Migrants into What? Integration Processes and Policies in Europe*. Cham: Springer.
Sides, J. and J. Citrin (2007). "European opinion about immigration: the role of identities, interests and information", *British Journal of Political Science* 37: 477–504.
Strömblad, P. and B. Malmberg (2016). "Ethnic segregation and xenophobic party preference: exploring the influence of the presence of visible minorities on local electoral support for the Sweden Democrats", *Journal of Urban Affairs* 38: 530–545.
Ucarer, E. M. (2013). "The area of freedom, security and justice", in M. Cini and N. Pérez-Solórzano Borragán (eds) *European Union Politics*. Oxford: Oxford University Press.
Weldon, S. A. (2006). "The institutional context of tolerance for ethnic minorities: a comparative, multilevel analysis of Western Europe", *American Journal of Political Science* 50: 331–349.
Zimmermann, K. (2017). "Refugee and migrant labour market integration: Europe in need of a new policy agenda", in R. Bauböck and M. Tripkovic (eds) *The Integration of Migrants and Refugees. An EUI Forum on Migration, Citizenship and Demography*. Firenze, Italy: Robert Schuman Centre for Advanced Studies.

APPENDIX

The following variables, based on information from the European Social Survey, round 7, are utilised in the empirical analyses.

Subjective Evaluation of Immigration (SEI)

SEI is the dependent variable in the estimated regression models. The SEI is an additive index based on three survey questions: (1) "Would you say it is generally bad or good for [country]'s economy that people come to live here from other countries?"; (2) "Would you say that people who come to live here generally take jobs away from workers in [country], or generally help to create new jobs?"; and (3) "Most people who come to live here work and pay taxes. They also use health and welfare services. On balance, do you think people who come here take out more than they put in or put in more than they take out?" Responses were given using equivalent 11-point scales, anchored in: 0 = "Bad for the economy" vs. 10 = "Good for the economy"; 0 = "Take jobs away" vs. 10 = "Create new jobs"; and 0 = "Generally take out more" vs. "Generally put in more", respectively. The additive index is finally rescaled to, again, range from 0 to 10.

Explanatory and control variables

Skills qualification

An additive index based on three survey questions, with the common introduction: "Please tell me how important you think each of these things should be in deciding whether someone born, brought up and living outside [country] should be able to come and live here [...], how important should it be for them to..." (1) "...have good educational qualifications?"; (2) "...be able to speak [country's official language(s)]"?, and (3) "...have work skills that [country] needs?". Responses were in each case given using an 11-point scale, anchored in 0 = "Extremely unimportant" vs. 10 = "Extremely important". The additive index is finally rescaled to, again, range from 0 to 10.

Cultural qualification

Collected from the same part of the survey, with the same introduction as the questions utilised for "Skills qualification", this variable is based on the question: “How important should it be for them to be committed to the way of life in [country]?” Responses were thus also in this case given using an 11-point scale, anchored in 0 = “Extremely unimportant” vs. 10 = “Extremely important”.

Migrant

A dichotomus variable based on the question “Were you born in [country]?” Respondents answering “yes” are classified as migrants.

Labour market position

A set of dummy variables based on (ESS administrated) post-coded classification of respondents’ reports on main activity “in the last 7 days”, according to:

– Employed, represents the answers “In paid work (or away temporarily) (employee, self-employed, working for your family business)”, or “In education, even if on vacation (not paid for by employer)”, or “In community or military service”;

– Unemployed/Early retirement, represents the answers “Unemployed and actively looking for a job”, or “Unemployed, wanting a job but not actively looking for a job”, or “Permanently sick or disabled”;

– Pensioner, represents the answer “Retired”;

– Housework/other, represents the answers “Doing housework, looking after children or other persons”, or “Other”.

Education

A continuous variable, based on the survey question “About how many years of education have you completed, whether full-time or part-time? Please report these in full-time equivalents and include compulsory years of schooling.”

Female

A dichotomous variable based on interviewer coded sex of respondent.

Age

A continuous variable, calculated from respondents' reports regarding year of birth.

10. Entrepreneurship in times of crisis: a resilience perspective on the Greek wine sector

Evangelia Petridou, Maria Alebaki and Marie-Louise von Bergmann-Winberg

INTRODUCTION

In contemporary, diverse economies, entrepreneurship has been recognized as a catalyst towards growth and economic development. The term is elastic and its interdisciplinary roots underpin the diversity of the scholarship in entrepreneurship. Concomitantly, the research on political entrepreneurship has also attracted considerable scholarly attention in recent decades (for a comprehensive review see Petridou, 2017; Petridou et al., 2015).

This edited volume adopts a narrow view on political entrepreneurship, taking "an actor and structure perspective by focusing on politicians/public servants/bureaucrats/institutions within the publicly funded sector that with innovative approaches encourage entrepreneurship/business and where the goal is, in this particularly study, growth and employment" (see Chapter 1 in this volume). The focus is on institutions and actors who work towards policies aimed at fostering market entrepreneurship in EU countries in light of the recent crisis. Crises and the management of crises have attracted significant attention amongst academics and practitioners for several decades. The altering nature of social conditions, the decrease of an actor's power and the eventual emergence of others at the international level as well as the increasing complexity of domestic politics in an interdependent system have necessitated a constant evolution in theorizing crises, their causes, evolution, and management. This scholarly attention has engendered research in adjacent concepts, such as resilience.

The concepts of resilience and entrepreneurship have potential interlocking theoretical points as noted already by Miles and Petridou (2015) and Williams et al. (2013). However, the theoretical and analytical interconnections between political entrepreneurship and resilience and the impact these might have on the resilience of firms remain under-researched and opaque. The aim of this chapter is to investigate the interconnections between political entrepreneurship and resilience with a focus on the ways that politically entrepreneurial strategies might promote resilience, especially in times of crisis. In particular, we employ a qualitative research design in order to empirically investigate the wine sector in Greece as an example of an emerging sector that has proved particularly resilient despite the adverse performance conditions caused by the economic crisis in the Eurozone. The research questions that guided this study are the following:

1. In what ways has the crisis impinged on wineries and how resilient was the Greek wine sector in the face of the economic meltdown?
2. Who was affected the most and which (if any) were the sources of resilience?
3. Which strategies did the wineries mainly use in coping with the challenges associated with the crisis and what was the link between resilience and political entrepreneurship within this framework?

Further to this introduction, the chapter is structured into six sections each dealing with: (i) the relationship between resilience and political entrepreneurship; (ii) a history of the EU Agricultural Policy with an emphasis on common wine policy; (iii) the economic crisis and its impacts on the Greek wine sector; (iv) extroversion as a resilience strategy; (v) the role of networks, and (vi) concluding comments.

RESILIENCE AND POLITICAL ENTREPRENEURSHIP

Though the research on resilience is vast and growing, Miles and Petridou (2015) (based on McAslan, 2010), posit that resilience is generally understood to include the ability to bounce back from a jarring extraordinary instance (see, for example, Holling, 1973; Wildavsky, 1988); the ability to be prepared to handle extraordinary events, potentially causing major discontinuity (see, for example, Bhamra et al., 2011); the ability to adapt to a new and arduous environment (see, for example, Davoudi, 2012); perseverance and will to survive (see, for example, Norris et al., 2008), and a willingness of community members to mobilize for a common cause (Linell, 2014).

In this theoretical analysis, we privilege agency, as opposed to structure, as we seek to understand the mechanisms through which the former contributes to a resilient system. The economic crisis plaguing Greece for the last decade, or rather its long aftermath, provides the opportune space for the emergence of entrepreneurial action (Miles and Petridou, 2015). Crises, providing opportunities in the midst of disasters (Dror, 1993), "contribute to the loosening of institutional rigidities and organizational interests" (Petridou and Sparf, 2017; see also Cohen et al., 2006; Kingdon, 1984/2003). This in practice may result in the acceptance of actions that would not have been considered during more stable periods. They contribute to an environment where entrepreneurial agents may bring their ideas before a larger and, more than usually, attentive public, forcing the leadership to take action by rendering inaction costly for politicians (Cohen et al., 2006; Donnelly and Hogan, 2012; Hogan and Feeney, 2012; Kingdon, 1984/2003).

In this chapter, we take an instrumental view of political entrepreneurship as a means of achieving resilience. In addition to the definition posited above and generally speaking, we view resilience as "the capacity to cope with unanticipated dangers after they have become manifest" (Wildavsky, 1988). Early scholarship on the resilience concept theorized that a resilient system "bounced back" (see, for example, Wildavsky, 1988), however Boin et al., (2005) point out that returning to an earlier state is not only unrealistic, but also not desirable as the internal triggers that led to the crisis to begin with would still be present. Thus, resilient systems are able to "bounce forward" (Davoudi, 2012). The concept of resilience, beyond the early notions of it being a strategy towards safety (Wildavsky, 1988), is rather a desired state of affairs which, much like sustainable development, is sort of a "guiding fiction" (McCool and Moisey, 2001) and not necessarily an achievable societal equilibrium. Indeed, resilience is another way of conceptualizing change (Miles and Petridou, 2015). The concept of change is integral in political entrepreneurship (Petridou, 2017).

We thus investigate concepts common to both political entrepreneurship and resilience and we use the tools of the former as a strategy towards the latter. Wildavsky (1988) quite clearly called for entrepreneurs to act in order to promote resilience. He envisioned entrepreneurs as anticipators of unknown dangers, creative enough to construct future scenarios and act upon them. Creativity is a core concept of (political) entrepreneurship and a tool that may promote resilience in imagining possible futures. These entrepreneurs must also bear the cost for the implementation of any of these scenarios and for attempting to change a policy, an institution, or a rule in order to be prepared for an eventuality or to combat a malaise that has already taken place. Moreover, political entrepreneurs embrace risk rather than avoid it and use it for creating new alternatives and for gains, the latter stemming from successfully effecting change and in this case for promoting resilience.

EU AGRICULTURAL POLICY

The Common Agricultural Policy (CAP) is one of the cornerstones of EU policy, accounting for 39 per cent of the total EU budget for the period 2010–2014 (Gaeta and Corsivoni, 2014). The CAP came into force in 1962, after the definition of the general objectives of a CAP already present in the Treaty of Rome in 1957. Three major principles were established: market unity, community preference and financial solidarity. The six member states had different intervention principles in their respective agricultural sectors in terms of production, organization of farming and maintaining of prices. Article 39 of the Treaty of Rome outlines the objectives of the CAP, including increasing productivity through modernization of equipment, optimally utilizing factors of production, market stabilization, a better living standard for farmers and reasonable prices for consumers (Gaeta and Corsivoni, 2014). According to Lowe et al. (2010), despite wide-ranging criticism of agricultural policy, especially within Western industrialized countries, new frameworks of justification are emerging and new hybrid policy fields have been established to tackle some of the externalities of agricultural support. Having said that, institutional frameworks are proving slower to change. This is partly due to the fact that institutional change requires coordinated action across different levels of governance. The authors point out that previously marginalized environmental concerns have successfully gained entrance to agricultural policy networks, while the intersection of trade liberalization and rural diversification has undermined the dominance of the productivist mindset in government. This gives rise to a plurality of policy actors and actions, which defy the conventional categories of agricultural policy, calling for changing frameworks of the polity of agriculture (Lowe et al., 2010)

A first implementation was realized through the Mansholt Plan in 1960, based on a two-pronged approach: improving the agricultural infrastructure and regulating prices so the disparities between member countries would be alleviated. The first agricultural products to be covered under the CAP were cereals, sugar, dairy products, beef, poultry, eggs, fruits and vegetables, and wine. The years between 1973 and 1985 saw increases in expenditure and the build-up of great surplus, so reforms in the 1980s attempted to reconcile demand and supply (Gaeta and Corsivoni, 2014).

Recent reforms have followed traditional lines with diminishing production and subsidies, though not showing any real innovative or entrepreneurial characteristics. Given the long chain of formal decision-making, the question that emerges is whether it is possible to find political entrepreneurs amongst the EU officials, or amongst the national, regional or local officials, who might open up space for entrepreneurial action. Some voices called for change from below, in accordance with the principle of subsidiarity. For example, Harvey (2006) found the historical legacy of mandatory CAP spending, exclusively financed from the EU budget, to be no longer legitimate or sensible. More specifically, in the case of Eastern European transition economies, a gradual restructuring of their national economies did not always bring about a higher level of urbanization and overproduction is still a problem.

More recently, the Agenda 2000 reforms divided the CAP into two pillars: production support and rural development. Agri-environmental schemes became compulsory for every member state (Dinan, 2005: 367). The launch of the Rural Development Regulation (RDR) as part of the Agenda 2000 reform was seen by many to herald a new approach – the Second Pillar (Dwyer et al., 2007). One of the EU Commission Reports (that of 2003), which largely dealt with alternative measures more useful to the EU, rather than discussing the CAP, suggested that farm aid would be administered more effectively by member countries on an individual basis. The Sapir report laid the foundation of local agrarian entrepreneurship, pointing out new categories of agrarian entrepreneurs, according to the principle of subsidiarity, but did not operationalize or suggest either new modes or substance. The findings of the report were mostly ignored, and CAP spending was kept largely unchanged. The need for profound change thus remained.

A recent comparative study (Dwyer et al., 2007) assessed the efficacy of the Agenda 2000 reform in terms of sustainable rural development. The authors found large variance in the results. Some countries spent almost half of the finance on Less Favoured Areas and agri-environment (Austria, Sweden), whereas others (Spain, France) put the majority of funding on agricultural modernization and infrastructure development. Some countries simply rolled forward to the RDR programmes, acting as pragmatic drivers of conservatism (Dwyer et al., 2007). Dwyer et al. (2007) note that special efforts and programmes show innovative regional experiments, and adoption of best practices. These experiments may be entrepreneurial, with regional and local officials cooperating with farmers to start new projects, answering the call for bottom-up change. New groups of competent actors, that question the former closed policy communities, emerge and mark the way polity is transformed. A change from centralized to decentralized policymaking, and from command and control to contextual steering, implies more participatory policymaking and channels more decisions via market mechanisms, including the change in the agri-food sector from production-driven to consumer-driven (Lowe et al., 2010).

The farm structure, and especially the small and semi-subsistence farms, shows a split between the small farms, engaging 42 per cent of the labour force, but representing only 7 per cent of output in 2010. Davidova (2014) notes that it is crucial to subsidize, at least partially, farmers and their households in rural areas that might otherwise further depopulate. She discusses three possible scenarios with policy implications. First, the disappearance of the small farms due to absorption into larger commercial farm holdings, or to land abandonment, especially in sparsely populated areas; second the transformation into small commercial farms via greater market integration, with increasing farm output sales and reduced subsistence dependence, a path in line with EU policy, and third, the long-term survival of small farms through diversification, part-time farming and non-agricultural wage employment or "forced" succession.

Specifically regarding the wine sector, the Common Market Organization (CMO) for wine (developed in the 1960s) has comprehensively regulated and thus influenced different aspects of wine production in the EU, such as the quality, quantity and price of wine grapes. More specifically and in addition to quality regulations, since the implementation of the Common Wine Policy in 1970, the EU has imposed minimum prices for EU wine, tariffs on imported wine and has intervened in the market to deal with surpluses (Meloni and Swinnen, 2016). A major reform in 2008 restricted the amount of land that growers were allowed to use to grow grapes (Balogh and Jámbor, 2017; Meloni and Swinnen, 2016) by paying them to remove vines (Anderson and Jensen, 2016).

Several regulatory forces and external contingencies have affected the comparative advantage of European wine producers. Meloni and Swinnen (2016) report that the EU produces and consumes about 60 per cent of the wine produced worldwide and it does so in a highly regulated environment. For example, regulatory intervention has resulted in the destruction of the equivalent of 3 billion to 6 billion bottles yearly for the past three decades. The authors contend that regulatory policies have exacerbated rather than ameliorated problems by creating distortions in the wine sector and often reducing overall welfare and efficiency.

Balogh and Jámbor (2017) report that between 2000 and 2013, only Bulgaria, Cyprus, France, Greece, Italy, Portugal and Spain had comparative advantage in the world market, albeit declining for all countries bar France, Italy and Spain. Financial support for generic promotion of EU wines continues to increase (Anderson and Jensen, 2016). Concomitantly, New World wine producers have increased their share of the world market (Balogh and Jámbor, 2017; Meloni and Swinnen, 2016). Additionally, the economic crisis has negatively affected the production and consumption of wine in Europe in general (Balogh and Jámbor, 2017) and Greece in particular (Iliopoulos and Theodorakopoulou, 2014; Vlachos, 2017), though Meloni and Swinnen (2016) report that it has been since the 1980s that overall wine consumption within the EU has decreased.

European Commission reforms in 2016 liberalized the planting rights system, which resulted in the increase in that amount of land. However, opponents of this decision made in 2007, organized and lobbied heavily for its reversal. This has resulted in the reversal of this decision by the European Commission, the Council, and the European Parliament. Instead, it was decided that the current system would stay in place until 2016, at which time it would be replaced by a system of authorizations for new plantings (Deconinck and Swinnen, 2015). Meloni and Swinnen (2016) note that the political forces against planting rights liberalization were very strong and that liberalization has historically occurred only under such extreme events like revolutions and wars. The system in force until 2030 remains restrictive.

THE ECONOMIC CRISIS AND THE GREEK WINE SECTOR

An economic crisis "refers to an interval of decline in a long period of steady growth and development" (Boin et al., 2005). The economic crisis in Greece is a "slow burning" crisis ('t Hart and Boin, 2001). This is because, instead of constituting a one-and-done affair as compared to one of the recent strings of terrorist attacks in Europe, for example, it creeps up, lingers, and rather it being resolved, it fades away—though admittedly very few Greeks would attest to the recession having faded away so far. Indeed, resolving such crises is very difficult and often resolution is forced through top-down processes, such as, for example, the imposition of austerity measures on Greece by the troika (i.e. the European Commission, the European Central Bank, and the International Monetary Fund).

The Greek economy in general adheres to the Mediterranean model characterized by firms owned and managed by families or individuals with power, with a large percentage of very small, independent family-owned firms (Amable, 2003). In fact, 57 per cent of working people in Greece are either self-employed, or work in firms that have 10 or fewer employees (Adamides and Tsinopoulos, 2015). Agriculture holds a predominant share in the economy with a structure including fragmented, non-adjacent lots, ageing farmers, and a disconnect between arranging life in farming in combination with non-farming occupations (Ribeiro, 2015). Drawing from Kasimis and Papadopoulos (2013), Ribeiro (2015: 79) distils a recent re-imagining of rural Greece, a "new rurality" to three trajectories: "deagriculturalization of the countryside; the perplexity of rural mobilities, and rural resilience during [the] economic crisis".

The wine industry in particular is controlled by a small number of large firms with the ability to market their products through extensive networks. A host of medium-sized and small wineries and associations of agricultural cooperatives also comprise the wine industry in Greece. Smallholdings in Greece are found to not be included in data banks comprising the FADN (Farm Accountancy Data Network), which analyses the income of European agricultural holdings (Pappalardo et al., 2013; Vlachos, 2017). The number of wine enterprises as well as people employed in them in 2013 is approximately the same as 2003 levels: 406 enterprises (compared to 400 in 2003, and a peak of 528 in 2011) employing 2980 people (compared to 2772 in 2003, with a peak of 3363 in 2010). In fact, since 2010, the average annual production has dropped by 20 per cent, a corollary of the economic crisis, which has also meant that consumers buy less expensive bottled wine and/or cask wine (Vlachos, 2017). At the same time, Pappalardo et al. (2013) report that the Greek wine industry has undergone somewhat of a revolution during the past two decades, with an emphasis on quality, individuality and history.

Empirical data for this study were collected using a field survey. In particular, 39 in-depth interviews were conducted by the second author, in the five-month period between December 2014 and April 2015. The interviews were semi-structured, carried out in Greek, and took place in Athens and Thessaloniki. The mode of discussion was face-to-face with the exception of three cases, where two interviews were conducted over the telephone and skype, and one informant chose to communicate via email. All interviews were recorded and transcribed, while the participants were guaranteed anonymity and labelled as "Respondents" (i.e. R1, R2, R3 … R39).

In order to capture the nuances of the Greek wine sector, we appealed to a diverse group of stakeholders, including winemakers; enologists; wine distributors and exporters; representatives of wine tourism associations and wine clubs; wine writers and wine tourism bloggers; wine restaurant owners and tourism entrepreneurs; viticulture/wine/tourism academics; wine/tourism officials, and policymakers. These were elite interviews; following Flint et al. (2011), the wine producers selected for this study were chosen because they were key decision makers. The participants were recruited through snowball sampling. As a first step, we contacted each participant to explain the project's objectives. Once they accepted the invitation to take part in the research, an interview date and place were set. We then sent a confirmation email with a covering letter and the interview guide. Interviews lasted between 20 minutes and 2.5 hours. Thematic Analysis was used to analyse the qualitative data collected from the interviews. Through the use of this method we were able to tease out prominent themes and categories in the responses of the participants through a series of iterative readings (Liu and Tsaur, 2014).

With respect to the first research question posed in the introductory part of this chapter, results indicate that the impacts of the economic crisis on the wine sector would seem to be inextricably related to sociological dimensions of the product itself: "… when the economic crisis emerged, wine producers got a little panicked because wine was considered a kind of luxury" [R14]. Interestingly, one of the respondents, who represented the public sector, was rather pessimistic, arguing that "the economic crisis has affected all three parties: the consumer, the winemaker and public administration. I am not very sure that we will come back" [R32]. However, other respondents stated that the economic downturn of 2008 did not cause much disturbance to the industry, because it "shrinked the middle class out of existence, it did not affect wine" [R8]. R36 further explains:

> The wine sector has not suffered, but it did slow down because of the crisis. The target clientele of bottled wine was a relatively small portion of people. This market segment remained loyal, and therefore the economic crisis did not greatly affect the industry's performance. Of course, there has been a shift towards the consumption of cask or anonymous wine; yet, this shift did not trigger a deep crisis with long-term consequences, compared to what happened to other primary sectors. The wine sector may have faced a setback compared to the progress it had made over the past few decades but not to an extent that one can doubt the sector's future. [R36]

Some respondents expressed a moderate level of optimism: "… there is now a clear picture of what Greek wine is" [R37]; with other interviewees stating that "the financial crisis affected the industry in a positive way, since it forced us to a self-criticism" [R22] and "another good thing that the crisis has done is the decline of imported wines consumption. We sort of returned to locality" [R25].

Specific impacts caused by the crisis included a decline in product sales (R9, R15, R23, R26), particularly those of bottled wine (R23, R25, R36), as well as problems in liquidity (R15, R22, R24, R36). The latter have subsequently led to a stagnation in terms of investments. As one respondent reported, "lack of liquidity means, I try to survive by making cuts and being very careful but I do not invest. You do not have added value, so you remain stagnant" [P36]. The crisis has also affected wine tourism, in terms of both visitation numbers and cellar door sales (R24). In addition, the recession had a great impact on the investments the wineries had to make in order to engage in wine tourism activities (R34). When asked who the crisis had affected the most, R8 stated that "the crisis, one way or another – has affected every winery". R34 explained further:

> All wineries lost income during the recession, with only few exceptions; mainly wineries selling very cheap wine in 1.5-liter plastic bottles, etc. Such companies saw their turnover growing. All other businesses, members of the Greek Wine Federation, suffered losses. The crisis has mostly damaged bottled wine. What gained ground was the very low category, what we call uncontrollable, bulk wine.

Product diversification was another factor of resilience, since "consumption of red wine was more severely 'hit' compared to the one of white" (R9). As R22 also posits, "during the crisis, white wine producers did better, because white wines are fresh and usually consumed immediately".

With respect to business size, respondents have varied perceptions. According to a number of interviewees, the larger winemakers were more severely affected by the crisis, "because of the parcel tax" [R14]; "because they had loans" [R14], or "because they faced a bigger drop (turnover, etc.), and they had to make drastic cuts in spending, borrowing, production; which are not easy things" [R37]. On the contrary, smaller wineries with lower fixed costs were more resilient … [R22]. As R34 also emphasized: "boutique wineries, with owned vineyards and developed exports are obviously not affected by the internal recession". However, R20 argued: "smaller wineries faced much more difficulties in adapting to the economic crisis", while R18 further said: "10–15 larger wineries, as well as some smaller: there are robust companies in Greece, it is not a matter of size. These (wineries) have no wine to sell for four to five months annually. Because they have found the solution, a balance with their exports, everything. Everything counts".

Notably, despite the multiple challenges the wine industry has endured, "no winery has closed down due to the crisis" [R3, R15, R22, R37]. The reasons behind this strength are clear in the following statements: "I do not think that any winery will ever close down. I think it's a job that can always spur someone into investing. It may change hands, but that is all" [R22]. "Even though they struggled, wine entrepreneurs were not defeated. Most of them have the mentality that they must continue producing a high quality product" [R15]. As stated:

> A winery represents a long-term investment that you make for your children. Thus, you have no choice. Once you have planted 10 hectares Athiri [i.e. a local Greek variety], even if things *do not work out in your favour*, you will fight until there is nothing left. This is the reason why no winery has closed down due to the crisis. The motivation for someone who makes wine is very deep, compared to those who produce olive oil or cereals. [R2]

Several respondents mentioned the positive role of the wine bars (R9, R13, R14, R24), which resulted in boosting domestic consumption and "created a fashion, making a trend and supporting quality wine" (R14). Other resilience strategies included a shift in production from expensive, bottled to cheaper bottled or bulk wine (R14, R15, R25, R31); turning to rosé ("due to direct profit, the style of rosé has changed; it began to resemble white, this trend began by France" (R15); and wine tourism, which was considered to be "the life jacket that provided wineries with liquidity" (R23).

EXTROVERSION AS A RESILIENCE STRATEGY

Notably, the large majority of the respondents stressed the importance of exports (R14, R18, R20, R22, R25, R26, R28, R31, R37) as a vehicle to deal with the decrease in domestic consumption. Indicatively, informants stated: "… the sector is resilient at the moment, which is largely due to extroversion" (R20) and "… those who turned abroad showed greater resistance to the financial crisis" (R28), as well as "winemakers who exported to a lesser extent were more affected. Those whose exports accounted for less than 40 per cent of the total turnover had a problem" (R8). Nevertheless, as R34 argued: "it is not easy for a Greek winery to hold a large share of exports". Thus, several respondents highlighted the crucial role of political entrepreneurship and the utilization of CAP programmes for wine:

> The crisis has positively affected wineries because, combined with European Union programs, it has enhanced extroversion. This resulted in an increase in exports. It is very difficult to get into foreign and dynamic markets. Before the crisis, most winemakers had their wines in Greece and were sitting back. [R20]

In addition, "thankfully the Ministry, in the midst of the crisis, put out a program of extroversion for third countries and not only did we maintain but we also increased our sales" [R31].

It would appear that the five-year strategic plan for the Greek wine, conducted by the National Inter-professional Organization of Wine and Vine (EDOAO), helped exports (R37). It is important to note that the aforementioned body represents "the only Greek inter-professional organization which has arranged collectively a strategic plan of collaboration, unique for the Greek standards" (New Wines of Greece, 2012: 6). Recently, EDOAO has been working together with Enterprise Greece, which is the official agency of the Greek State, under the supervision of the Ministry of Economy and Development, aiming to promote investments and exports (Enterprise Greece, 2017).

THE ROLE OF NETWORKS

Respondents (R5, R20) underlined that the crisis has strengthened collaborative activities: "… in the case of Greece, winemakers' associations have played a key role. Wine tourism was mainly the result of the creation of networks. They made wine tourism popular" (R20). It is important to mention that the first organized scheme towards the promotion of wineries resulted in the creation of the "Wine Producers Association of the Macedonian Vineyard" in 1993. This is a non-profit, non-stock corporation established by the joint efforts of the 15 members of the Macedonian vineyard. In 2002, wineries from the regions of Epirus, Thessaly and Thrace joined the association, which was renamed the "Wine Producers Association of the Northern Greece Vineyard". In 2008, the network grew further to include, apart from wineries, several other associated companies (Alebaki and Iakovidou, 2011). Today, Wine Roads of Northern Greece include 28 wineries and 58 cooperating members.

In the two decades that followed, winemakers in the regions of Peloponnese, Attica, Central Greece, Crete and the Aegean Islands followed suit and established their own associations. In addition to the seven regional networks, there were also joint initiatives at the local (prefectural) level. These include the Association of Winemakers of Nemea in Peloponnese (2011), of Naoussa (2014) and Drama (2015) in Macedonia (Alebaki and Ioannides, 2018). However, small "networks set up at the level of the region [i.e. Drama, Naoussa] so far are in the direction of projection, not production" (R20). R33 also expressed some concerns: "we create local networks in the context of exploiting some programs. For some of them, it would probably make sense to have a follow-up to these programs" [R33]. R20 emphasized the need for further collaboration amongst winemakers at various levels as a means to pool resources:

> Where smaller networks could be set up, it is in the supply. That is, all the small winemakers in Goumenissa [i.e. a wine region in Northern Greece] make a small network and through it buy corks, labels, have machinery together, squeezing production costs. Then, they could also do promotion actions. I have the feeling that the new EU programs are set in this direction. It is good to have regional local networks. [R20]

However, "not all networks are equally successful" (R20). Within this context, results indicate a difference in the way various networks have responded to the crisis. For instance, in the case of Northern or Central Greece, the current economic downturn is severely constraining some members' ability to pay their annual subscription, forcing them thus to exit the Association (R28, R35). R20 further emphasized:

> networking is often a luxury. In times of crisis, what you cut is luxury. You prefer with the money you spend to be a member of the Association to cover other needs (buy caps and corks). That is why most wineries who left the network are small, family-owned operations.

R28, representing the newly established (2008) network of Central Greece, described a more unbalanced situation:

> Over the last years, a large number of wineries have taken a hit by the crisis, so what more could you ask from them to pay? We did not have the opportunity to organize many events. We were the only ones sponsoring promotional activities. All these difficulties have led to a relative stagnation. [R28]

Notably, there are others who leave the network (in the case of Northern Greece) because "they do not find it to be of benefit" (R37) or "disagree with the decisions of the administration" (R35). More specifically:

> They believe that the Association does not serve our original purposes. We must note that when the network started, its main objective was to develop the Wine Roads. However, in the course of time and – partly – due to the crisis, we have engaged into other activities. We developed programs to promote our wines, and this seems to have dropped wine tourism out of our priorities for a while. This bothered two members. They said, "We are not a trading company, we are Wine Roads." But I do not know for sure why they left. [R35]

R11 further supported this view:

> The market punishes inaction. If networks do not evolve, they will lead to fatigue among members. When a network is established, an expectation is created for members, the key is the proper management of expectations. If there is no result in 2–3 years, the first problems begin. [R11]

In the case of Crete, there are two distinct networks: one in the western part of the island, which was founded in 2006 and includes 24 wineries of the Herakleion and Lasithi districts, and another one in the eastern part of the island, founded in 2009, which incorporates eight wineries located in the wine regions of Chania and Rethymno. Even though these two associations coordinate and jointly organize their actions, they remain two separate entities. The reasons behind this choice were articulated by one of their representatives:

> The two networks are like two legs that walk together and have a common head, which is the brand "Wines of Crete". We have not joined into one Association for tactical reasons. There are European programs in which eligible entities are in Chania, and others in which eligible entities are in Heraklion. If we were together, there would be a difficulty in terms of eligibility. [R24]

Wineries – members of "Wines of Crete" consider the network's contribution to the development of the Cretan wine sector as "being very important" (R23). More specifically,

> the fact that we are doing well in the field of wine tourism is due to the network. The effort that everyone does on their own is not enough. If the network had not existed, we would not have done well either in sales or exports. [R23]

Despite its recent history, the Cretan network seems to be more resilient in the face of the current crisis. One respondent stated that they doubt the crisis affected the association and went on to say:

> We undertake now more actions than we did before. I do not know if there was no crisis, and we had the possibility, for example, to hire another person to work for us, maybe we could multiply our actions and possibly do more things. What I think is really interesting is that in the last 3–4 years, despite the economic crisis and the difficulties, no one has ever turned back. They are all supporters. They consider it necessary. That they are members of a family who must go ahead. [R24]

We should note, however, respondents from other regions in Greece accredited Cretans' resilience to the financial support received by their regional public authorities:

> The Cretans have extremely important funding from the Region; Central Macedonian winemakers, for example, have no financial support from their Public Authority. The Cretans participate in wine exhibitions and the Region covers the expenses. This has never been the case here. Each winemaker has to pay. The cost for participating in wine events is much higher for a Northern Greek winery compared to what the Cretans have to afford. You do not want to find a program occasionally. You want the aid from state bodies, who are completely absent. [R20]

Access to monetary resources remains a critical success factor for the long-term prosperity of such ventures, since "most networks are depended to external funding" (R10). The latter, as R35 argued, "has not been affected. We always had programs, although there is a delay in payments at this time". What seems to be a major issue is the lack of a stable tax system in Greece: "we have no financial stability, these are other problems. These are institutional problems, which are also very serious" (R18).

Other primary concerns expressed by the interviewees were the lack of executives to assist in management and the need "to set some qualitative standards for networks upon registration" (R19) and the need for coordination and planning at a central (national) level (R8, R11, R19, R37). Finally, respondents also discussed specific European policy measures, that is, the reduction of vineyards, which might lead to the country's self-sufficiency in wine (R34). R22 further emphasizes:

> The abandonment of the vineyards was a wrong measure, it should never be implemented in the case of Greece. The reduction of vineyards has been caused by administrative mistakes. People want to plant vines. There is

simply a problem due to planting rights ... As far as I know, this policy measure will be in force until 2020. Essentially, here the decision makers are the large producers, namely, France, Italy and Spain. However, since the 1960s when the EU initiative for the uprooting of vineyards has been undertaken, the Ministry ought to have responded by establishing a "Bank of Planting Rights". [R22]

CONCLUSIONS

In this chapter we set out to tease out the linkages between political entrepreneurship and resilience in times of crisis. The case study chosen to illustrate these was the Greek wine sector because it allowed for an examination of the effect of CAP, as well as the effects of the economic crisis on a sector that had seen much progress since the early 1990s. A survey of CAP as it relates to wine production does not demonstrate politically entrepreneurial action. For example, in an assessment of the 2016 decision on planting rights, Meloni and Swinnen (2016: 404) conclude that "the new authorization system could be more restrictive than the previous one". Conversely, the deep seated economic (and some argue political) crisis Greece has faced for over ten years combined with the short-sightedness of the public sector, a lack of continuity, and an absence of stability in the tax system does not provide substantial support to the wine growers.

At the same time, crises (as Dror [1993] contends) may provide opportunities and spur (entrepreneurial) action. Faced with decreased bottled wine consumption in Greece, wine producers turned to exports and wine tourism. Most importantly from a theoretical perspective is the collaborative action, the creation of networks, which is a well-established strategy of political entrepreneurs (Petridou et al., 2015). At the same time, the notion of a bottom-up, community resilience is based on collaboration and the pooling of resources, in other words, on network arrangements.

Our findings indicate that the wine producers formed associations early on, in an effort to strengthen the sector and to create a counterweight to EU and national policies affecting the production of wine. This was a politically entrepreneurial strategy by a stakeholder (though others contributed and developed the networks) who has been an important player in the sector for decades, but has also been part of the public sector at different times and in different capacities. Not surprisingly, the networks pooled financial, social and political resources of a sector heavily dominated by small, family enterprises. These networks also took advantage of European regional development initiatives designed to foster regional development.

Having said this, networks are not uniform arrangements with predictable results. Research in network arrangements in risk governance, for example, has shown that the effectiveness of a network depends on a variety of factors, including the presence of an entrepreneurial actor acting as a glue, increasing the cohesion of the network (Petridou and Olausson, 2017). Further research is required on the networks in the Greek wine sector to reveal what factors enable these networks to contribute to the overall resilience of the wine sector under crisis.

REFERENCES

Adamides, E. D. and C. Tsinopoulos (2015). "Survival in economic crisis through forward integration", in R. Bhamra (ed.), *Organisational Resilience: Concepts, Integration, and Practice*. Boca Raton, FL: CRC Press.

Alebaki, M. and O. Iakovidou (2011). "Initiatives towards wine tourism development in Greece", *Enometrica*, 3(2), 15–25.

Alebaki, M. and D. Ioannides (2017). "Threats and obstacles to resilience: insights from the Greek wine tourism sector", in J. Cheer and A. A. Lew (eds), *Tourism and Resilience: Transnational and Comparative Perspectives. Routledge Advances in Tourism*. New York: Routledge.

Amable, B. (2003). *The Diversity of Modern Capitalism*. Oxford University Press: Oxford.

Anderson, K. and H. G. Jensen (2016). "How much government assistance do European wine producers receive?", *Journal of Wine Economics*, 11(2), 289–305.

Balogh, J. M. and A. Jámbor (2017). "The global competitiveness of European wine producers", *British Food Journal*, 119(9), 2076–2088.

Bhamra, R., S. Dani and K. Burnard (2011). "Resilience: the concept, a literature review and future directions", *International Journal of Production Research*, 49(18), 5375–5393.

Boin, A., P. 't Hart, E. Stern, and B. Sundelius (2005). *The Politics of Crisis Management: Public Leadership Under Pressure*. Cambridge: Cambridge University Press.

Cohen, D. K., M.-F. Cuéllar and B. R. Weingast (2006). "Crisis bureaucracy: homeland security and the political design of legal mandates", *Stanford Law Review*, 59(3), 673–759.

Davidova, S. (2014). "Small and semi-subsistence farms in the EU: significance and development paths", *EuroChoices*, 13, 5–9.

Davoudi, S. (2012). "Resilience: a bridging concept or a dead end?", *Planning Theory and Practice*, 13(2), 299–333.

Deconinck, K. and J. Swinnen (2015). "The economics of planting rights in wine production", *European Review of Agricultural Economics*, 42(3), 419–440.

Dinan, D. (2005). "Governance and institutions: a new constitution and a new commission", JCMS: *Journal of Common Market Studies*, 43, 37–54, doi: 10.1111/j.0021-9886.2005.00575.x.

Donnelly, P. and J. Hogan (2012). "Understanding policy change using a critical junctures theory in comparative context: the cases of Ireland and Sweden", *Policy Studies Journal*, 40(2), 324–350.

Dror, Y. (1993). "Steering requisites for crises-opportunities: on-going challenges", *Journal of Contingencies and Crisis Management*, 1(1), 13–14.

Dwyer, J., N. Ward, P. Lowe and D. Baldock (2007). "European rural development under the common agricultural "second pillar": institutional conservatism and innovation", *Regional Studies*, 41(7), 873–887.

Enterprise Greece (2017). Accessed 1 September 2017 at http://www.enterprisegreece.gov.gr/en/about-us-/profile.

Flint D., S. Golicic and P. Signori (2011). "Sustainability through resilience: the very essence of the wine industry", in Conference Proceedings, *The Faces of Wine Sustainability*. Bordeaux: The 6th AWBR International Conference, 8–11 June.

Gaeta, D. and P. Corsivoni (2014). *Economics, Governance, and Politics in the Wine Market*. New York: Palgrave Macmillan.

't Hart, P. and A. Boin, (2001). "Between crisis and normalcy: the long shadow of post-crisis politics", in U. Rosenthal, R. A. Boin and L. K. Comfort (eds), *Managing Crises: Threats, Dilemmas, Opportunities*. Springfield: Charles C. Thomas.

Harvey, D. (2006). "The EU budget and the CAP: an agenda for the review?", *EuroChoices*, 5(1), 22–27.

Hogan, J. and S. Feeney (2012). "Crisis and policy change: the role of the political entrepreneur", *Risk, Hazards & Crisis in Public Policy*, 3(2), 1–24.

Holling, C. S. (1973). "Resilience and stability of ecological systems", *Annual Review of Ecological Systems*, 4, 1–23.

Iliopoulos, C. and I. Theodorakopoulou (2014). "Mandatory cooperatives and the free rider problem: the case of Santo wines in Santorini, Greece", *Annals of Public and Cooperative Economics*, 85, 663–681.

Kasimis, C. and A. G. Papadopoulos (2001). "Rural transformation and family farming in contemporary Greece", *Research in Rural Sociology and Development*, 19, 263–293.

Kingdon, J. W. (1984/2003). *Agendas, Alternatives, and Public Policies* (2nd ed.). Boston, MA: Longman.

Linell, M. (2014). "Citizen response in crisis: individual and collective efforts to enhance community resilience", *Human Technology*, 10(2), 68–94.

Liu, J. S. and S. H. Tsaur (2014). "We are in the same boat: tourist citizenship behaviors", *Tourism Management*, 42(1), 88–100.

Lowe, P., P. H. Feindt and H. Vihinen (2010). "Introduction: Greening the countryside? Changing frameworks of EU agricultural policy", *Public Administration*, 88(2), 287–295.

McAslan, A. (2010). "The concept of resilience: Understanding its origins, meaning and utility", accessed 10 March 2016 at http://torrensresilience.org/images/pdfs/resilience%20origins%20and%20utility.pdf.

McCool, S. F. and R. N. Moisey (eds) (2001). *Tourism recreation and sustainability: Linking culture and the environment.* Wallingford: CAB International.

Meloni, G. and J. Swinnen (2016). "The political and economic history of vineyard planting rights in Europe: from Montesquieu to the European Union", *Journal of Wine Economics*, 11(3), 379–413.

Miles, L. and E. Petridou (2015). "Entrepreneurial resilience: role of policy entrepreneurship in the political perspective of crisis management", in R. Bhamra (ed.), *Organisational Resilience, Concepts Integration and Practice*. Boca Raton, FL: CRC Press.

New Wines of Greece (2012). Newsletter, November, accessed 2 September 2017 at www.newwinesofgreece.com/assets/media/.

Norris, F. H., S. P. Stevens, B. Pfefferbaum, K. F. Wyche and R. L. Pfefferbaum (2008). "Community resilience as a metaphor, theory, set of capacities, and strategy for disaster readiness", *American Journal of Community Psychology*, 41, 127–150.

Pappalardo, G., A. Scienza, G. Vindigni and M. D'Amico (2013). "Profitability of wine grape growing in the EU member states", *Journal of Wine Research*, 24(1), 59–76.

Petridou, E. (2017). "Political entrepreneurship in Swedish: Towards a (re)theorization of entrepreneurial agency", (Doctoral Dissertation), Mid Sweden University, Östersund.

Petridou, E. and P. M. Olausson (2017). "Policy entrepreneurship and policy transfer: flood risk governance in Northern Sweden", *Central European Journal of Public Policy*, 11(1), 1–12.

Petridou, E. and J. Sparf (2017). "For safety's sake: the strategies of institutional entrepreneurs and bureaucratic reforms in Swedish crisis management, 2001–2009", *Policy and Society*, 1–19.

Petridou, E., I. Narbutaité Aflaki and L. Miles. (2015). "Unpacking the theoretical boxes of political entrepreneurship", in I. Narbutaité Aflaki, E. Petridou and L. Miles (eds), *Entrepreneurship in the Polis: Understanding Political Entrepreneurship*. Burlington, VT: Ashgate.

Ribeiro, J. D. M. (2015). "Between Bacchus and Dionysus: European Union policies on rural development – the cases of Nemea and Basto wine regions", (Doctoral Dissertation), Aveiro University.

Vlachos, V. A. (2017). "A macroeconomic estimation of wine production in Greece", *Wine Economics and Policy*, 6, 3–13.

Wildavsky, A. (1988). *Searching for Safety*. New Brunswick, NJ: Transaction Books.

Williams, N., T. Vorley and P. H. Ketikidis (2013). "Economic resilience and entrepreneurship: a case study of the Thessaloniki City Region", *Local Economy*, 28(4), 399–415.

PART IV

Case studies on local political entrepreneurship

11. The legitimacy of political entrepreneurs in networks: lessons from local development projects in Swedish municipalities

Albin Olausson and Elin Wihlborg

INTRODUCTION

Local and Regional policy is a complex area. Its aim is both to promote economic growth and to help achieve a more sustainable society. However, the concept of regional or local development has no agreed-upon definition. Mainstream policies in this area focus on traditional business and economic growth; others take a more holistic approach. Achieving the 2030 development goals set out by the United Nations (UN), for example, requires policies of the latter kind (United Nations, 2017). In addition, the allocation of tasks regarding local and regional development, in the Swedish multilevel governance system, is unclear (Tillväxtanalys, 2014, 2017), as the pervasive discourse on cross-sector collaboration and network governance would seem to suggest (Olausson and Syssner, 2017; Wihlborg, 2015). These unclear conditions make local and regional development a messy field with unclear institutional arrangements. In this chapter, we look at how civil servants in Swedish municipalities – who are embedded in these messy institutional arrangements – act as political entrepreneurs and how they succeed or fail in gaining legitimacy. More specifically, we examine and discuss the importance of networks for the legitimacy achieved by political entrepreneurs. Taking a critical perspective, we show that political entrepreneurs do not always succeed; nor are they always perceived as legitimate.

Local development is a task for local policymaking, but there are also global aims in this area, as well as European policy initiatives and support structures. Regional development appears as a main issue on the European policy agenda, among other things through the European

Regional Development Fund, which addresses not just less developed regions but also the 'growth engines' of Europe (European Commission, 2014). Thus interpretations, meanings, and structures of local development in both policy and practice are formed and embedded within local contexts and arrangements. This yields a demand for local political entrepreneurs, and an arena where they can combine overarching aims with local change. Such entrepreneurs can translate general policy aims into local practices to improve living conditions for their neighbours in the local community (Assmo and Wihlborg, 2016).

In these times of structural change in Europe, there are indeed demands for change at the local level. The need for economic growth and entrepreneurship must be expressed locally, and translated into new support structures and projects at the local level. In this chapter, we focus on one such national support scheme for enabling political entrepreneurs to work for regional and local growth in networks. The three projects we have chosen address varied needs and produce differing outcomes, which is why we look into how they generate legitimacy for their activities. They also address different political challenges: in the first case, structural changes towards a more resilient local economy; in the second, demographic changes and urbanization; in the third, a post-Fordist response to attract investors, entrepreneurs, and visitors to the city centre (Franzén et al., 2016).

Political entrepreneurs are embedded in policy networks, and they make changes through these networks. One of their many strengths is to bridge the gap between different networks, thus pooling resources and ideas for change. Through such processes, they not only convey meanings, they also translate them, often by bringing resources and competences into local networks and making them useful in the specific setting (Wihlborg and Söderholm, 2013). However, forming and combining local networks is a challenge, involving a wide variety of actors from different sectors. Thus, legitimacy is critical for political entrepreneurs' ability to build networks and to contribute to policy change for local development. While we cannot measure legitimacy, it is obvious that a lack of it poses a challenge to networks and projects, and indeed to local development as such. Legitimacy is a key to making networked governance function smoothly to implement policy aims; moreover, it has to involve both legality and trustworthiness (Sørensen and Torfing, 2007).

In this chapter, then, we discuss legitimacy for local political entrepreneurs through an analysis of three local development projects. Our focus is on how political entrepreneurs can gain legitimacy through collaboration in networks. The overall aim of the chapter is to show empirically, and to discuss theoretically, how relations in policy networks impact upon the legitimacy of political entrepreneurs. Three specific interests guide our analysis of the empirical cases. Thus we ask:

1. How do political entrepreneurs navigate through 'messy' institutional arrangements, in order to establish collaboration with external networks?
2. How do they mobilize resources through networks?
3. How do they manage serving as a link between the municipality and networks of external stakeholders?

The remainder of this chapter contains four sections. In the first, we present our research design and the case setting. In the second, we explain our theoretical focus on legitimacy for political entrepreneurs. In the third, we present and analyse the results of the case studies. Finally, in the fourth section, we discuss the lessons learned from these cases, and we explore some general implications for the legitimacy of political entrepreneurs.

FIELD STUDIES OPENING UP FOR NEW INTERPRETATIONS – RESEARCH DESIGN, METHODS AND THE CASE SETTING

Our analysis is based on field studies from three municipalities in Sweden. The cases form part of an ongoing longitudinal study, in which one of the authors (Olausson) is following a development project in a total of ten municipalities. The research project takes an inductive and explorative approach. Here, however, we analyse a number of findings more explicitly in relation to the legitimacy of political entrepreneurs building networks for local development within the project setting.

The ten municipalities included in the long-term study have all been selected to take part in a national programme for knowledge development in connection with local and regional development policy. That means that the municipalities have applied on their own to take part in the programme and that the Swedish Agency for Economic and Regional Growth follows, observes, and supports them in order to learn from the processes taking place. Each of the ten municipalities has formulated its own project plan, based on its own local context and its own way of concretizing the holistic meaning of local and regional development. Here we include the processes both before and after the municipalities applied to take part in the national programme and to get co-funding for their local projects. Out of these ten municipalities, we have specifically chosen to analyse three, due to their particular interest in connection with theories of network governance and legitimacy.

The three cases chosen are distinctly different from each other in regard both to (1) specific *local conditions* and (2) *outcomes* (i.e. success or failure for the project managers; see Table 11.1). We analyse both the trust dimension and the legal aspect of legitimacy, and we consider both inputs and outcomes in connection with local processes. Despite the variations between the three cases, there are certain core common features. All include a civil servant who is acting in an entrepreneurial way – through networks outside the public administration – in order to promote his or her own meaning of local development. In sum, we would contend, this strategic case selection yields solid data from which we can learn more about the legitimacy of civil servants who serve as political entrepreneurs.

This chapter builds on in-depth interviews with the civil servants who are also project managers in the national development programme. Each project manager was interviewed twice: first in the spring of 2016, and again in the winter–spring of 2017. The mayors[1] and chief executives in two of the municipalities were also interviewed in the spring of 2016. All interviews were conducted within the municipality in question, and all were recorded and transcribed. In order to triangulate and create a thick description of the process, we also carried out a textual analysis of policy documents, working materials, and articles in local newspapers relating to the projects. We also made follow-up calls to the project managers after the interviews. Since the projects are all part of a national funding scheme, there have also been national meetings for all project leaders, which we have attended as well. Taken together, these elements form the basis for our case descriptions.

All informants have been promised personal anonymity. One major reason for this is that we wish to uncover the networks, resources, and power relations surrounding the projects. This necessitates the building of trust. Acquiring sensitive information on various matters is important for the validity of our study. Since we talked to the project managers on several occasions, as well as meeting them in specific programme conferences arranged by the Swedish Agency for Economic and Regional Growth, we needed to gain their trust and to persuade them to talk honestly about challenges and tensions in their projects. Therefore, we refer to all of the project managers here by fictive names (all of them

---

[1] Chair of the municipal executive committee.

female). For the sake of this anonymity, moreover, the specific documents and newspaper articles analysed in this study are not cited explicitly.

In the table below, we present the three local development projects and the municipalities in which they are located.

Table 11.1 Core characteristics of the political entrepreneurs under study and their local setting

	Mill Town	Small Town	Suburb
Aim of the project for local development	To give better municipal service to local trade and industry, and to promote the development of small firms.	To collaborate with civil society in order to develop rural development strategies favouring a rural lifestyle.	To transform the suburban centre into a regional city centre, and to strengthen the trademark of the municipality in order to attract entrepreneurs and investors.
Key municipal characteristics	10,000 inhabitants. The local economy has been dominated by a single big industry.	10,000 inhabitants. A large rural population and a small municipal centre.	80,000 inhabitants. A suburb on the outskirts of a metropolitan area.
Employment status of the project managers	Contracted by the municipality as consultant in charge of development of trade and industry.	Long-time member of the municipal staff, in charge of rural and small-firm development.	Project employee by the municipality; positions funded half by the municipality and half by property owners.
Key networks of the project managers	Local trade and industry in general.	Village associations, in particular those in rural areas.	The largest commercial property owners in the city.

POLITICAL ENTREPRENEURS IN OR OUTSIDE POLICY NETWORKS – OUR THEORETICAL FRAMING

In this section, we set our framing of the problem – how we analyse the legitimacy of political entrepreneurs in relation to policy networks and local political processes. We proceed from the premise that networked governance provides a context for the operation of political entrepreneurs, at the same time that the latter – by knitting the networks together – generate networked governance in turn. Our focus here is on how legitimacy is formed through the policy processes supporting the entrepreneurs as well as their networks. Thus, we start out this section with a brief overview of networked governance, after which we present a general conceptualization of legitimacy. The purpose of the latter is to combine these theoretical tracks – network governance and legitimacy – in relation to political entrepreneurs: first, through a conceptualization of formal and informal legitimacy; second, through an explication of input and output legitimacy. Finally, we relate these theoretical approaches to the research questions posed in our introduction.

Networked Governance as the Context for Political Entrepreneurs

Policy networks are the context for political entrepreneurs, since it is the latter that actually form and develop the networks (Kingdon, 1995; von Bergmann-Winberg and Wihlborg, 2011; Narbutaité et al., 2015; Peters and Pierre, 2004). Policy networks are kept together by common meanings, formed by the core values held by actors who, through their networks, can share and coordinate resources so as to attain their aims more easily (Rhodes and Marsh, 1992). Policy entrepreneurs are the ones who knit policy networks together. They are actors, most often single individuals; but they can also be organizations or groups of individuals. They possess essential resources, as well as the ambition to take on particular roles so as to influence and thus to direct the governing process. In another line theory, they function as meta-governors in processes of networked governance (Sørensen, 2006).

When policymaking takes place in a networked governance setting, there are many openings for how, when, and where to make decisions and to formulate policies. Kingdon (1995) identified the networked process of policymaking as a process combining the three streams of: problems, politics and policies. He showed that policy changes take place when the three streams are coordinated. A new *policy* can address a *problem* when being managed through the *political* context of norms and values that are embodied in the specific structure for decision-making. This process of policy change takes place, he claimed, when a policy entrepreneur manages to get all three streams through the policy window (a specific window of opportunity).

Kingdon used the concept of 'policy entrepreneur'; however, in line with the introduction to this edited volume, we use the term 'political entrepreneur' (see Chapter 1 in this volume). Kingdon (1995) distinguished clearly between 'policy' and 'politics' in his discussion of different 'streams' that must pass through a common policy window if a policy change is to occur. A policy, in Kingdon's terms, refers to the content and meaning of an issue in a specific field. He used the term 'political', on the other hand, in reference to the political game of actors and their norms and values. Combining this distinction with the meaning of entrepreneurs as critical actors in the game, we get policy entrepreneurs, who focus on the matters that they aim to change; and political entrepreneurs, who focus – almost independently of the issues at stake – on the political game and on how coalitions and networks can be formed (for a more exhaustive discussion of these different concepts, see Assmo and Wihlborg, 2016). Then, when using political entrepreneurs, we also include policy entrepreneurs – who are the main focus here, since they are driven by an interest in the policy aims of local and regional development.

The setting of networked governance also ranges across traditional levels of government in the multi-level government structure. In areas which are experiencing lower growth there is a particular need for building networks to promote growth, to make policy changes and to achieve real local development (Assmo and Wihlborg, 2016). In times when public policy is implemented through networked governance, there is a need for local actors to take responsibility for ensuring the implementation of policies all the way to the end user, where policies can make a change (see Chapter 2 in this volume; Vedung, 2016). Thus, policy entrepreneurs have to gain legitimacy in the processes of networked governance taking place on several levels of the multi-level government system.

The Legitimacy of Political Entrepreneurs

Legitimacy has been described as a rather fuzzy concept. In an effort to make legitimacy more graspable, Bekkers and Edwards (2007) pointed out that it presupposes authority. Legitimacy must be related to an actor, an institution, or a system that can exercise authority. It is thus common to understand legitimacy in terms of acceptance for authority. In other words, an authority can promote legitimacy even among those who disagree with the decisions it makes. Legitimacy can be portrayed in two ways: as closely related to legality, or as based on trust among stakeholders (cf. Bekkers and Edwards, 2007). In the first case, something is legitimate if it is lawful. Legality is often seen as a basic precondition for legitimacy, since it makes analysis on the basis of formal conditions and decisions possible.

The second understanding of legitimacy fastens on informal arrangements of trust. Legitimacy here builds on the perceptions of different stakeholders. In other words, legitimacy is in the eye of the beholder, and it is something conferred by others (Bekkers and Edwards, 2007). Actors can have different interpretations of the authority in question, and so may experience legitimacy in different ways. According to this view, then, legitimacy is about trust and acceptance rather than legality. This kind of legitimacy can be gained independently of whether or not the exercise of authority is in accordance with the law. This informal and constructivist approach to legitimacy builds on the activities and interpretations of the actors who constitute the community.

Both of these approaches to legitimacy portray it as contextual – as arising in relation to the authorities that form the policy networks. Thus, political entrepreneurs can gain legitimacy both by acting in line with the legal framework and by gaining trust among stakeholders. The two forms of legitimacy co-construct each other; and, in the most favourable case, they support each other. However, an activity can be legitimate in legal terms yet still be seen as illegitimate among the actors in question. This may be the case, for example, if the actors do not trust the legal arrangements in the area, as when people openly share pictures online in spite of copyright laws. It can also be the other way around: that is, that the actors regard the lawful provisions as legitimate, but lack trust that the local context is in line with those provisions (as when the legitimacy of the police is under challenge in some socioeconomically deprived suburbs). In sum, legitimacy is formed in the interplay between formal and informal arrangements, and it takes shape in the local context.

In the literature on political entrepreneurs in the context of networked governance, the political entrepreneur identifies and defines problems that have to be addressed. The motives of political entrepreneurs may be altruistic in part; that is, they may wish to promote new policies and to facilitate the operation of networks; however, they may also benefit individually if such policies and innovations prove successful (Mintrom, 1997; Wihlborg, 2000). Policy entrepreneurs do not necessarily act on the basis of a single organizational foundation; instead they may show flexibility, rearranging their networks for each policy issue (Mintrom and

Norman, 2009). The legitimacy of political entrepreneurs and of similar actors has been discussed in various ways in the literature. In a discussion of institutional theory, Fligstein (1997) pointed out that critical individual actors can gain legitimacy through their social skills, which in turn can endow them with direct authority as well as with more subtle forms of agenda-setting power. Weber saw charisma as a specific source of legitimacy (Weber, 1978). Research on institutional entrepreneurship (see Chapter 3 in this volume) has shown how entrepreneurs can use the quantification and measurability of local conditions to gain legitimacy for their activities. For instance, individual entrepreneurial actors can use rankings and output measurements to make legitimate institutional changes (Déjean et al., 2007). Other scholars have stressed the subject position of entrepreneurial actors as a source for their legitimacy. Factors such as background, personal experience, and previous career can play a critical role for the ability of individual actors to come across as legitimate (Maguire et al., 2004).

Our focus is on how the legitimacy of political entrepreneurs is formed through the interplay of legality and trust. Policies are formed in processes in which political entrepreneurs, interacting in networks, play a crucial role. If we are to understand how political entrepreneurs do or do not achieve legitimacy, we need to problematize the process of networked governance and the content of that process. What does it mean to be legitimate? If we are to grasp how political entrepreneurs form policy networks and policy changes, we must appreciate that legitimacy arises differently on the political system's input side from how it comes about through implementation at the output side.

Networks are a specific source of legitimacy, and they relate to the political system in two quite different ways: they provide inputs into it, and they enhance the outcomes produced by it. The structural setting in the two cases differs, and the legitimacy arising from the two processes differs as well. Easton (1965) described *inputs* as the norms and values expressed by the electorate; and *outputs* as the decisions, public services, and infrastructural arrangements provided by the government. We use this distinction between inputs and outputs to analyse the concept of legitimacy, since researchers in the field have applied it extensively (Schmidt, 2013; Rothstein, 2009). In relation to local policymaking, Evans (2014) showed that legitimacy in local government has been defined in two different ways. Input legitimacy, his overview revealed, has been defined as transparency, accountability, responsiveness, and electoral representation as brought into policymaking through the political decision-making structure. Input legitimacy is based on how the public perceive decision makers, and whether the power wielded by the latter results from fair and democratic elections. Output legitimacy, by contrast, is more 'functionalist'; local government is seen here as 'a service provider with efficient service delivery being the main objective' (Evans, 2014: 44). Output legitimacy has figured centrally in the 'quality of government' research field (Rothstein, 2009; Rothstein and Teorell, 2012). But as we see it, and as Evans (2014) emphasizes, local politics is indeed constructed in the interplay between input and output legitimacy.

Analysing the Legitimacy of Political Entrepreneurs in Local Development

Our interest in this chapter is in the legitimacy of specific political entrepreneurs in their local networks. Summing up the theoretical discussion above, we can say that we are working along two dimensions. First, we understand legitimacy in terms of a combination of legality and trust; or, in other words, as consisting of formal and informal components. Second, we see these two components in terms of the process leading from inputs to outputs in the political system. Both dimensions are represented in the model below (Table 11.2).

Table 11.2 The combination of formal and informal legitimacy and of input and output legitimacy

		Phase of the policymaking process	
		Input	Output
Components of legitimacy	Formal legality		
	Informal trust		

Since these cases are set within a formal and political structure (the municipality, as shown in Table 11.1), our focus is on the interplay between external networks and internal organizational actors involved in both the input and output phases of the policymaking process. We show hereby the complexity of the concept of legitimacy, and how it implies that there are several ways of gaining legitimacy. We shall use our three research questions for this analysis, and shall embed them in these two aspects of legitimacy.

The first and second questions focus on the input phase of the policymaking process. Political entrepreneurs must navigate through a field of 'messy' institutional arrangements in order to establish collaboration with external networks. They attempt to do this by gaining trust, even while still staying within the legal framework of the municipal policymaking process. They also mobilize resources, such as funding and other support, through networks. At the same time, there are clear legal norms about what kinds of resources can be mobilized; otherwise, suspicions of corruption are bound to arise. The focus of our third research question, relating to the output phase, is on how political entrepreneurs manage to maintain a link based on trust between the municipality and external stakeholders, without departing from the legal framework of local politics.

LOCAL AND REGIONAL DEVELOPMENT IN A MULTILEVEL SYSTEM OF GOVERNANCE – FROM THE EU TO SWEDISH MUNICIPALITIES

There has been a clear shift from providing support to lagging areas to pursuing a more general policy for economic growth. This policy shift has affected both the content and the organization of regional policy in Sweden, as well as in other countries of Western Europe (sees Keating, 1998). The new orientation has predominated in the policy debate since the late twentieth century. In more recent years, furthermore, it has functioned as a guide for practical implementation strategies. Hadjimichalis (2011) argued that the policy agendas of the European Union have laid down a more general approach aimed at enhancing growth in all regions on the basis of their own resources, without external support. This is in contrast to the large structural-fund projects that guided EU enlargement in the 1980s. This focus on the use and development of local resources to achieve growth has found expression in the term 'endogenous approaches' (Tödtling, 2011).

The idea of new regionalism has been prominent in the UK, as a way of addressing increased regional differences and related political and social divides. It has been shown, however, that it is a highly political discourse aimed at reframing the function of local governments and at promoting networked governance (Deas and Ward, 2000). There are cases where the new regionalism has encouraged development in new sectors through the activities and networks established by political entrepreneurs. An example can be seen in the rural parts of western Kansas, in the US, where a programme based on the idea of new regionalism was established. The focus was on supporting new forms of leadership, encouraging value-added agriculture, and promoting local business. A new website was set up to publicize job opportunities and to promote networking. Projects have included voluntary regional grass-roots initiatives and collaboration among public actors (Lu, 2010). This indicates the importance of networking for making the new regionalism work. In sum, there is an emphasis on economic growth and development in both Swedish and European discourses. However, it is worth noting that regional and local development can include more elements than those featured in models of economic growth. The cases included in our analysis are taken from a national programme striving for a broader understanding of growth – beyond the single metric of easily measured economic growth.

In line with the developments noted above, there has been a similar trend at the national level in Sweden, with a clear shift from a selective policy focused on support for less favoured regions to a general policy for economic growth in all regions (Johansson, 2013; Nilsson, 2012). There has also been a shift from national programmes to a more decentralized approach. Local and regional actors have therefore assumed a more important role as policymakers in the area of local and regional development. The formal responsibility for regional development has been transferred into the hands of regional governments.[2]

Thus, local governments in Sweden have assumed a key role as actors in an overall national strategy for achieving sustainable growth in all regions (Swedish Government, 2015). As compared with their counterparts in other European countries, moreover, Nordic municipalities have a long tradition of engaging in local community development (Aarsaether and Ringholm, 2011). Furthermore, Swedish municipalities have contributed even more actively over the last 30 years to local development in a broad sense (Nyhlén, 2013; Wihlborg, 2015). This has particularly been the case when it comes to taking the initiative for public–private partnerships to promote local economic growth (SOU, 1997: 77; Pierre, 1998; Persson, 2010). In this context, we can expect political entrepreneurs to have become increasingly important in mobilizing and coordinating the resources of different actors.

Legally speaking, Swedish municipalities enjoy considerable discretion when it comes to local and regional development. Unlike their counterparts elsewhere in Europe, Nordic municipalities are free to undertake such policies as they might wish, as long as these are not expressly

[2] Lag (2010: 630) om regionalt utvecklingsansvar i vissa län [Swedish legislation on the responsibility for regional development in certain counties].

prohibited (Lidström, 1996). Furthermore, Swedish municipalities have far-reaching financial and fiscal autonomy (Sellers and Lidström, 2007). These factors yield favourable conditions for active and creative local development policies.

Two central functions in the Swedish municipal context are those of the municipal chief executive (hereafter 'chief executive') and the chair of the municipal executive committee (hereafter 'mayor') (Jonsson and Arnell, 2006). The chief executive is the head of the municipal administration. The mayor is the highest elected politician; in many small municipalities, moreover, he/she is the only full-time paid politician. Thus the mayor has a special role: in one way or another, he/she is involved in all strategic decision-making in the municipality (Karlsson, 2006). The function of the chief executive, finally, is politically very important, with a considerable influence on strategic decision-making (Högberg, 2007; Jonsson, 2012; Lennqvist Lidén, 2010).

Stories from Three Municipalities

In this section we present results from our three case studies, and we analyse how political entrepreneurs strive to gain legitimacy through their activities in policy networks. Each case presentation is paired with an analysis. In the subsequent section, we carry out some cross-case analyses in relation to our research questions.

Sara in the Mill Town

As our story begins, a civil servant in charge of development of trade and industry is about to quit. Before doing so, however, she ensures that Sara is asked to contract for the job. Sara has been an entrepreneur for many years, and she now runs her own firm offering consulting in business development. She is a well-known person in local networks in trade and industry. Sara sees an opportunity to make real improvements for local trade and industry and the municipality engages her as a consultant – through her firm – to do the job.

Sara starts working with great enthusiasm, in the hope of transforming the municipality's attitude to small business from the inside. Local politicians and municipal officials, she contends, don't understand or value how much small business affects local job prospects and economic development. Her main mission is to strengthen contacts and collaboration between the municipality and local business. This, she believes, is a job for which she is well-suited: 'I find it easy to get in contact with entrepreneurs in the market. I find it easy to get them to trust me and what I stand for. In addition, I have many former associates in local business' (Interview Sara, 2016).

To begin with, Sara gets solid support for her new ideas from local politicians. However, administrators and specifically the chief executive is somehow sceptical of Sara's ideas. The first step in Sara's long-term strategy is to produce a development plan for local trade and industry, in collaboration with the stakeholders – the local entrepreneurs. The main purpose of her plan is to produce a picture of the problem that illustrates the need for change. Although the plan involves strong criticism of the municipality, the municipal assembly does adopt the plan. The mayor, who is not as critical of the municipality's work as Sara is, agrees to some extent, saying that 'contacts between the municipality and local trade and industry have not been bad, but they have been few' (Interview Mayor, 2016). The plan now forms – especially in its criticism of the municipality – the basis for Sara's forthcoming work.

In order to strengthen her own position and to facilitate the efforts of the municipality vis-à-vis local trade and industry, Sara applies to take part in a national development programme.[3] The application is granted, which means that Sara now has access to greater resources. She is able to start a more formalized project based in part on project funding from the national agency. Sara has stressed the need to include the stakeholders – local trade and industry – in the project. A steering group is therefore constituted, composed of Sara, the mayor, the chief executive, and representatives from local trade and industry.

Eventually the work of the steering group seems less and less satisfactory. For the local representatives of trade and industry, who for a long time have distrusted the local government, the steering group becomes a forum for voicing various complaints about the municipality. 'It's a lack of trust that makes a constructive dialogue impossible', Sara points out (Interview Sara, 2017). It is particularly the chief executive and the representatives of trade and industry who have a hard time understanding one another. It is not just the representatives of trade and industry, however, who are a problem in the eyes of the chief executive. As he sees it, namely Sara, too, is one of the problematic stakeholders. Sara, for her part, sees the chief executive undermining the project. Behind Sara's back, moreover, the mayor even calls her 'the consultant', and implies that she is not loyal to the municipality (Interview Sara, 2017).

---

[3] The programme is administered by the Swedish Agency for Economic and Regional Growth.

A year after the project has started, it all seems to have reached its end. The mayor – who in Sara's view is under strong influences from the chief executive – announces that the project will be shut down. Extensive protests from local trade and industry then follow, as well as attention in the local newspapers. The mayor then backs down. Still, Sara feels that her job at the municipality is threatened. She sees an opportunity to save her own position, and the core of the project, by getting the representatives of trade and industry removed from the steering group. In agreement with the mayor and the chief executive, therefore, the representatives of local trade and industry are kicked out of the project – a project which had been meant to strengthen dialogue and collaboration between the municipality and local trade and industry. By this means, however, Sara's legitimacy as the project manager is at least temporarily saved.

Jenny in the Small Town

In the Small Town, Jenny has worked in the municipal administration for several years. As a civil servant, she is in charge of rural affairs and development of trade and industry. Improved public and commercial service in the countryside is the particular task to which Jenny feels most dedicated. She describes herself as a 'doer', with an ability to gain people's trust and to push changes through:

> I find it very easy to pay a visit and to speak with people in the village communities and the local associations, as well as with the politicians. It is all about building relations and persuading people to play a part. Getting people to understand that nobody is going to make these changes for us. It is up to ourselves to get things done. (Interview Jenny, 2016)

According to Jenny, the politicians have some vague ambitions to develop the rural part of the municipality and to improve rural living conditions. But no strategic work is being done in the municipality to realize these ambitions – there is no diagnosis of the problems, no concrete goals, no plans. The lack of systematic work along such lines is frustrating to Jenny. She understands, however, that the resources of the municipality are small, and that she has to be smart if she is to make some real change.

Jenny sees an opportunity to strengthen her position by applying to take part in a national development programme, and the programme is still open for applications.[4] In her application for the programme, she

---

[4] The programme is administered by the Swedish Agency for Economic and Regional Growth.

stresses the need to approach rural development systematically, and to collaborate with the village associations and other stakeholders. The village associations have partnered with Jenny on previous development projects, and she describes herself as a link between the stakeholders and the municipal administration and the politicians.

> I think I'm good at listening, and maybe I'll become a spokesperson for [the village associations] in the local government sector, with the politicians. I also have a relationship of trust with the leading politicians. (Interview Jenny 2016)

The chief executive, however, tells Jenny that she cannot apply for the national development programme. That kind of work is not a part of Jenny's duties, as he sees it. The mayor, on the other hand, listens to Jenny and urges her to apply and to keep up the good work. The mayor appreciates Jenny's creativity and her good relations with important stakeholders. Jenny also gets good news from the national development programme: her application has been accepted. Bolstered by the supportive mayor, Jenny starts sending invitations to what she calls 'dialogue cafés' – public citizen deliberations based on dialogue meetings. The aim of the 'dialogue cafés' is to establish a common understanding and to create a platform – for the municipality, for stakeholders, and for citizens – upon which further collaboration can be built.

However, the 'dialogue cafés' attract no more than a few persons, which is a big disappointment to Jenny. For the next 'dialogue café', she tries sending special invitations through the village associations to selected actors in the countryside, but with no result. Jenny feels growing frustration, as do the municipal officials, including the chief executive. Jenny argues that she does not get the needed support from the municipal administration. They don't support her in her efforts to be creative and to improve living conditions in the rural part of the municipality. The chief executive is now clear about his disagreement with Jenny, and says to her that the project she is running is not furthering the development of the municipality at all. As the chief executive sees it, the project is consuming resources without giving anything back. This is especially true, in his estimation, of Jenny's attempt to mobilize resources from the network of village associations.

Now even support from the municipality's leading politicians is about to break down. For Jenny, the disappointment is overwhelming. She feels undermined by the officials and betrayed by the politicians who had previously supported her. Furthermore, the failure of the 'dialogue cafés', where Jenny did not manage to mobilize the network of village-association volunteers, is a real setback. Taken together, these developments make Jenny feel marginalized. As she sees it, she has not been granted the discretion or the resources needed to fulfil her commitment to rural development in the Small Town. Ultimately Jenny chooses to quit, and to start working in another municipality instead.

Caroline in the Suburb

In the strategy for regional development adopted in 2010 by the county council, the Suburb's city centre was highlighted as one of eight city centres in the expansive region. But such an assessment is not, according to citizen surveys, shared by the Suburb's inhabitants, nor by local leaders in trade and industry when they look for areas in which to establish new businesses. The city centre of the Suburb is seen as highly anonymous. Thus, if expectations for the regional development strategy are to be fulfilled, changes will have to take place in planning, in practices, and in attitudes towards the Suburb's city centre.

In 2012, the municipality starts addressing the largest owners of commercial properties in the city centre. The ruling coalition wants to start some kind of collaboration with these property owners, in order to develop the city centre. In what way this is to be done, however, is unclear. From the municipality's point of view, the Suburb's city centre can't be developed without a commitment from the property owners. A dialogue begins, in a tentative way, with a network consisting of six of the largest property owners. The vague ambitions of the municipality make it clear there is a need for some kind of link between the municipality and the property owners – a link that can facilitate dialogue and identify a way forward. With funding drawn in part from the property owners, Caroline is now employed by the municipality as project manager. Despite her very special employment status – with unregulated and informal commitments from the property owners – in the municipality Caroline is seen as just a normal municipal civil servant.

Caroline herself has years of experience in urban development and project management, both as a public official and as a consultant. She soon understands she will need a clear mandate from the municipality, in order to strengthen her own position and to inspire commitment from the property owners. After attending the municipal executive committee, Caroline gets what she wants: a clear mandate to produce, in collaboration with the property owners, a *new* development plan for the city centre. Due to Caroline's clear mandate, the property owners feel confidence in the project's great potential for them. Now she has a platform on which to stand. She describes her work this way:

> My task is to get others involved in developing the city centre. I can never do this alone; I have to get other key actors to join in. Thus, my work is very much about gaining acceptance for the issue, and nagging. (Interview Caroline, 2017)

Some years later, Caroline successfully applies to take part in a national development programme.[5] She describes participation in the national programme as giving the project a positive aura. Through Caroline's successful project management, collaboration between the municipality and the property owners is clearly formalized. Rather surprisingly, however, Caroline's legitimacy is never challenged. Caroline finds that her colleagues treat her no differently, despite the fact that half her salary is paid by the property owners. She uses her networks and her various skills to muddle through and to get the project to work. The project is proving a success, and she is aware of her own role in the process. She explains: 'I could never have had this as my first job. You have to have been in the business of networking to know how to manage, how to get things through, how to build relationships' (Interview Caroline 2017).

For Caroline and some of her colleagues at the municipality, the work with the development plan for the city centre is proceeding. The property owners take an active part in workshops arranged by Caroline, and she is able to balance and to calibrate their influence on the development plan. Eventually a draft of the plan is presented to the municipal committee and the chief executive, and it is well received. The chief executive urges that the plan be given the status of a supplement to the comprehensive municipal plan,[6] and the municipal committee agrees. A vague idea about establishing some kind of collaboration with property owners ends up as a supplement to the comprehensive municipal plan. This must be seen as definitive recognition for Caroline's legitimacy, and for the success of her project management.

Lessons Learned from Across-Case Analysis

All of the cases are embedded in processes rooted in local Swedish governmental settings. The institutional framework is thus common to all of them, even if the outcomes differ. In addition, all of the projects have

---

[5] The programme is administered by the Swedish Agency for Economic and Regional Growth.

[6] The comprehensive municipal plan is a legally established plan, and the most important strategic plan for Swedish municipalities, see Plan – Swedish Planning and Building Act, 2010: 900.

during the processes become a part of a programme for regional development managed by a national governmental agency. A cross-case analysis is therefore needed (see Table 11.3). In this section, we compare the three cases and the role of political entrepreneurs in each one. To guide this discussion, we return to the three research questions presented in our introduction. The two first questions relate to how input legitimacy is formed; the third concerns output legitimacy, as discussed in the theoretical section above.

Our analysis indicates that trust in the outcome of the process – that is, output legitimacy – is indeed dependent on the process having started with a clear formal input legitimacy.

In the *Mill Town*, the initial input legitimacy is formed primarily through the networks; thus, the legal arrangements are not explicitly addressed. This fuzziness on formal and legal questions undermines the legitimacy of the project. However, after some challenges that risk putting a halt to the project, the PE puts an effort into clearing up these matters and gaining greater formal input legitimacy for the project. The main output legitimacy thus far gained for the project is achieved through improved networks and new collaboration.

In the *Small Town*, Jenny does not manage as the political entrepreneur to bring together the formal municipal administration with the network of village associations. Thus, she never becomes the link they had expected; nor is she able to share resources among the actors. This can be explained by the lack of formal support from the municipal administration (legality) during the input phase of the process. Without the formal input legitimacy and a clear mandate within the municipal organization, Jenny had a hard time attracting potential members to form a policy network. Jenny therefore leaves the project, never having gained the necessary legitimacy among the stakeholders.

In the *Suburb*, Caroline achieves legitimacy in the network of stakeholders (the property owners), among the members of the municipal committee, and among the municipal administration. In the initial phase, however, she has no clear formal input legitimacy, as there are no specific expectations for the project at this stage. In order to gain formal input legitimacy, Caroline addresses the municipal committee, thereby obtaining a clear mandate for change. Through her formal legitimacy in the municipal organization and her informal legitimacy in terms of trust among stakeholders, Caroline has a platform on which to stand. By showing results and building trust, she acquires considerable legitimacy.

Table 11.3 Overview of the results in the three local projects

	Mill Town	Small Town	Suburb
How do Political Entrepreneurs (PEs) navigate through 'messy' institutional arrangements in order to establish collaboration with external networks?	The PE uses benchmarking and a self-authored study to gain acceptance for the need for public–private collaboration. However, the PE has an unclear position and mandate.	The PE wants to establish collaboration with a network of village associations, but lacks support from the municipal administration. Instead, she seeks and gets strong support from the mayor as the political leader. Still, the chief executive's disapproval persists.	At the very beginning, the network gains acceptance in the municipal committee. In addition, however, the PE actively seeks and gets further discretion, as well as a clear mandate from the municipal committee to grant the property owners an influential role.
How do PEs mobilize resources through networks?	The PE elicits a commitment from local trade and industry. From the chief executive's point of view, however, the representatives of local trade and industry do not contribute any resources.	The PE doesn't manage to mobilize resources or to obtain support through the already established network.	The network of property owners is considered a valuable resource. The members of this network contribute resources without asking for 'too much' influence.
How do PEs manage serving as a link between the municipality and networks of external stakeholders?	The PE initially loses legitimacy when the network fails to generate any resources. The PE is seen as part of the network of trade and industry, rather than of the municipal network. The PE later establishes a more explicit connection with the municipal network, thereby gaining legitimacy in the eyes of the municipality.	The PE does not manage to engage the network of village associations, and so is not considered a link to valuable networks with resources.	Clear support from the municipal council bolsters the PE's legitimacy among the property owners. In a similar way, the PE earns legitimacy within the municipal organization, due to the support she enjoys from the property owners as well as the smooth way in which she handles them.

Note: PE = Political entrepreneur.

In concluding this section, let us look at the model above. As our cases have shown, it is critical for political entrepreneurs to gain formal and legal input legitimacy. Without a clear legal mandate, it seems hard to act entrepreneurially. Following the formal input way of account legitimacy, political entrepreneurship would always be legitimate, as long as the political entrepreneur acts in line with legal arrangements, their remits and responsibilities in the input phase and follow it through the project. One obvious problem lies in the difficulty of defining what, in terms of legality, is in accordance with the role of civil servant. On the one hand, the national programme in question seeks entrepreneurial civil servants; on the other, legitimacy for civil servants in municipalities is often perceived as something static and universal.

However, legitimacy of political entrepreneurs can't be created just from legal aspects in the input phase. Rather, output as a source of legitimacy lays in the nature of entrepreneurship. In the output phase, drawing from the case studies, it appears that trust among stakeholders and other informal aspects of legitimacy are the most critical. Through the analyses of the case studies, we can see how trust in outcome is critical among both the municipality and the external networks and stakeholders. Thus, legitimacy of political entrepreneurs seems to be created in an interplay between formal input and informal output aspects of legitimacy.

CONCLUSIONS

Aspirations for local development in these times of European and global crisis open up a space for political entrepreneurship when new ways are being sought to solve local problems and to coordinate the use of resources. However, messy institutional arrangements in the area of local development policy offer few clear structures on which to rely; instead, legitimacy for local projects and for political entrepreneurs has to be gained in each and every case. Legitimacy is formed through a balance of legality and trust among stakeholders. Legitimacy both forms the action space for political entrepreneurs and is formed by the latter's activities, networks, as well as their personal competences and skills.

Based on the case studies above, we argue that it is almost impossible to separate the actors totally from the *form* of public decision-making and the *policies* that are formulated. Political entrepreneurship, we contend, is a form of public decision-making. If political entrepreneurs in the public sector are given discretion and a mandate to operate in entrepreneurial fashion, a decentralized form of decision-making results. Likewise, political entrepreneurs want change – it lies in the nature of political entrepreneurship – so it is hard to separate the actors themselves from the change driven by them. Our way of understanding legitimacy as something conferred by others implies that the observer can find it very hard to separate the policy changes proposed by political entrepreneurs from the political entrepreneurs themselves.

The motives for political entrepreneurs to get engaged in projects for local development seem to lie in the informal legitimacy they can achieve among stakeholders, and the trust that the latter may place in them as people. But, as we have seen above, it is the formal legitimacy in the input phase of the project that is critical for the outcome. This, however, presents a challenge in the context of local and regional development policy, since processes like these can never be planned and started by just a formal decision. There must also be informal legitimacy – an entrepreneurial person enjoying trust among stakeholders who takes the lead in the messy institutional setting.

Many scholars emphasize the importance of output legitimacy for trust in the political system in general (Rothstein, 2009; Rothstein and Teorell, 2012). In the local cases we have examined, however, the opportunities for output legitimacy were dependent on input arrangements and on the efforts expended to make the process legally correct and informally trustworthy. This may, however, reflect the fact that all of these projects were far from 'business as usual' in the context of municipal service provision. All of the projects sought to stretch the formal arrangements of municipal policymaking and to extend municipal policies for local development. What we learn, then, is that political entrepreneurs must remember the importance of input legitimacy if they are to gain output legitimacy.

Theoretically, one can argue, there is a tension between formal input legitimacy and entrepreneurship. Rather than clear mandate and formal decision-making, the concept of entrepreneurship is associated with informality, 'thinking outside the box' and output. Entrepreneurship is a fragile process. Drawing from the case studies in this chapter, we argue that a more complex accounting of legitimacy of political entrepreneurship is needed. Fragile entrepreneurial development projects, within the public founded sector, cannot only be built from an informal and output-based legitimacy; there is also a need to clarify the formal and input-based legitimacy to create a platform from which entrepreneurial processes can be built.

REFERENCES

Aarsaether, N. and T. Ringholm (2011), 'The rural municipality as developer – entrepreneurial and planning modes in community development', *Lex Localis*, 9(4), 373–387.

Assmo, P. and E. Wihlborg (2016), 'Political entrepreneurship and sustainable growth in rural areas', in C. Karlsson, C. Silander and D. Silander (eds), *Political Entrepreneurship: Regional Growth and Entrepreneurial Diversity in Sweden*. Cheltenham: Edward Elgar Publishing.

Bekkers, V. and A. Edwards (2007), 'Legitimacy and democracy: a conceptual framework for assessing governance practices', in V. Bekkers, G. Dijkstra, A. Edwards and M. Fenger (eds), *Governance and the Democratic Deficit*. London: Ashgate.

Deas, I. and K. G. Ward (2000), 'From the "new localism" to the "new regionalism"? The implications of regional development agencies for city–regional relations', *Political Geography*, 19(3), 273–292.

Déjean, F., J.-P. Gond and B. Leca (2007), 'Measuring the unmeasured – an institutional entrepreneur strategy in an emerging industry', *Human Relations*, 57(6), 741–764.

Easton, D. (1965), *A Systems Analysis of Political Life*. New York: Wiley.

European Commission (2014), *European Regional Development Fund*, accessed 27 October 2017 at http://ec.europa.eu/regional_policy/en/funding/erdf/.

Evans, M. (2014), 'Democracy, legitimacy and local government electoral reform', *Local Government Studies*, 40(1), 41–63.

Fligstein, N. (1997), 'Social skill and institutional theory', *American Behavior Scientist*, 40(4), 379–405.

Franzén, M., N. Hertting and C. Thörn (2016), *Stad till salu – entreprenörskap-surbanismen och det offentliga rummets värde*. Göteborg: Diadalos.

Hadjimichalis, C. (2011), 'SME, entrepreneurialism and local/regional development', in A. Pike, A. Rodriguez-Pose and J. Tomany (eds), *Handbook of Local and Regional Development*. London and New York: Routledge.

Högberg, Ö. (2007), *Maktlösa makthavare: en studie om kommunalt chefskap*, Diss, Linköping: Linköpings Universitet.

Johansson, J. (2013), 'Regionalpolitikens utveckling: mellan politisk kamp och ekonomisk nytta', in T. Mitander, L. Säll and A. Öjehag-Pettersson (eds), *Det regionala samhällsbyggandets praktiker*. Göteborg: Diadalos.

Jonsson, L. (2012), 'The Swedish municipality director: a managerial function between politics and administration', in S. Tengblad (ed.), *The Work of Managers – Towards a Practice Theory of Management*. Oxford: Oxford University Press.

Jonsson, L. and S.-I. Arnell (2006), *Att organisera kommuners ledning*. Nora: Nya Doxa.

Karlsson, D. (2006), *Den svenske borgmästaren. Kommunstyrelsens ordförande och den lokala demokratin*. Göteborg: Förvaltningshögskolan.

Keating, M. (1998), *The New Regionalism in Western Europe – Territorial Restructuring and Political Change*. Cheltenham and Northampton, MA: Edward Elgar Publishing.

Kingdon, J. W. (1995), *Agendas, Alternatives and Public Policies*. New York: HarperCollins College Publishers.

Lennqvist Lidén, A.-S. (2010), *Att lägga politiken till rätta. Kommunala chefers professionalisering*. Diss. Örebro: Örebro Universitet.

Lidström, A. (1996), *Kommunsystem i Europa*. Stockholm: Publica.

Lu, M. (2010), 'Thinking beyond political boundaries', *Planning*, 76(6), 24–26.

Maguire, S., C. Hardy and T. B. Lawrence (2004), 'Institutional entrepreneurship in emerging fields – HIV/AIDS treatment advocacy in Canada', *Academy of Management Journal*, 47(5), 657–679.

Mintrom, M. (1997), 'Policy entrepreneurs and the diffusion of innovation', *American Journal of Political Science*, 41, 738–770.

Mintrom, M. and P. Norman (2009), 'Policy entrepreneurship and policy change', *Policy Studies Journal*, 37(4), 649–667.

Narbutaité Aflaki, I., E. Petridou and L. Miles (eds) (2015), *Entrepreneurship in the Polis: Understanding Political Entrepreneurship*. London: Ashgate.

Nilsson, J.-E. (2012), *Från aktiv lokaliseringspolitik till regional tillväxtpolitik*, Tillväxtanalys PM 2012:18. Östersund: Tillväxtanalys.

Nyhlén, S. (2013), *Regionalpolitik i förändring: en fallstudie av regionalpolitikens aktörer och former i Åre kommun*, Diss. Sundsvall: Mittuniversitetet.

Olausson, A. and J. Syssner (2017), *Att stärka den lokala attraktionskraften – målbilder och genomförande i den lokala utvecklingspolitiken*. Norrköping: Centrum för kommunstrategiska studier.

Persson, B. (2010), *Lokal och regional näringslivspolitik – samarbete, konkurrens, utveckling*. Norrköping: Centrum för kommunstrategiska studier.

Peters, G. and J. Pierre (2004), 'Multi-level governance and democracy', in I. Bach and M. Flinders (eds), *Multi-level Governance*. Oxford: Oxford University Press.

Pierre, J. (ed.) (1998), *Partnerships in Urban Governance: European and American Experiences*. London: Palgrave Macmillan.

Rhodes, R. A. W. and D. Marsh (1992), 'New directions in the study of policy networks', *European Journal of Political Research*, 21, 181–205.

Rothstein, B. (2009), 'Creating political legitimacy: electoral democracy versus quality of government', *American Behavioral Scientist*, 53(3), 311–330.

Rothstein, B. and J. Teorell (2012), 'Defining and measuring quality of government', in S. Holmberg and B. Rothstein (eds), *Good Government: The Relevance of Political Science*. Cheltenham and Northampton, MA: Edward Elgar Publishing.

Schmidt, V. A. (2013), 'Democracy and legitimacy in the European Union revisited input, output and "throughput"', *Political Studies*, 61(1), 2–22.

Sellers, J. M. and A. Lidström (2007), 'Decentralisation, local government, and the welfare state', *Governance: an Institutional Journal of Policy, Administration, and Institutions*, 20(4), 609–632.

Sørensen, E. (2006), 'Metagovernance: the changing role of politicians in processes of democratic governance', *American Review of Public Administration*, 36(1), 98–114.

Sørensen, E. and J. Torfing (2007), 'Theoretical approaches to governance network failure', in E. Sørensen and J. Torfing (eds), *Theories of Democratic Network Governance*. London and New York: Palgrave Macmillan.

SOU (1999:77), Demokratiutredningens forskarvolym II. *Demokrati och medborgarskap.*

Swedish Government (2015), *En nationell strategi för hållbar tillväxt och attraktionskraft 2015–2020.*

Tillväxtanalys (2014), *Samverkan inom ramen för flernivåstyrning*. PM 2014:09.

Tillväxtanalys (2017), *Regionala tillväxtpolitiska utmaningar – behov av nya strukturreformer och nya samverkanslösningar*? PM 2017:10.

Tödtling, F. (2011), 'Endogenous approaches to local and regional development policy', in A. Pike, A. Rodriguez-Pose and J. Tomany (eds), *Handbook of Local and Regional Development*. London and New York: Routledge.

United Nations (2017), *Millennium Development Goals and Beyond 2015*, accessed 27 October 2017 at http://www.un.org/millenniumgoals/.

Vedung, E. (2016), *Implementering i politik och förvaltning*. Lund: Studentlitteratur.

von Bergmann-Winberg, M.-L. and E. Wihlborg (eds) (2011), *Politiskt entreprenörskap – kreativ problemlösning och förändring*. Malmö: Liber förlag.

Weber, M. (1978), *Economy and Society. An Outline of the Interpretative Sociology*. Berkeley, CA: University of California Press.

Wihlborg, E. (2000), *En lösning som söker problem: Hur och varför lokala IT-policyer utvecklas i landsbygdskommuner*, Diss. Linköping: Linköpings Universitet.

Wihlborg, E. (2015), 'Utvecklingspolitik på lokal nivå', in N. Bohlin, S. Nyhlén and P. Olausson (eds), *Lokalt beslutsfattande*. Lund: Studentlitteratur.

Wihlborg, E. and K. Söderholm (2013), 'Mediators in action: organizing sociotechnical system change', *Technology in Society*, 35(4), 267–275.

INTERVIEWS

Mill Town		
Project manager	March 2016	February 2017
Chief Executive	March 2016	
Mayor	March 2016	
Small Town		
Project Manager	March 2016	March 2017
Chief Executive	March 2016	
Mayor	March 2016	
Suburb		
Project Manager	May 2016	February 2017

12. Local cases of institutional entrepreneurship: change agents in regions facing demographic change

Birgit Leick and Susanne Gretzinger

INTRODUCTION

In spite of an abundant body of empirical research on institutional entrepreneurship, notably in management and organisational theory literature (e.g., Garud et al., 2002; Greenwood et al., 2002; Casile and Davis-Blake, 2002), far less attention to date has been devoted to cases of local institutional entrepreneurship outside organisational change and management processes. Recent empirical studies have begun addressing institutional change involving local actors such as local firms, public organisations and business clusters, for example, Sotarauta and Mustikkamäki (2015), Matthyssens et al. (2013), McCarthy (2012), Ritvala and Kleymann (2012), Hung and Whittington (2011), and Perkmann and Spicer (2007).

In this chapter, we aim to contribute to the latter strand of empirical research on local institutional entrepreneurs and describe two different case studies that represent local cases of institutional entrepreneurship (Maguire, 2008; Battilana et al., 2009), emerging through individual commitment and bottom-up approaches (see Anderson, 2008). Both case studies highlight the process of influencing institutionalised practices through the so-called institutional entrepreneurs in regions across Germany that face important demographic challenges such as persistently steady population decline, the emigration of young people and population ageing (European Union Committee of the Regions, 2016).

The first case study specifically points out the strategic capabilities of institutional entrepreneurs who engage in network-building and sense-making in order to change the institutionalised practices of firms and public organisations in the light of population ageing and population decline. By contrast, the second case portrays in more depth a local initiative for age-friendliness in the public administration of an East German municipality; it describes local institutional entrepreneurship from a process perspective, showing the triggers for and characteristics of such bottom-up activities, as well as their impact on the municipality. The chapter concludes by stressing two main governance implications of local institutional entrepreneurship as lessons learnt from the cases, lessons that can also be considered as future research avenues.

LOCAL INSTITUTIONAL ENTREPRENEURS AND DEMOGRAPHIC CHANGE IN GERMANY: BACKGROUND AND CONTEXT OF THE CASE STUDIES

The following case studies present anecdotal evidence from empirical field research that has taken place in different regions across Germany between 2011 and 2015. In these regions, the local economies are characterised by long-term demographic ageing and population decline (see Leick, 2017; Matuschewski and Leick, 2012). Based upon a series of interviews, the context for the institutional entrepreneurs can be described as follows: local companies across industries and sectors in the regions have been increasingly pressurised by emerging and over time, rising, shortages of labour in local markets, as well as the ageing of their employees, including managerial staff and owner-managers. However, small companies in particular apparently found it very hard to cope with these developments, notably, the tremendous uncertainty associated with the market changes in the longer run. Although long-term demographic projections exist at the level of regions and municipalities (for example, www.regionalstatistik.de and www.wegweiser-kommune.de), many firms in the regions, where the interviews were conducted, considered the adaptation of their operations and strategies towards more demography-sensitive business models as an enormous challenge (see Leick, 2017).

Against the backdrop of these observations, narrative interviews (Boje, 2002; Czarniawska, 1998) were conducted with individuals or groups associated with private or public organisations that worked to change the dominant practices of firms in light of the regional demographic challenges. Methodologically, a qualitative research approach was applied in accordance with the recommendations provided by Eisenhardt (1989), Eisenhardt and Graebner (2007), and Siggelkow (2007), with regard to both the research design and the coding and thematic analysis.

With regard to the first case study (see Table 12.1), the interviews focused on representatives of local business communities, business clusters and public-policy agencies (such as regional development agencies and educational organisations) and provided specific evidence about the challenges – for local firms – that are associated with regional demographic challenges. As the interviewees consistently report, these challenges generate considerable uncertainty for individual firms, while, at the same time, putting pressure on their established practices in the area of human resources/recruiting, health and safety in the workplace, and training and further education. Hence, the first case study gives an impression of the networking activities, strategic-political commitment, and sense-making capabilities of these actors who represent local institutional entrepreneurs in their endeavours to change the firm practices.

Table 12.1 Key respondents and their characteristics of local institutional entrepreneurship

Key respondent	*Case region in Germany*	*Main areas and responsibilities*	*Affiliated organisation*
A	Thuringia	Education and training	Network of training and educational agencies
B	Rhineland Palatinate	Regional and tourism management; Business development	Municipality; Association of local municipalities
C	Schleswig Holstein	Regional and tourism management	Municipality; Business association
D	Schleswig Holstein	Business development	Chamber of Commerce; Business association
E	Saxony Anhalt	Applied research	University College

The second case study focuses on another bottom-up initiative that represents such local institutional entrepreneurs (see also Leick, 2017); it gives an in-depth portrait of the process of institutional entrepreneurship, including the triggers and impact of the change agents (Cels et al., 2012) on the local practices. All interviews have been conducted with key informants in the initiatives (A–E).

Case Study 1: The Strategic Networking and Sense-Making Capacities of Institutional Entrepreneurs

In the following, we present selected findings from interviews with representatives from private or public organisations that show proactiveness and commitment for the local economy and thus qualify as local institutional entrepreneurs (Table 12.1). An important activity of these local institutional entrepreneurs is the building of alliances, coalitions and networks not only in accordance with the needs and challenges of the local business community, but also in line with their own agenda-setting. By adopting a proactive stance and setting impulses, these agents show leadership in developing such networks and, moreover, act strategically, because they intentionally include powerful players from the region whom they consider as multipliers for their work, as A and B stress:

> From the very start, we have been searching those who are active in the field … and have tried to bring the active people together. We have purposely asked ourselves: Which actors do what? Which firms are active? What do the other organisations offer the firms? How could we make our network attractive for them? … We also built up another circle, which we have called 'our strategic partners'. These were representatives of the regional policy and the government. (A)

And

> We said to ourselves: Yes, we will start a local training alliance to support the firms in our region. Then we went on a journey … Personally, I have all the contacts and I have my network. (B)

Multipliers are, for instance, large firms or key actors in the municipalities with dense ego-networks that might benefit the network or alliance of the institutional entrepreneurs. Therefore, these agents try to integrate such focal actors in their initiatives because they acknowledge their importance in achieving their own goals, including the interests of the local business communities that they wish to support. Hence, "bringing the right people together" (A) and building such alliances are important activities of local institutional entrepreneurs. Often, they possess the critical piece of knowledge about who might match whom and are able to deploy their knowledge strategically for the sake of benefiting themselves and the local businesses. Based upon their networking capacities, such entrepreneurs establish an infrastructure that enables knowledge flows among the business community. In addition, they manage and steer the knowledge flows according to their own agenda; however, at the same time, the institutional entrepreneurs are driven by demand from the local companies. B describes a prototypical context in which the potential institutional entrepreneur uses information advantages strategically as a critical resource for networking:

> For the project, there is no co-ordinator available to whom firms may turn and ask questions. But I know the ministry quite well and I contact the people that I need for the project. I know very well which department I shall approach. When I need specific support, I look for the right people there, and then I will get the support. (B)

Along with strategic networking, local institutional entrepreneurs offer convincing interpretations to their potential collaborators in the local communities. As knowledge managers, these agents apply framing techniques and translation in order to build common ground in the networks, for example, by taking into account different management and leadership cultures and, as a result, different languages between the industries or types of companies. An illustrative example is that C tries to adapt to the *non-academic* and more *basic* language that is common in small enterprises in order to communicate with them, which the interviewee considers as critical for identifying, framing and understanding the challenges or problems that such firms meet:

> If you do not understand the language of the firms, if you do not understand how they think, or how they have to struggle, then you do not understand which needs or problems they have (…) (C)

Therefore, the translation between different understandings and languages, along with the framing of both challenges or problems and potential "solutions", which local institutional entrepreneurs favour, are important activities. Local institutional entrepreneurs establish common understandings for all parties involved, for instance, to convey an idea of new challenges that the local businesses will encounter. This is the case for new policy instruments or external trends associated with demographic ageing and population decline that many small firms tend to adopt at a later point in time compared to large or globally operating companies, as B expresses:

> Family-friendly employers and employer branding … Work–life balance, health and safety in the workplace … The firms have not addressed these important trends. But we give them some ideas to think about. We are the ones pushing these ideas with the firms and the managers … This is what we are actually doing: picking up trends and giving firms ideas about them. And

> asking ourselves: how can we implement such trends locally with the firms and employers we have here in this region? (B)

Furthermore, the local institutional entrepreneurs interviewed are also able to recognise the need for framing and translation – not only when new trends emerge and contest the established practices of the local business communities, but also when the institutional entrepreneurs themselves recognise that these established practices are becoming challenged. Based upon this reflective attitude towards the local business environment, the institutional entrepreneur D, for example, describes how his approach to support the local businesses changed along with a twist in the local labour market. While there had been an excess supply of young trainees for many decades in the past, this has recently turned into a shortage:

> You know, in former times, we were known for our good deeds when we have been training young people to increase their chances to get hired locally, or when we introduced new professions to them, just to get them employed … Now the tide has turned, and firms are our target group, instead of young people. We have to tell the firms now how to hire young people and think about 'employer branding'. (D)

In such cases, local institutional entrepreneurs provide completely new interpretations, which help them introduce alternative practices with local businesses and get them institutionalised over time.

Case Study 2: Local Institutional Entrepreneurs – Insights into the Process of Promoting Institutional Change

The following case study focuses on the triggers, activities and impact of local institutional entrepreneurs. It describes the initiative *Age-Friendly Local Government Magdeburg* which was founded in 2011 by researchers from the department of sociology at the University College Magdeburg-Stendal in Germany. The research focus of the group has been the ageing society and they had already conducted several funded projects that deal with this topic. These researchers have been investigating the issue of age-friendliness for a long time and have become aware of both the huge potential and neglect of the topic in the public debate. Like many East German cities, Magdeburg has been coping with an ageing population, with the cohort of elderly residents visibly growing in numbers, and the outmigration (notably of young people) from the city and the region and, in part, suburbanisation occurring at the same time. For a long time, a major focus of the local government has therefore been the management of urban decline and renewal, and many political efforts were made in the past notably to attract younger residents (for example, families with children) and students to the city centre and counteract the ageing of the local population. Only recently did the city administration become aware of the fact that it not only needs to provide attractive living spaces for young adults, students and families, but also for the rising share of elderly people living inside the city area. This was the starting point for the city administration of Magdeburg to install a board for a so-called *senior citizen policy* that was formally responsible for elderly people in the city area and the quality of their lives.

Against this background, the local researchers who had been working on the topic of *age-friendliness* had begun to set up an informal collaboration with the city administration of Magdeburg. After some time, they successfully implemented the topic with the public administration and took the lead in establishing a more formalised collaboration with the city administration. In this project-based collaboration, the researchers wanted to find out how *age-friendliness* can be included in the operational routines inside the public administration, as the interviewee summarises:

> There had been a process in the city administration running in parallel. But we, the researchers, had been proactive and had shared the topic with those persons in the city administration who have also been working on the topic in various fields. (E)

Hence, the researchers had identified a vacuum, that is, that neither the topic of age-friendliness nor dealing with elderly citizens in the city had been addressed by the city administration, and that organisational specifications about how to include age-friendliness in their operations did not exist, either. Therefore, at that time, it was unclear for the city administration what age-friendliness actually means and how it could be operationalised, which was the initial stimulus or trigger for the researchers to work for change, as the key informants report:

> The representatives of the city administration saw that they had to offer a high quality of living not only for youngsters and families moving to the city but also to the rising number of elderly persons living inside the city area.
>
> Most persons in the city administration had not felt that age-friendliness was their responsibility.

Their push for an intensified and more formalised collaboration was based upon the group's vision that age-friendliness was a neglected topic for the city of Magdeburg and that it should gain more awareness and importance in a city, where population ageing was a visible and pressing problem. Indeed, they recognised the opportunity to bring the topic to the fore by establishing a formal collaboration with the city administration. The institutional entrepreneurs thus placed the topic with those local stakeholders who they wanted to influence, and they both argued and acted strategically in order to allocate resources to their project:

> 'Of course, we have argued that pressures will increase to adjust to the rising share of elderly persons in the city area.' (...) 'Our research had, at least in part, initiated an own process of dealing with age-friendliness on the part of the city administration.' ... 'The topic gained importance through our project efforts and our work'. (E)

Moreover, the researchers used public funding and a grant to achieve this. The funded project *Age-Friendly Local Government* deals with age-friendliness in the city of Magdeburg and addresses urban lifestyles for elderly persons and the role of the public administration. It conceptually explores what age-friendliness means for the local government, which spheres of activity are connected with the concept and how age-friendliness can be integrated into the work and operational routines of the city administration.

With their aim to place the topic high on the agenda of the city administration and increase awareness for age-friendly policies in a demographically ageing city, the researchers addressed circa 100 persons working in different units in the city administration and in related public organisations (for example, public real estate companies, educational agencies, etc.) by using exploratory interviews. Moreover, they aligned their project work to the newly introduced *senior citizen policy*, thereby safeguarding that all the interviewed stakeholders were open to the researchers' topic. The researchers intensively worked to gain network partners within the formal, project-based collaboration. The collaboration granted them legitimacy to approach all relevant people and units inside the city administration and motivate them to collaborate. More specifically, the researchers brought about collective action by bringing those stakeholders together in workshops, conferences, and more informal discussions in which the relevance of the topic has been repeatedly addressed, for example, by asking the following questions: What does it mean for your administration? How can it be included in the daily operations? Why is it important?

Through this communication, the institutional entrepreneurs promoted their agenda by talking to key persons, showing them the importance of their issue, and conducting workshops or small conferences in order to bring all the involved parties together. Indeed, they managed to raise awareness for the topic because they convinced the administration to acknowledge that age-friendliness is an important trend, which will affect their operations in various fields. Although most stakeholders had already felt the necessity to take action vis-à-vis the problems associated with demographic ageing, they had not been aware of their importance and the opportunity to envision *age-friendliness* as a positive change, rather than a problematic trend, as the interviewees' state:

> We actually showed the officials what could happen in the specific area that they were working in if they neglected age-friendliness. For instance when it comes to accessibility in the city. (E)

Indeed, the researchers created meaning about the topic and showed the administration how the concept can be used in everyday life and in the daily operational routines. The researchers benefited from both rising pressures created by ongoing demographical ageing in the city and from a political order to put emphasis on elderly citizens. Nevertheless, they managed to accompany the city administration during the process of learning about age-friendliness. For example, the researchers used *aha effects* in their interviews with responsible persons in the administration. The way in which they asked them about their perceptions and opinions led these local stakeholders to acknowledge, "Yes, I agree that, here, you are right. We did not think so far. But that is an interesting issue that we will have to think about." Another element of their political agenda was to promote their project continuously through presentations, talks and discussions in meetings, workshops and conferences. In this communication process, the researchers filled the vacuum that they had identified by creating meaning about age-friendliness, as the key informant tells:

> If you are talking and talking about a certain issue almost all the time and everywhere, you may gain more interested parties who promote the issue further and further. (E)

In the workshops, the researchers also presented solutions to some problems that are associated with ageing citizens. Since many persons and units in the city administration had a strong motivation to take part in these workshops, the institutional entrepreneurs benefited from their openness regarding the topic and potential solutions. Therefore, the researchers did not have to overcome resistance against the institutional change that they promoted. On the contrary, they could build on the self-interest of their partners to adopt, at least, *some* of the approaches to the problem-solving offered by the entrepreneurs as new routines or practices. An important impact of their work for change is that the city administration finally implemented new organisational specifications including age-friendliness across many departments and units in the public administration.

CONCLUSIONS

Using the concept of institutional entrepreneurship, the case studies portrayed in this chapter describe how influential actors, groups of actors and networks interact with firms and, more generally, organisations in the local economies, in order to influence their institutionalised practices to cope with demographic ageing and population decline. Informed by theoretical insights into institutional entrepreneurship (DiMaggio, 1988; Maguire, 2008; Battilana et al., 2009), the cases describe local institutional entrepreneurship as a process that is triggered by uncertainty and contested institutional practices of firms and public organisations in the wake of demographic change. Firms and public organisations face uncertainty in terms of questions of *what to do exactly* and *how to do this* (see Beckert, 1999). Often, there is also a lack of awareness on the part of the firms of the necessity to take action against such external challenges (Leick, 2017).

As new challenges, problems, or needs of the local business community or local residents emerge in the context of demographic challenges, local *change agents* enter the arena and promote new topics (Battilana and Casciaro, 2012; Cels et al., 2012). These agents are seeking opportunities and rewards in contexts when discourses about the specific facets of demographic challenges are missing, incomplete, unclear, biased or controversial. Therefore, entrepreneurial thinking and opportunity-seeking, proactive behaviour are central to local institutional entrepreneurs (Battilana et al., 2009; Henrekson and Sanandaji, 2011). However, the local agents portrayed do not work out of a sense of altruism. Instead, they want to promote and disseminate their institutional agenda across wider circles and networks. Therefore, local institutional entrepreneurship is associated with a strategic approach to bring to the fore a vision about a specific institutional setting, to forge coalitions and to mobilise resources in order to take on leadership and influence the participating actors.

As the cases portrayed illustrate, the building of alliances and coalitions (Battilana et al., 2009) is an important activity performed by local institutional entrepreneurs in the context of demographic change, along with communication and negotiation processes within these networks. By using their discursive and interpretative power (see Leick, 2017), local institutional entrepreneurs create meaning about new or alternative interpretations of the changing market and business environments in the wake of demographic challenges: for example, the newly-emerging issue of age-friendliness and the need to change the established recruiting and training practices. Sense-making (Sandberg and Tsoukas, 2015) occurs in a process in which local institutional entrepreneurs frame and visualise the challenges and problems and sort out *if–then* scenarios, thereby reducing uncertainty with the local businesses and organisations. Moreover, they also transfer fresh ideas about existing problems and solutions to the parties that they want to influence, that is, the local companies and public organisations that are confronted with demographic change. By disseminating knowledge about alternative ways of looking at these problems, local institutional entrepreneurs systematically establish and deploy knowledge bases as powerful resources and accompany, or even steer, learning processes (see Leick, 2017).

Taken together, the case studies provide two main lessons on the capacities of local institutional entrepreneurs, which can be considered as potential avenues for follow-up research. First, it seems necessary to empirically address and investigate in more depth the trade-offs and externalities that are inherent of institutional entrepreneurship. Such trade-offs arise from opportunism due to the reward-seeking behaviour of local institutional entrepreneurs. Because such agents operate strategically for the sake of capitalising on their *investments* in terms of time, energy, and resources, thus following their own agenda and self-interests, their opportunistic behaviour can adversely affect the networking and framing processes that they initiate. Therefore, local institutional entrepreneurship raises the question of how agent-based leadership can be balanced and controlled for the sake of governing local–regional networking without risking opportunism and its adverse effects (see Burdack et al., 2013; Sotarauta, 2009; Harmaakorpi and Niukkanen, 2007). As a matter of fact, it is necessary to internalise the potentially harmful effects of opportunistic behaviour on the part of the agents who are driving the process of institutional change. Local–regional collaboration and scale-crossing networks within local business communities can be considered as a public good if such alliances aim to bring about higher awareness of local problems and challenges, and support knowledge transfer in the context of demographic challenges. Hence, regional governance needs to be addressed as one future research area, which focuses on the defying of opportunism on the part of local institutional entrepreneurs.

Second, Kalantaridis and Fletcher (2012) criticise the concept of institutional entrepreneurship because, altogether, the capacity of single actors to change complex and stable institutions based upon entrepreneurial behaviour has been exaggerated. Therefore, another open question is how local institutional entrepreneurs can support and feed the existing elements of a local–regional governance infrastructure (Hill and Hupe, 2002: 41 ff.), which consists of various levels (see Chapter 1, in this volume, on governance, local, regional, national and supra-national levels) and both top-down and bottom-up elements of public-policy programmes. The case studies illustrate the leadership capabilities of local institutional entrepreneurs, including those who are located outside the mainstream organisations, and stress their potential to turn into promoters and facilitators of change who contribute to driving regional economic development. Therefore, from a normative standpoint, policy-makers should actively foster local institutional entrepreneurs and support their commitment because such agents complement the variety of existing tools and assistance at the regional level (for example, chambers of commerce, business development agencies, business and industry associations, etc.) with bottom-up initiatives that are closer to the business communities. Therefore, another research avenue refers to governance implications and questions of how to combine, or even reconcile, existing top-down programme structures with bottom-up initiatives of all kinds, both formalised and less formal ones, which qualify as institutional entrepreneurship in a multi-level governance scheme (see Leick and Lang, 2018).

REFERENCES

Anderson, O. J. (2008). 'A bottom-up perspective on innovations: mobilizing knowledge and social capital through innovative processes of bricolage'. *Administration and Society* 40(1): 54–78.

Battilana, J. and Casciaro, T. (2012). 'Change agents, networks, and institutions: a contingency theory of organizational change'. *Academy of Management Journal* 55(2): 381–398.

Battilana, J., Leca, B. and Boxenbaum, E. (2009). 'How actors change institutions: towards a theory of institutional entrepreneurship'. *The Academy of Management Annals* 3(1): 65–107.

Beckert, J. (1999). 'Agency, entrepreneurs, and institutional change. The role of strategic choice and institutionalized practices in organizations'. *Organization Studies* 20(5): 777–799.

Boje, D. M. (2002). *Narrative Methods for Organizational and Communication Research*. Thousand Oaks, CA: Sage.

Burdack, J., Kriszan, M. and Nadler, R. (2013). 'Networks of regional learning in rural Eastern Saxony'. In: C. Tamasy and J. Revilla Diez (eds). *Regional Resilience, Economy and Society. Globalising Rural Places*. Farnham: Ashgate.

Casile, M. and Davis-Blake, A. (2002). 'When accreditation standards change: factors affecting differential responsiveness of public and private organizations'. *The Academy of Management Journal* 45(1): 180–195.

Cels, S., de Jong, J. and Nauta, F. (2012). *Agents of Change. Strategy and Tactics for Social Innovation*. Washington, DC: Brookings Institutions Press.

Czarniawska, B. (1998). *A Narrative Approach to Organization Studies*. Thousand Oaks, CA: Sage.

DiMaggio, P. (1988). 'Interest and agency in institutional theory'. In L. Zucker (ed.). *Institutional Patterns and Culture*. Cambridge: Ballinger.

Eisenhardt, K. M. (1989). 'Building theories from case study research'. *The Academy of Management Review* 14(4): 532–550.

Eisenhardt, K. M. and Graebner, M. E. (2007). 'Theory building from cases: opportunities and challenges'. *The Academy of Management Journal* 50(1): 25–32.

European Union Committee of the Regions (2016). *The Impact of Demographic Change on European Regions*, accessed 20 September 2017 at http://cor.europa.eu/en/documentation/studies/Documents/The%20impact%20of%20demographic%20change%20on%20European%20regions/Impact_demographic_change_european_regions.pdf).

Garud, R., Jain, S. and Kumaraswamy, A. (2002). 'Institutional entrepreneurship in the sponsorship of common technological standards: the case of Sun Microsystems and Java'. *The Academy of Management Journal* 45(1): 196–214.

Greenwood, R., Suddaby, R. and Hinings, C. R. (2002). 'Theorizing change: the role of professional associations in the transformation of institutionalized fields'. *The Academy of Management Journal* 45(1): 58–80.

Harmaakorpi, V. and Niukkanen, H. (2007). 'Leadership in different kinds of regional development networks'. *Baltic Journal of Management* 2(1): 80–96.

Henrekson, M. and Sanandaji, T. (2011). 'The interaction of entrepreneurship and institutions.' *Journal of Institutional Economics* 7(1): 47–75.

Hill, M. and Hupe, P. (2002). *Implementing Public Policy: Governance in Theory and Practice*. Thousand Oaks, CA: Sage.

Hung, S.-C. and Whittington, R. (2011). 'Agency in national innovation systems: institutional entrepreneurship and the professionalization of Taiwanese IT', *Research Policy* 40(4): 526–538.

Kalantaridis, C. and Fletcher, D. (2012). 'Entrepreneurship and institutional change: a research agenda'. *Entrepreneurship & Regional Development* 24(3–4): 199–214.

Leick, B. (2017). 'Institutional entrepreneurs and small firms: how firm practices are being shaped in the context of demographic transformations'. *Journal of Small Business & Entrepreneurship* 29(1): 1–24.

Leick, B. and Lang, T. (2018). 'Re-thinking non-core regions: planning strategies and practices beyond growth'. *European Planning Studies* 26(2): 213–22.

Maguire, S. (2008). 'Institutional entrepreneurship'. In S. R. Clegg and J. R. Bailey (eds). *International Encyclopedia of Organization Studies*. Thousand Oaks, CA: Sage.

Matthyssens, P., Vandenbempt, K. and van Bockhaven, W. (2013). 'Structural antecedents of institutional entrepreneurship in industrial networks: a critical realist explanation'. *Industrial Marketing Management* 42(3): 405–420.

Matuschewski, A. and Leick, B. (2012). 'Wirtschaftsentwicklung in demographischen Schrumpfungsregionen. Unternehmerische Herausforderungen und Strategien am Beispiel von Oberfranken'. *Raumforschung und Raumordnung* 70(6): 515–530.

McCarthy, B. (2012). 'From fishing and factories to cultural tourism: the role of social entrepreneurs in the construction of a new institutional field'. *Entrepreneurship & Regional Development* 24(3–4): 259–282.

Perkmann, M. and Spicer, A. (2007). '"Healing the scars of history": projects, skills and field strategies in institutional entrepreneurship'. *Organization Studies* 28(7): 1101–1122.

Ritvala, T. and Kleymann, B. (2012). 'Scientists as midwives to cluster emergence: an institutional work framework'. *Industry and Innovation* 19(6): 477–497.

Sandberg, J. and Tsoukas, H. (2015). 'Making sense of the sensemaking perspective: its constituents, limitations, and opportunities for further development'. *Journal of Organizational Behavior* 36(51): S6–S32.

Siggelkow, N. (2007). 'Persuasion with case studies'. *The Academy of Management Journal* 50(1): 20–24.

Sotarauta, M. (2009). 'Power and influence tactics in the promotion of regional development: an empirical analysis of the work of Finnish Regional Development Officers'. *Geoforum* 40(5): 895–905.

Sotarauta, M. and Mustikkamäki, M. (2015). 'Institutional entrepreneurship, power, and knowledge in innovation systems: institutionalization of regenerative medicine in Tampere, Finland'. *Environment and Planning* 33(2): 342–357.

Internet resources:

http://www.wegweiser-kommune, accessed 18 October 2017.

https://www.regionalstatistik.de/genesis/online/, accessed 18 October 2017.

PART V

Concluding remarks

13. State of the union for a prosperous Europe

Daniel Silander and Charlotte Silander

There is a long scholarly tradition of describing and explaining European integration in terms of crises and challenges. If the 1990s and early 2000s were dominated by scholarly work on why more integration had developed, the last decade or so has consisted of an increasing number of studies on European recession, stagnation and disintegration. However, one of the founding fathers of European integration, Jean Monnet, once stated that he believed that "Europe would be built through crises, and that it would be the sum of their solutions" (Monnet, 1978: 417) and how "... people only accept change when they are faced with necessity, and only recognize necessity when a crisis is upon them" (Monnet, 1978: 109).

On 1 March 2017, the European Commission published its White Paper on the Future of Europe. This paper addressed European changes and challenges and set the agenda for the state leaders of the EU to meet and celebrate 60 years of unity since the Treaty of Rome in Italy. The European Commission stated how European challenges had historically been overcome based on shared norms and values, but also how the anniversary called upon Europe to handle new challenges. As stated:

> As a result, our troubled past has given way to a peace spanning seven decades and to an enlarged Union of 500 million citizens living in freedom in one of the world's most prosperous economies. The current situation need not necessarily be limiting for Europe's future. The Union has often been built on the back of crises and false starts. From the European Defence Community that never got off the ground in the 1950s, to the exchange rate shocks of the 1970s, through to aborted accessions and rejections in referenda in recent decades, Europe has always been at a crossroads and has always adapted and evolved. (European Commission, 2017: 5)

In addition:

> Like generations before us, our response to the task ahead cannot be nostalgic or short term. It should be built on a common perspective, and on the shared conviction that by coming together, each of us will be better off. (European Commission, 2017: 6)

The Commission argued that Europe had historically faced many crossroads, but has been able to adapt and evolve (European Commission, 2017: 6). The global economic crisis of 2008 and forward was one such major challenge that hit hard in terms of European economic growth and employment, political stability and social integration. As stated in this study, the EU immediately called for bold and innovative leadership and actions to protect Europe from further economic harm and to promote a competitive and prosperous European economy. On 13 September 2017, the president of the European Commission, Jean-Claude Juncker, presented the annual State of the Union 2017, addressed at the European Parliament in Brussels. The president declared the future objectives for Europe after numerous meetings, discussions and debates from a governance perspective to engage European citizens; the European Parliament; member state parliaments; local, sub-regional and regional public authorities; civil society organisations and social movements. The State of the Union was followed by a debate amongst all members of the European Parliament to ensure transparency and political accountability.

President Juncker acknowledged that the EU had faced a crossroads in previous years in terms of returning to isolation or promoting a future-looking European agenda, "a Europe that protects, a Europe that empowers, a Europe that defends" (Juncker, 2017). President Juncker further stressed the importance of collaboration amongst EU institutions and welcomed the work done by the European Parliament and the Council of Ministers with member states and how such collaboration had led to a needed economic recovery in Europe. He further argued how "Growth in the European Union has outstripped that of the United States over the last two years" and how "It now stands above 2% for the Union as a whole and at 2.2% for the monetary area". In addition, he stated that "Unemployment is at a nine-year low. Almost 8 million jobs have been created during this mandate so far. With 235 million people at work, more people are in employment in the European Union than ever before" (all cited in Juncker, 2017).

The economic change in recent years was, according to Juncker, a result of what this study has referred to as European governance. President Juncker stressed the important role played by all European institutions and member states and how determined action, the ability to catch the wind in our sails and to see the window of opportunity (Juncker, 2017), that is, political entrepreneurship, may provide for a united, stronger and more democratic Europe (Juncker, 2017). President Juncker explicitly acknowledged five necessary reform proposals for a prosperous Europe. First, the European trade agenda had to be strengthened. Trade, the president argued, provides jobs, creates new businesses and promotes European norms and values, and Europe today is facing a growing number of partners around the world that are seeking trade agreements with the continent. A recently signed agreement with Canada, a political agreement with Japan on an economic partnership in the near future, ongoing talks with Mexico and South American countries and future trade negotiations with Australia and New Zealand are all beneficial for Europe.

Second, President Juncker argued for reforms to create stronger and more competitive industry. The manufacturing base, with specific attention to the car industry, was mentioned, including how the car industry had to take immediate action to improve its legitimacy amongst European car consumers and transform its industry towards clean car production. Europe's new industrial policy has to be based on innovations, digitisation and decarbonisation to promote a greener economy.

Third, in relation to the industrial reforms, President Juncker stated the importance for Europe to become the global leader in fighting climate change. In a world where the US is reluctant to participate in international talks on climate change and in signing global climate change agreements, Europe must stand up for our planet to safeguard humanity's heritage. Such leadership is all about reducing carbon emissions from the transportation system and finding new forms of carbon-free production, based on green innovations.

Fourth, President Juncker further argued for the protection of Europeans' online security in the digital age. The ongoing efforts to protect intellectual property, cultural diversity and personal data have to continue, and Europe's fight against terrorism, terrorist propaganda and hate and radicalisation online, as well as cyber-attacks, must be prioritised. The increasing threat from cyber-attacks challenges the fundamental cornerstones of Europe's democracy and market economy and is today a real threat to European companies.

Fifth and finally, President Juncker called for ongoing action on migration. Europe's external borders must be protected, and support to Greece, Italy, Bulgaria and Spain must continue along with ongoing activities in the Mediterranean Sea. In addition, human rights standards must be improved in neighbouring states regarding migration, and the internal burden-sharing of migration flows must be improved.

An improved Europe of the future has to implement the five reform proposals above and must do so based on the values of the Union. In his concluding remarks, President Juncker explicitly called for European action to strengthen Europe and the EU. As argued:

> Honourable Members, Europe was not made to stand still. It must never do so. Helmut Kohl and Jacques Delors, whom I had the honour to know, taught me that Europe only moves forward when it is bold. The single market, Schengen and the single currency: these were all ideas that were written off as pipe dreams before they happened. And yet these three ambitious projects are now a part of our daily reality. Now that Europe is doing better, people tell me I should not rock the boat. But now is not the time to err on the side of caution. We started to fix the European roof. But today and tomorrow we must patiently, floor by floor, moment by moment, inspiration by inspiration, continue to add new floors to the European House. We must complete the European House now that the sun is shining and whilst it still is. Because when the next clouds appear on the horizon – and they will appear one day – it will be too late. So let's throw off the bowlines, sail away from the harbour and catch the trade winds in our sails. (Juncker, 2017)

This study has explored one major challenge to European integration, the EU and member states in how European governance and political entrepreneurship have handled the European economic crisis of 2007/2008 and forward. Chapter 1 on "European governance and political entrepreneurship in times of economic crisis", by Daniel Silander, addresses the economic crisis as being the worst crisis since the Great Depression of the 1930s. Despite European efforts to protect European economics from the global crisis, it hit hard economically, politically and socially. Economically, Europe saw a major decline in gross domestic product (GDP), employment and business activities; politically, it saw nationalism, populism, protectionism and citizen distrust of European integration; and socially, it saw curtailed welfare benefits, poverty and social despair. In 2009, the European Commission called for coordinated European efforts to not only combat the ongoing recession, but to build a better Europe. Europe saw great need for European governance and political entrepreneurship to handle the economic, political and social challenges that came with the economic crisis. This study set out to explore how European politicians, public servants, bureaucrats and institutions acted to promote economic growth and entrepreneurship in Europe. It was argued that the European economic crisis may have provided a window of opportunity for entrepreneurial political measures.

Based on this approach, this study was organised into three major themes: Framework of the Study (Chapters 1 to 3), European Institutions on Entrepreneurship and Regional Growth (Chapters 4 to 6), Embedded EU Policies on Entrepreneurship and Regional Growth (Chapters 7 to 10), Case Studies on Local Political Entrepreneurship (Chapters 11 and 12) and finally Concluding Remarks (Chapter 13).

In Chapter 2, "Political entrepreneurs as actors in governance networks: conceptualising political entrepreneurs through the actor-network approach", Elin Wihlborg extended the concept of political entrepreneurship by adding the sociological literature of actor-network theory to enhance the actor-oriented analysis of political entrepreneurship. This contributes to the understanding of how political entrepreneurs can be included in the analysis of policy networks and how an analysis of political entrepreneurs needs to include a network analysis. Actor–network theory extends the meanings of actors, stating that they can only be understood in relation to the network. In a similar way, the network is nothing without its actors. Furthermore, by adding an analysis of power, actor-network theory helps to highlight how actors have the power to influence the consequences of policy processes.

In Chapter 3, "Institutional entrepreneurship: a different perspective on political entrepreneurs?", Birgit Leick and Susanne Gretzinger presented a literature review on institutional entrepreneurship as a complementary perspective to political entrepreneurship. They argued that the bulk of studies on institutional entrepreneurship focus on different types of agents with the interest and capacity to change institutions and institutionalised practices. The main focus of the chapter was to describe triggers, activities and effects of institutional entrepreneurs as well as how a perspective of institutional entrepreneurship complements a perspective of political entrepreneurship. The authors argued that political entrepreneurs can be institutional entrepreneurs and that institutional entrepreneurship provides a broader perspective by focusing on the transformative process of institutional change both within and outside a policy arena. Both institutional entrepreneurship and political entrepreneurship provide insights into change agents that seek new opportunities to change the institutional setting. However, political entrepreneurship is about the public sector and how to provide new windows of opportunity for entrepreneurial activities.

In Chapter 4, "The European Commission: the EU as agenda-setter for economic growth and entrepreneurship", Daniel Silander and Charlotte Silander analysed the important role of the European Commission as a driving engine and agenda-setter for entrepreneurship. The DG for Growth has explicitly and repeatedly stated how Europe's economic growth and job creation depend on the development of entrepreneurship and SMEs. In line with previous research, which has shown how crises can be opportunities for change, examples of how the Commission has acted as a political entrepreneur were presented. In a time of long-term economic crisis, the Commission has approached entrepreneurship and the promotion of entrepreneurial activities through different initiatives, such as the Small Business Act for Europe and the Entrepreneurship 2020 Action Plan. Entrepreneurship is viewed as necessary to create companies and job opportunities, to identify and enter new markets and to promote new know-how and skills. An important part of promoting entrepreneurship is introducing entrepreneurship into all areas of education. Education as a political concern is linked to EU policy in relation to its growth policy ambitions and is influenced by the economic motives underpinning entrepreneurship education. The economic crises of 2008 have served as a "window of opportunity" (Kingdon, 1984) for making changes possible. In the European reform initiatives of the Lisbon Strategy and Europe 2020, education issues are linked to an economic growth discourse in which knowledge is regarded as the very foundation of intended growth.

In Chapter 5, "Entrepreneurship policy in the Council of the EU: reaching consensus among member states?", Brigitte Pircher analyses the Council's debates on the main entrepreneurial action plans: the Small Business Act for Europe and the Entrepreneurship 2020 Action Plan. The chapter shows how the Council has acted as a political entrepreneur by initiating and adopting policies and policy measures that are favourable to entrepreneurs. As institutions determine the set of rules, they therefore have an important impact on entrepreneurship and entrepreneurial possibilities and can therefore be regarded as key to the foundation of entrepreneurship and self-employment. In responding to the 2008 crisis, the EU has tried to support innovative policies and measures for economic growth. The assumption that entrepreneurship is the basis for a growing economy has led the EU and national governments to promote entrepreneurship. The analysis shows that the Council has acted as a political entrepreneur by using the crises as a window of opportunity for placing entrepreneurship on the political agenda and by bringing ready-made plans to the decision-making stage. An important reason for success was the common understanding of entrepreneurship as being vital for economic growth and for lifting the EU out of the crisis. Most important, the chapter shows how an institution as a whole can serve as an entrepreneur by introducing entrepreneurial policies.

In Chapter 6, "Debating the economic crisis in the European Parliament: enriching the discourse", Brigitte Pircher discusses how the European Parliament (EP) has addressed the issue of entrepreneurship. In contrast to the European Commission or the Council of the European Union, the EP is a more heterogeneous institution constituted by different political parties, committees, politicians and bureaucrats. By analysing parliamentary debates, the author demonstrates how the EP has used its policy-influencing instruments to act as a political entrepreneur and to define entrepreneurship in a broader sense. The debates on the Small Business Act and The European Private Company (EPC) Statute show that the EP has extended the discussion on entrepreneurship by introducing legal and social aspects which have led to innovative approaches to promoting the common good. In addition, the EP has been able to influence the decision-making process and enhance the open method of coordination. However, the debates show that the possibility for the EP to act as a political entrepreneur is, in the end, determined by its political majorities, which will give the direction of its entrepreneurship policy.

In Chapter 7, "Industrial policy in the post-industrial society: is the EU on the right track?", Charlie Karlsson and Sam Tavassoli discuss the controversial area of industrial policy which, after the 2008 crisis, faced the reaction that markets do not always perform optimally for society, generating a demand for new policy models. The chapter shows how the views on industrial policy have changed from a long-term perspective, with a special focus on the post-war period up to the current post-industrial society. The authors argue that industrial policies should be placed at the regional level and that small- and medium-sized regions need different policies than large urban regions. In addition, this chapter briefly evaluates the EU's current approach to industrial policy – the so-called smart specialisation – and sheds light on the problems related to this policy initiative, which include the idea that one policy model should fit all regions, a persisting focus on existing industries, a lack of focus on structural transformation in many regions and finally the focus on large administrative regions instead of on functional economic regions.

In Chapter 8, "The social efficiency of entrepreneurship education", by Charlotte Silander and Caroline Berggren, EU policy towards entrepreneurship education is analysed from an ideological perspective. The authors discuss how EU policies have influenced the direction of higher education. Increasing expectations on higher education graduates to contribute to welfare and economic growth through self-employment have pushed the development of entrepreneurship education at European universities. They show how the EU is striving to introduce entrepreneurship education into the education system through policies to improve entrepreneurial performance, both vertically and horizontally. The authors also show how the social efficiency perspective dominates, under which the overall purpose of higher education is to efficiently and scientifically contribute to economic growth and fight unemployment. This represents an instrumentalist view on education that focuses on the individual entrepreneur as a hero figure and in which entrepreneurship education is often expected to present role models to students and teach them the proper behaviour to become successful.

Chapter 9, "Exploring preconditions for political entrepreneurship and integration in European societies", by Anna Parkhouse and Per Strömblad, analyses the institutional preconditions of political entrepreneurship for EU migration and integration policies. The main focus of this chapter is to identify the potential roles that European political entrepreneurs may play, including supranational, intergovernmental and non-governmental actors. In addition, based on information from the European Social Survey, this study also explores Europeans' attitudes towards migrants along with cross-national institutional differences in focus. The authors argue that immigration and migration to Europe are necessary to handle Europe's demographic challenges. However, the large influx of refugees in 2015 created political overload on individual member states and the Common European Asylum System (CEAS), resulting in the reintroduction of territorial border controls and restrictive migration policies. As stated in the chapter, the 2015 refugee crisis has also been referred to as a migration governance crisis. As a consequence and as this chapter identifies, EU institutions such as the Commission have acted entrepreneurially to assist member states with improving the integration of potential labour migrants and refugees in Europe. Individual member states have implemented integration programmes with educational objectives and reforms to facilitate employment, but there have also been major structural hindrances to integration. Further, this study also argues for the importance of changes in European mindsets, leaving this study to identify necessary top-down and bottom-up changes to promote European integration.

Chapter 10, "Entrepreneurship in times of crisis: a resilience perspective on the Greek wine sector", co-authored by Evangelia Petridou, Maria Alebaki and Marie-Louise von Bergmann-Winberg, provides a case study on crises and the management of crises by conceptualising and exploring the interconnections between resilience and entrepreneurship. The main focus in this chapter is how politically entrepreneurial strategies might promote resilience in times of crisis. The case study explores the emerging wine sector in Greece as an example of a sector that is resilient despite major economic challenges. The authors seek answers to three questions: (i) In which ways has the crisis impinged on wineries, and how resilient was the Greek wine sector in the face of the economic meltdown? (ii) Who was affected the most, and what (if any) were the sources of resilience? (iii) Which strategies did the wineries mainly use to cope with the challenges associated with the crisis, and what was the link between resilience and political entrepreneurship within this framework? The authors argue that the economic crises may become a trigger factor in entrepreneurial activities. Faced by economic challenges due to decreased wine consumption in Greece, many Greek wine producers decided to focus on wine exports and wine tourism. In addition, the crises also triggered collaboration amongst the wine producers through associations and networks to counterbalance EU and national policies that have negatively affected the conditions for wine production. These networks consisted of public and private actors that pooled financial, social and political resources and were able to use European regional development projects for regional development.

Chapter 11, entitled "The legitimacy of political entrepreneurs in networks: lessons from local development projects in Swedish municipalities", co-authored by Albin Olausson and Elin Wihlborg, provides case studies by exploring the legitimacy of political entrepreneurs in Swedish local development projects. The main focus is to explore how civil servants in Swedish municipalities act as political entrepreneurs and whether they succeed or fail in gaining legitimacy in the municipal setting. The authors argue that successful political entrepreneurship is based on legitimacy and that networks are crucial for gaining legitimacy. Whilst political entrepreneurs are embedded in and make changes based on networks, legitimacy is a crucial aspect within networks. Political entrepreneurs may receive legitimacy from stakeholders within networks through collaboration and trust. However, they also argue that such informal legitimacy must be complemented by formal legitimacy as inputs to projects. As a result, local political entrepreneurs are not always successful in their endeavours and are not always perceived as legitimate, which becomes a hindrance for implementing local and regional policies for growth and sustainable development. By focusing on one national support scheme for helping political entrepreneurs to promote regional and local growth in networks, this chapter explores three projects with different outcomes, levels of legitimacy for their activities and political challenges.

In Chapter 12, "Local cases of institutional entrepreneurship: change agents in regions facing demographic change", Birgit Leick and Susanne Gretzinger address the urgent need in an increasing number of European regions to counter demographic challenges to economic growth and development. The authors argue that initiatives from local change agents, as institutional entrepreneurship, are important for supporting local economies and for the survival and development of local firms. The discussion on local institutional entrepreneurship is applied to three selected bottom-up initiatives in Germany, analysing how actors, groups of actors, networks, firms and organisations in the local economies interact and collaborate to improve the local institutionalised practices for handling demographic ageing and population decline. Based on theoretical perspectives on institutional entrepreneurship, as set out in Chapter 3, the three cases of local institutional entrepreneurship shed light on the roles of and actions taken by change agents that seek windows of opportunity, in times of uncertainty, to promote and diffuse their institutional agenda in alliances and coalitions to become influential. Local institutional entrepreneurs may successfully set such agendas by using discursive and interpretative power in negotiations within existing networks and thereby present new ideas on how to define and handle local challenges.

REFERENCES

European Commission (2017). *White Paper on the Future of Europe – Reflections and scenarios for the EU27 by 2025*. Brussels: European Commission.

Juncker, Jean-Claude (September 13, 2017). *State of the Union Address 2017*. Brussels: European Commission, accessed 3 November 2017 at http://europa.eu/rapid/press-release_SPEECH-17-3165_en.htm.

Kingdon, J. W. (1984). *Agendas, Alternatives, and Public Policies* (2nd ed.). Boston, MA: Longman.

Monnet, Jean (1978). *Memoirs*. London: William Collins.

Index